DIGITAL INFORMATION AND RESEARCH SUPPORT

Transforming Library and Information Services in Knowledge Society

DIGITAL INFORMATION AND RESEARCH SUPPORT

Transforming Library and Information Services in Knowledge Society

SHIVA SUKULA

Ess Ess Publications
New Delhi

DIGITAL INFORMATION AND RESEARCH SUPPORT
Transforming Library and Information Services in Knowledge Society

ISBN : 978-93-87698-85-7

Price : Rs. 1250/-

First Published 2021

Published by:
Ess Ess Publications
4831/24, Ansari Road,
Darya Ganj,
New Delhi-110 002.
INDIA
Phones: 23260807, 41563444
Fax: 41563334
E-mail: info@essessreference.com
www.essessreference.com

Cover Design by *Patch Creative Unit*

Printed and bound in India

To my father!
Who shared with me
that

Your work is to discover your world and
then with all your heart give yourself to it
as said by Buddha;

Learn as if you were to live forever
as told by Mahatma Gandhi;

But still try for who knows what is possible!
As experimented by Michael Faraday

Because spirituality and humanity need to collaborate together
with science & technology!

Foreword

Academic libraries and higher education have become synonymous with the highly sophisticated information services and learning ecosystem. In India, the universities and academia are overwhelmingly utilizing advanced libraries and their services which are unique sometimes keeping in view reaching the remotest user from a diverse academic and social background. Recent developments in the technological sphere have been creating niche in research arena of higher education. Innovative library services have been discovering methods to support academicians, researchers and scholars in learning settings. Alternatives in knowledge resources in the form of customized information products and also that of digital channels have transformed the way researchers and libraries used to interact to academic and organizational persuasions.

Experiencing the knowledge journey spread over the large span of researching and professing the subjects, the domain of learning and research depends upon the swift information retrieval andnumber of smart tools in libraries. Sinceadvancements over last couple of years in the social science research has opened new vistas such as digital platform to share and showcase the research output. Researchers across the world are well-acquainted with the research tools, applications and implications. Various concepts have emerged due to the refined practices in research; such as research collaboration, understanding of internationalization of research along with the roles of libraries in knowledge society. The ubiquitous nature of data and its needs among the people in higher education system have been felt strongly and governments have come forward to provide solutions for such needs.

While going through the contents of the present book, the connection with present research scenario is visualized in the form of various postulations and notions discussed in conceptually sound chapters where conceptions have been well organised to facilitate learning. The abstractions of knowledge in different directions are delineated in the chapters as Knowledge Society and Digital Environment; Library and Information Services in the Digital Age; Digital Libraries in Current Scenario; Information Management; Library and Research Support; Collaborative Research; Open Data; and Digital Humanities. I am sure that Dr. Shiva Kanaujia Sukula has made accomplished scholarly efforts and it could be evidenced by the configuration of concepts. In my opinion, the book would prove to be an instrument of enhancing learning among the research scholars, library professionals and academicians.

Prof. Virendra Kumar Malhotra
Member Secretary
Indian Council of Social Science Research
JNU Institutional Area
Aruna Asaf Ali Marg
New Delhi-110067

Preface

There have been tremendous waves of ICT developments and inclusion in the way libraries operate and serve the research quest in current learning environment. Research and innovations are the most essential components in higher education, especially in University academic scenario. The entire spectrum of challenges and growth in library services, different tools and sophisticated nature of users' academic requirements has provided a mechanism to indulge in updated visuals of technological practices. Since the last decade, the upsurge in ICT implementations is observed in university libraries. Various areas such as interactive library websites, open movements in the form of open access, open resources, open data, digital humanities, etc. have tried to reshape the knowledge society. The recent interests and curiosities in the provisions of information services have motivated the librarians to observe more into the unconventional methods of serving the users.

To discern the spaces and roles of digital technologies and their extension in the plethora of disciplines have transformed the aims and ways to library practices. The need to study the relationship between various subjects' needs and technology has augmented our imaginations with the questions to map and understand the increased interest and scope. The specific contexts of library and information services in the knowledge society are in critical phase as the continuous changes are components of the process. Academic and research practices in the current times have a focus upon efforts to create smart and sophisticated consensus on myriad approaches to serve the diverse needs of users in academic scenario. The aspects related to definition, structure, ontology, and mechanisms are pertinent to recognize the context in the global narratives. Reiterating the predominantly ICT narrative endeavors the reach to some solution in higher education and research scenario.

The notion of 'digitality' in the information scenario has been observed and there have been requirements to be redefined due to adoption of digital technologies. Each sphere from academic to research innovation has pushed towards a digital economy with the tremendous investment in various stages of education. The advancements, implementations, and the altering higher education as well as research system in India have unveiled the current practices in university libraries. The efforts to map intersectional perspectives have been providing inspirations and further, insights to narrate the discourse around the various components. As a practicing library professional, it seems as a significant opportunity to contextualise the concepts, debates, transitions in the knowledge society.

The growth of digitally-engaged libraries and services provide pertinent scope in context of "digital turn" well established with possibilities to engage with alternative practices in mainstream academia. Several challenges along with a closer look on various tools, resources and skills, and the context that shapes the current libraries have expanded roles and responsibilities expressed in the present book; Knowledge Society and Digital Environment; Library and Information Services in the Digital Age; Digital Libraries in Current Scenario; Information Management; Library and Research Support; Collaborative Research; Open Data; and Digital Humanities. The author hopes that the book would prove as an efficient tool for the scholars, practitioners, and university libraries rushing towards embracing the "digital" facilities; the reconfigurations, infrastructure and practices of research scholarship and pedagogy in higher education.

— Shiva Sukula
JNU, New Delhi

Contents

Chapter One

Knowledge Society and Digital Environment

SUMMARY : The chapter is moving along with the concepts woven over a long journey spread across the centuries and development in the world. Various steps for the framework are as following:

- Introduction
- How the Concept emerged!
- Knowledge Society
- Definitions
- Understanding the Knowledge Society
- Existence of Knowledge Society
- The Information Society or the Knowledge Society
- Information society
- Origin of Knowledge society
- The Earlier Initiatives
- Building Knowledge Societies
- The Digital Divide in the Knowledge Society
- The initial stages
- Mobilizing structures
- The Network Society
- Digital Society
- Digital Economy
- Framing processes in Information Society
- Librarians in a Knowledge Society
- Towards a Knowledge Society
- Role of Knowledge in Development
- Research and Development in Knowledge society

INTRODUCTION

A knowledge society is about people with similar interests, who endeavoured to create impact of knowledge processes about their areas of interest and in the process, contribute to this knowledge. Knowledge society as a society operates within the paradigm of the economics of information. Knowledge society is that kind of society which has emerged as outcome of the current societal changes induced by technological innovation. This knowledge society is inclusive of technological innovations as well as the most essential components "human beings". The human element has certain characteristics and attributes such as individual growth, creativity, life-long experiences and contributions in the generation and dissemination of knowledge. The growth of knowledge society depends upon the transfer of knowledge into future generations. These contributors have another role along with being participant; the commitment of being "knowers". The evolution reflects the "information society" (IS), is followed by Knowledge Society. The emergence of IS happened due to unimagined flow of information. The advent of computers, and data processing systems flooded the information. In the knowledge society, knowledge, and not mere information, is the most valuable asset. The information societies or knowledge societies are "advanced societies reaching a stage of development predominantly based on production and utilization of knowledge". It can be considered as a society where people take the path of progress through the creation, sharing and use of knowledge. Knowledge Society is understood as the ability to process, and use of the information to develop a reflective competence, to establish connections with the surrounding knowledge.

HOW THE CONCEPT EMERGED!

During early twentieth century in the year 1914, "post-industrial society", emerged. Later during 1958, Daniel Bell and 1960's, Alain Touraine revived this term in America and France, respectively. But the term "information society" emerged in "Japanese social sciences" during early years of 1960's. In the year 1961, during the conversation between Kurokawa, and Umesao (an anthropologist) the expression emerged. Later during 1980, the terms such as automation, cybernation merged into the concept of information and society. With the advent of personal computer (PCs) in early eighties (1981), the innovations were added in the information society due to rapid restructuring and global growth. The developments took place due to knowledge skills, capacity building, competitive advantages and transformation. Since the early 1990's, the telecommunications networks facilitated universal access beyond geographic and cultural boundaries. The changed shape of information society emerged due to advances of World Wide Web since 1994. After beginning of new millennium, the "International Telecommunications Union's World Summit on the Information Society" in Geneva (2003) and Tunis (2005) became instrumental for advanced policy making in the areas of promotion, infrastructure, and access of ICTs for development. The cultural, ethnic, and linguistic diversity are also components of policy considerations. In the past, Bell's theory of "information society" exists sue to presence of "information workers" and their growth performing the various kinds of information processing in different occupation. The division of information society theories can be broadly differentiated as observing the "technology as the driving force" as "social factors as shaping technology" and society. Picard and Grönlund (2003) tried to find answers for the "means for overall assessment of cultural life and measuring the involvement of the cultural sector in the information society".

The concepts, "Post-industrial society" (Daniel Bell) emerged as "Liquid modernity" (Zygmunt Bauman), later developed into a "Network society" (Manuel Castells) and finally, "New Information Society" (given by Frank Webster); very close to Knowledge society leading towards globalization and characterizing contemporary social transformations. Later during 1970s and 1980s, the "Third Wave" emerged as post industrial developments in the information-based services. The aspects of society in the perspectives of economic developments and changes were revolutionized. This was followed by generation and flow of information, an outcome of combination of computer technology and communications technology in the words of Masuda in Japan. He described various phases of innovative and technological changes brought by technology through automation, knowledge creation, and new innovations. Though, Daniel Bell (1973) stated: "In the pre-industrial society life is a game against nature where one works with raw muscle power; in the industrial era where machines predominates in a technical and rationalized existence, life is a game against fabricated nature. In contrast to both, life in the post-industrial society based on services, is a game between persons. What counts is not raw muscle power or energy but information."

The later 1990s witnessed the information age, with the intricate knowledge society. The multilayered foundation by linking "economic-and political" with the technological grips have created a new social structure and services. The productivity and powers are based on information processing and transmission. Three independent processes are responsible for new structure of society. Imbibing new technologies and changes in ICTs, the information society is related with the various aspects and measures of information, its flow and information industries. The information is responsible for the quality of society and everything associated through the mechanisms, share and application of information in the society. Since in his belief, the notions of information society are directing towards an innovative platform.

Development of a typology in context with

technological, cultural, economic, and spatial factors to discern the information society aspects has taken place. The expanding role in all directions of social existence with social structures resulted in rapid changes in life. Many OECD and EU documents stressed about the "occupational aspect of the information society". The information processing related with "white-collar society" is an indicator of an information society. The transformative power of information has altered the scenario of occupation and generation of service sector.

KNOWLEDGE SOCIETY

Knowledge Society can be described as the types of societies that possess the characteristics of capacities and potential for creation of scientific and technological knowledge. The data-processing technologies have emerged as a common factor in utilizing the knowledge in a strategic manner as a mean of economic competition. This kind of scenario has taken place among various nations, organizations and corporate sectors. The strong connection between research and development is playing a significant role in framing the knowledge as specific commodity. The investment in the education sector has been a key area in building up the resources of human capital. The human capitol and innovations are interrelated in knowledge societies. Combination of such elements supports the expectations from societies which are based on knowledge attributes. Significant facets of knowledge society are as following:

a. networking among knowledge producers,

b. effectiveness in applying,

c. controlling and

d. evaluating and learning.

The dependence and role of education is related with understanding the comparison between quality of knowledge and the knowledge imparting organizations; the relativity of social status of a person with the educational qualification and achievement. The reflexive conscience has been attached with the constructional as well as methodological processes. The lifelong learning intrigues the expectations of pedagogical consequences associated with acquiring new knowledge. The extraordinary augmentation of complex nature of knowledge impacts the people at global level. The infrastructural and technological developments have been welcomed by individuals as well as educational curriculums.

Definitions

Few definitions are explaining more about information and knowledge society:

"A new type of society, where the possession of information is the driving force behind its transformation and development where human intellectual creativity flourishes" (Masuda, 1980).

"The information society is an economic reality and not simply a mental abstraction. The slow spread/ dissemination of information ends new activities; operations and products gradually come to light" (John Naisbitt, 1984).

The information society can be considered as a society which involves creation, diffusion, and usage of information in the context of economic factors, political and social aspects.

UNDERSTANDING THE KNOWLEDGE SOCIETY

The term knowledge society can be defined as a society that considers the creation, dissemination, and utilization of information and knowledge as the most significant factor of production. The role of knowledge as assets in producing the wealth in comparison with other conventional ways such as estimating the value of land, etc. along with the physical or financial capital. To understand it in more simple words and contexts:

a. At the outset, the use by social scientists for describing and analyzing the transformation toward the much talked "postindustrial society".

b. Next, it refers to a normative vision of the countries that is envisioned to achieve.

c. Established as a metaphor which encapsulates a number of concepts.

Sometimes the phrases, such as "knowledge economy" and other ideas relate to "knowledge driven economies", "economies of innovation" with the most popular one, "information society". So, all the discussed terms and phrases relate to two integral elements which can be categorized as "a formal association of people with similar interests" involved in use and application of combined knowledge towards creation of "knowledge society". The mechanism of working of Knowledge society relate to a paradigm in which the economics of information operates. The prime input to the production and innovation in knowledge society is human capital, based on ICTs for accessing the relevant information. The significance of ICTs is indispensable in underpinning the knowledge economy.

EXISTENCE OF KNOWLEDGE SOCIETY

The continuous re-imagination of knowledge society has taken place during last couple of decades, shaping the current times and future aspects. The various steps are used in "economic reasoning" with the help of strategy and creativity. The use and application of data along with designing, the developments in knowledge society take place. The innovation cast away myths and ambiguity. The existence of Knowledge Society has strengthened innumerable organizations, knowledge systems and corporate scenario at global level. The enthusiasm behind growing knowledge based economy and creating value have been intertwined to improve the knowledge system in the form of education sector. The economic revolution is also augmented by knowledge society. The education system in knowledge society is evolved and imparting learning through use of evidence and human-centered design. The education system can change the way of learning. The mechanism of improvement depends upon innovation for transformation. The deliverance of education and academic services is an integral part of knowledge society to induce innovation and improvement. Knowledge society paves way for innovation for growth. The creation of new "market opportunities" and models emerge to provide the sources of profit in the perspective of knowledge economy. The knowledge society may include the national innovation based on science advancements and actions taken for development strategy. The intricate relationship with digital paths has been instrumental in supporting the education and literacy.

THE INFORMATION SOCIETY OR THE KNOWLEDGE SOCIETY

The recent times have witnessed the continuum of change in the information society itself. The characteristics of transformations are found associated with catalytically presence and invasion by artificial intelligence. Few terms such as "Global village", "technotronic era", "post-industrial society", "information society" or "information age", and "knowledge society" have been redefining the shape and structure of current societies. These new coined terms are reflecting the changes, developments and transformation taken place in the information society, various areas which were earlier just few facets of growth. The strong connection of social media and such changes are supporting each other in spreading the awareness about transformation. Each phrase or term related with information society has distinct meaning expressing the specific context related with perception of people. Specific "ideological baggage" emerges related to each term, which functions as the focal point of the information society. The World Summit on the Information Society (WSIS) has come up with the emphasis on "information society and knowledge society" as two major terms having few more variants.

Information Society

The "information society" has been an expression denoting phases of changes and development due to industrial and ICTs advancements. While understanding the history of the term, the literature shows the events initiated during 1973, when in United States, famous sociologist Daniel Bell mentioned the "information society" in "*The Coming of Post-Industrial Society*" a book that introduced this concept first time. The reflection then was the initial argument of making knowledge in pivotal role for all-directions of society, especially the economic and development contexts. The arrival of knowledge based services will be cause of change in the information driven society. During the decade of 90s, the advent of proliferating World Wide Web and ICTs have been major causes of reentering of this term in information literature. In 1995, inclusion in the agenda of the G7 meetings has been powerful appearance. The same was part of G8 meetings as well. The concept of information society was later became part of discussion and addressed at the platforms of "European Community and the OECD - Organization for Economic Cooperation and Development". It is well understood that information society was being discussed not only among the group of developed nations but also developing countries. The adoption in US government system, UN agencies as well as the World Bank Group has expressed the central as well as powerful significance of information society at global level. The highly discussed topic, during 1990s, was selected for the "International Telecommunication Union" (ITU) and later by the UN, in 2003 and 2005. In the neo-liberal globalization, the "information society" has become a "construct" in order to accentuate the platform for the open as well as "self-regulated" world market. The possibility of such initiatives could happen due to collaboration among international agencies such as "World Trade Organization" (WTO), the "International Monetary Fund" (IMF), and the "World Bank". The multilingual aspect of these organizations has played a central role among the developing countries to encourage such policies which can minimize the digital divide.

The adoption of ICT infrastructure development policies in the developing and weak nations has paved way for a rise in the economy. The close relationship among economic globalization, the World Wide Web, Internet based phoning and satellite television, etc. have made possible this image of information society.

ORIGIN OF KNOWLEDGE SOCIETY

The "knowledge society" relating to "*sociedad del conocimiento*" came into scenario during the end of the 90s. Very soon it became a significant component among the academicians and academic society in the shape of "information society", which is a variant of the former notion. The role of UNESCO due to adoption of the term "knowledge society", or "knowledge societies" has made it one facet of various policies. The integrity of this concept can be found as: "*Information society is the building block for knowledge societies,*" *the link of 'information society' with 'technological innovation', have various facets which are social, cultural, economical, and political in nature. The relation of institutional transformation is basic idea which is prevalent in many components of governance and societal structure. The overall approach is pluralistic in vision. The complex and dynamic nature of information society paves way for economic as well as other areas growth of society.*

The following components are associated with the characteristics of information society:

a. practical certainties

b. analytical comprehensiveness

c. formal targets

d. intuitiveness

e. capacity to combine intelligence with other ideas

The interchangeability of economic growth and practical capacities is also observed in knowledge and information society. The policies and actions related with the concepts of knowledge society and information society are few of the governing factors to define these concepts in current times. The term "informational society" relating to "information society", thus makes it possible to understand the difference between the action and result. According to Manuel Castells "the term informational indicates the attribute of a specific form of social organization in which information generation, processing, and transmission are transformed into the fundamental sources of productivity and power, due to the new technological conditions that arise during this historic period." The characteristics of technological innovations and revolutions are the outcomes of applications of information in the process of knowledge generation. The innovation and its application is another facet towards transformation of knowledge society. The technology diffusion empowers the users of information. The ICT tools are not only supporting machines but also devising new mechanisms for productivity. As for the knowledge society, the knowledge generation and process are based on ICTs applications and revolutions. In this context, the Geneva Declaration of Principles has been adopted by many governments, has declared as:

> *"We... declare our common desire and commitment to build a people-centered, inclusive, and development-oriented Information Society, where everyone can create, access, utilize, and share information and knowledge, enabling individuals, communities and peoples to achieve their full potential in promoting their sustainable development and improving their quality of life, premised on the purposes and principles of the*

Charter of the United Nations and respecting fully and upholding the Universal Declaration of Human Rights."

In this context, further the Civil Society Declaration has expressed its vision as following: "*We are committed to building information and communication societies that are people-centered, inclusive, and equitable. Societies in which everyone can freely create, access, utilize, share and disseminate information and knowledge, so that individuals, communities, and peoples are empowered to improve their quality of life and to achieve their full potential.*" The addition of social and economic justice in this Declaration has included provisions for capacity building of people. The objectives of knowledge society such as sustainable development, equality, democratic developments are among few of the fundamental rights. The knowledge society facilitates the platform for equitable distribution of resources.

THE EARLIER INITIATIVES

The WSIS convocation was successful in developing the vision of the information society. There was little significance given by many governmental delegations along with the corporate and private sectors in this context, yet the civil society behaved more proactively. The approaches in this key issue have been about the new development paradigm which is based on technology and with the help of technological tools, the social order and economic development are driven. In developing countries, the transition phase has been a matter of time along with the governmental decisions. These factors have been responsible for creation of adequate "empowering conditions". The emphasis on removing the digital gap has been a great action to facilitate the "universal access programs". The technological advancements and availability of such programs have been crucial components of the information society development. The industrial developments are causes of services generation and dependence upon information. Another style of approach concentrated upon "human development" which is again revolving around usage of information, communication and the economy within they survive. The predominance of information is found to be major characteristic element in information or knowledge society. The 'technological supports' are accelerators of this process.

The information society growth and development has shifts of focus towards the human beings' needs for development in all directions including social justice. This style focuses on society instead of technological innovations and their applications. The tools and technological supports are components in first type of approach while the last one is related to living components of information society. The data, various communication and transmission channels are part of first style; and the human development and equality, in the other one. The campaign for Communication Rights in the Information Society -CRIS- points out in the document on the WSIS, "*The Question for Civil Society*": "*If civil society is going to adopt and recover the notion of an information society, it should return to these basic notions, posing the correct questions about:*

- generation and ownership of information and knowledge
- assessment and valued of information and knowledge
- dissemination and distribution of information and knowledge
- restrictions and use of knowledge

The term information society has relation and context with the "uniform world society". Several UNESCO documents mention and provide reference to "knowledge societies". Relating to "information", the debate taken up by the "knowledge society", has an integral vision including human process; the relation of knowledge with the economic context for the people's knowledge), such as objective, scientific, and digitizable in nature. This concept gives opportunity of "shared knowledge society (ies)". The use of information for information, communication and knowledge is done for a purpose not only for dissemination in the shared knowledge society.

Technocentric Concept of Society

The term "societies" are to be understood in the plural sense, understanding the heterogeneity, diversity and reaffirmation of the interest in context with the appropriating technologies for their specific development priorities. The information societies are utilizing disruptive technologies, for example, artificial intelligence. The phenomenon of self-driving cars is discussed and will be a part of our society in future soon. The rapid technological changes are priorities of the information society. Along with the developing countries, least developed countries (LDCs), and the landlocked developing countries are in constant need of high connectivity and deliverance in the form of ICT trainings. Developing digital skills for economy in information society are incubators for skills development. The digital transformations are revolving around the artificial intelligence, the Internet of Things, Big Data analytics, etc. The significance of digital skills is observed in information society. The multi-stakeholder approach is used in order to enhance the digital skills; it involves various sectors such as governments, academia, corporate sectors and research institutions.

The observations reflect that great service isn't delivered by chance (the credit goes to its design). The crafting of meaningful and long-lasting service experiences are outcome of collaboration between strategic thinking and human beings. In the knowledge society, the service design is the outcome of bringing together various components such as human beings, digital technologies, and physical interactions, the knowledge society provides windows for close collaborations to minimize the gap between the strategic actions and the demands within the society. The information society has the service sector as the outcome of various complex planning. The relation of rethinking services, organizations, and people are basic elements in information society. The identification of significant service moments of clients, based on creation of the human components, digital technologies and physical interactions is challenging as deliverance of great service.

BUILDING KNOWLEDGE SOCIETIES

The lives of people in society are highly touched by the knowledge and information. The roles of ICTs in sharing and disseminating the knowledge as well as information are powerful, in context with economy and societal transformation. The responsibility taken up by UNESCO has been tremendous in empowering the local communities and greater societies by way of facilitating access to information and preserving for the future generations. The preservation of knowledge is significant in both the areas; the education and cultural heritage. Knowledge societies are being built upon following components of strength:

a. freedom of expression;

b. universal access to information and knowledge;

c. respect for cultural and linguistic diversity; and

d. quality education for all

Building knowledge society is a lengthy and complex process. The implementation of bold strategies is found to be helpful in creating value. The value creation requires a constant focus through great strategy. One of the characteristics of Knowledge Society is to support the organizations to create bold strategies to yield value for strategic businesses ventures, clients, and citizens. A great strategy defines where an organization will play and outlines a clear vision that its people can rally around. The information society involves the role of delivered information in context with tangible results and, further seeking impact. The use of various processes is found in information society:

a. evidence synthesis

b. data analytics

c. design thinking

d. prototyping to create services

The measurable impact is achieved by combining the strategic challenges and delivery capability inducing actions. The Knowledge Society supports various organizations to improve from within; by engagement of information in the organization and applying insight in the organizational structure, targets and methods of work. The concept of co-designing the solutions works in the conditions where the environment is collaborative and target-oriented. The information plays the role of an expert yet augmented like a beginner's mind. The understanding of problems as well as related challenges is something that invites attention to apply a fresh approach with clarity. The outsiders' approach brings spectacular solutions due to combination of information power and the curiosity. The information society focuses on deep human needs as the human society revolves around eternal human needs. The information society uses human-centred design techniques in various areas. The focus on the strategies, and applications has been created for improving services, economy and development at global level.

The information society facets are very closely related; these are–sincere planning, authentic information, integrity. The capacity to judge and implement right decisions based on correct information is the continuous actions in information society. The information society focuses upon specific areas, problems where the improvements and innovations for a larger group of people can be done. The impact of such improvement or innovation is beyond a particular task, the emulation of progress follows as true measure of success in the knowledge society. The information society involves various components such as a transformational strategy not only for the innovation but also the education system, organizations and action strategies. The social impact is visualized once the action strategies are in vogue. The role of information and services bring radical improvement while achieving the new goals with the application of knowledge-based strategies and approaches. The problem solving approaches are significant in knowledge society which is a unique style of its own nature. Information based strategies, empirical research become the mechanism to address the issues in human society.

THE DIGITAL DIVIDE IN THE KNOWLEDGE SOCIETY

The role of ICTs in the development of modern economies is central as it is required in many diverse ways to participate fully in a modern society. The profound implications for education are the facilities provided innovative forms of learning. ICTs current forms have been showing the potential in education. The exposure towards the technology and usage supports the achievement of learning results. The three interrelated facets such as learners, policy framers and the corporate executives work together towards the knowledge economy. The knowledge society as well as digital economy drive is associated with knowledge-based activities. The implications of knowledge based steps for business, and society are discernible. The knowledge society concentrates on the divide between speed of ICT inclusions and the speed of industrial development and policy framing. The previous perceptions about the knowledge society show the historical trajectories with the early mentions of knowledge society.

a. During 1858 in the writings of Karl Marx;

b. In the writings of Schumpeter (1930s and 1940s);

c. Later on in the views of Masuda's 1980 (Japan);

d. Drucker's 1993 Post-Capitalist Society.

THE INITIAL STAGES

After a duration and gap of three decades in Japan, Yoneji Masuda (1980) prepared the idea of planning for the information society in context with new millennium. He also discussed about the developments in the human society taken shape in the form of hunting, agriculture and industry. The factors for social transformations include the innovation of the "social technology system" approached towards productivity. Later on this material productivity shifted towards the information productivity. This exponential growth of information has brought changes in human and social values, politics, ideological and economic aspects. The difference between industrial societies, and information society reflects the dynamism of various facets such as material productivity, and transport; the 'information revolution' due to ICTs making the production of systematized information, and knowledge for the society. Masuda emphasized in the concept of the information society as following:

a. Information is the "axis of socio-economic development". The production of information will be in the hands of organizations which would use information for routine tasks on the basis of ICT applications.

b. There will be increase in user-generated information. The growth of information will take place through "synergistic production and sharing."

c. The society will observe the economy shifting from the previous "structured exchange" to "synergistic" system of economy.

The industrial society was composed of actions which were enterprises and economic groups. These groups were categorized as public sector, private enterprise and government owned enterprises. Opposite to this, the information society is composed of "voluntary communities" which are socio-economic groups categorized as local communities, followed by information communities. The information society focuses on the revival human mind, in context with basic human rights, equality, spreading globalism, self-discipline leading towards the social contribution. Later in the business historian Peter Drucker (1993) perpetrated knowledge economy and digital society. The concept of "Post-Capitalist Society" (1993) given by him was based upon socio-economic evolution. Peter Drucker stated about the significance of knowledge. The significance of communication is related with knowledge to be communicable and the same is communicated. In this context, knowledge application has been considered as a significant tool for the development of developed economies.

MOBILIZING STRUCTURES

The knowledge society has witnessed various structures and levels to relate with among themselves. The components such as ICTs, people and creativity are highly influenced and responsible to generate the developments in the knowledge and information society. The information society has the mobilizing structures and relationship. The influence of ICTs on social movements and participation is dependent upon reduction of participation costs, promotion of collective identity and creation of community". Such mechanisms are directly affecting the participation in the information society due to increased usage of ICTs. The aspects such as the publishing and access costs are responsible for participation of people. Reidenberg (1997) stated that "for the information infrastructure, default ground rules are just as essential for participants in the Information Society as ... Lex Informatica intrinsically links rule-making capabilities well suited for the Information Society with substantive information policy choices". Various information movements have facilitated the maximum flow of information with increased access for the people. The reductions in the information production, distribution, dissemination and access can be possible due to new publication, business and access models. These steps have contributed in the augmented participation and generation of more information. To increase participation, a model including the attributes of decreasing the ICT coordination costs, ICTs facilitations expenditures and efficiency. Leizerov (2000) has been able to shape and increase the dynamism of participation in information society. The participation has contributed in many ways among the society in the form of political engagement through enhanced communication capacity and expansion formal education level. The impact of Internet has been observed in several forms of communication and information activity. The lack of systematic absorption among people and society has been visible and instrumental in identifying the areas to augment the access to information and participation. The technology and participation has been combined in order to increase in collective identity due to common ideas. The collective action from the collective identity in the society is possible due to ICTs (Arquilla and Ronfeldt, 2001). The role of mass media and common platforms to share ideas among small groups of people has been crucial in the information sharing and participation. The problems due to geographical and industrial reasons have been overcome by ICTs at a larger level to increase the peoples' participations in the information society. Towards contribution of knowledge, Delanty (2001) views "the university as a key institution of modernity and as the site where knowledge, culture and society interconnect" with the assessment of "issues such as globalization, the information age, the nation state, academic capitalism, cultural politics and changing relationships between research and teaching" in context with the university's role in knowledge society. The argument is that "in the knowledge society of today a new identity for the university is emerging based on communication and new conceptions of citizenship. It will be essential reading for those interested in changing relationships between modernity, knowledge, higher education and the future of the university."

The role of ICTs' facilitation by augmented participation in community creation is observed in reinforcing the social networks and providing them different levels, platforms and facilities for connection. The facilitation by ICTs for geographically dispersed location by channel of "face-to-face networks" has provided a strong medium to inform about the common ideas yet without the assessment of their strength and contribution in information society. The expansion and extension of ICTs in the information society has been dependent on the nature (Diani, 2000) of the social movement organization (SMO). The mobilization of professional resources by SMOs can bring transformation in the virtual communities.

The role of knowledge society as intellectual device has provided a platform where various components in the shape of knowledge, and knowledge production, are significant to organizations in context with industrial production, economics of contemporary societies. To debate the status of knowledge as private or public good, Marginson (2006) has intrigued the language, 'know-how', and other aspects of knowledge while comparing with the text-communication. The value of knowledge is beyond the limitation of number of use; "Nor are its benefits confined to individuals for long: knowledge can only ever be a temporary private good". The ownership of knowledge has become a significant area of concern around the globe in knowledge societies due to commodification of knowledge as "attempts at the commodification of information are probably less problematic than attempts to commodify knowledge, pedagogy and assessment" (Naidoo and Jamieson, 2005) due to ownership of innovation(s) and price of education (Etzkowitz et al., 2000). Välimaa and Hoffman (2008) have opined about the conventional approach of knowledge as "knowledge itself and the uses of knowledge are nothing new for mankind which understands itself through languages which are themselves symbolic systems for cultivating and transferring knowledge". The roles of knowledge in the capacity to collect, evaluate and use in future are the attributes in knowledge society by assessing the productions, quantity and use of information and ICT. The vastly availability of communication facilities is an instrument to create issue-based communication, among the people. The diverse mechanisms for interaction have strengthened and expanded the relationships and transnational organizations.

THE NETWORK SOCIETY

The shape of network society is outcome of interconnected people due to ICTs. The social uses of network society and ICTs have contributed in shaping the information society based on framing and structuring the policies. The network society is comprised of users who are the producers of technology and information. The diffusion of networking is a basic component in the network society, which is a type of information society due to new technological paradigm. The networking technologies in digital context are powerful and efficient to enable networks and move beyond the past practices carried on during industrial and post-industrial societies. The flexible and adaptive nature of technologies has the capacity and objective to decentralize the system to establish better coordination among the components of information society. The network society is based on communication networks which transcend and traverses through boundaries on global level. The globalization is considered a form of network society on the greatest level with more descriptive nature (Manuel, Wallis and Barcelona, 2006). The existing gap between knowledge and consciousness has been filled by the ICTs. The network society can be considered as a social structure which operates on networked based information through digital computer networks. This network functions to process and disseminate the information in the shape of formal structure of network in the information society.

THE DIGITAL SOCIETY

The initiation of the knowledge society through technological advances emerged after the World War II when the Japanese government identified power of knowledge as a resource to convert the nation into a "great economic power." Reiterating in Drucker's (1993), "the relationship between knowledge workers and organizations" depends upon knowledge workers responsibility meet the goals while the organizations serve as platforms. According to him, knowledge is a tool of economic resource as the knowledge-based economy changed in practice as the changes happened due to altered business equations around the globe. During this era, knowledge started to behave as a factor of production. This concept of knowledge made the capitalism obsolescent. The knowledge society has been considered as phenomenon of growth. The emergence as intellectual device has stirred a debate in last decade. The knowledge society has appeared as multi-dimensional entity during post-industrial times and regarded as "simultaneous growth of the internet, mobile telephony and digital technologies with the Third Industrial Revolution—which, at first in the developed countries, has seen much of the working population migrate to the service sector—has revolutionized the role of knowledge in our societies" (UNESCO, 2005).

DIGITAL ECONOMY

The knowledge society is inclusive of digital society, known as post-capitalist society, and the digital transformation has the knowledge society converted into the "knowledge economy or the digital economy", the e-government system, online education. The "Post-capitalist society", (as in Peter Drucker's work), refers to the notion that knowledge is a significant component in the production and supply-chain management. The roles of knowledge and information workers are expanded. While "Industry 4.0" is indicating that digitalization of manufacturing, such as robotics, the new economy is reflecting the visible changes due to factors such as digitalization and information explosion. New Economy is related with "dematerialization of daily life" (Magee and Devezas, 2017), where the commercial activities are dependent upon the data encryption with the sufficient knowledge of IPRs in digital context. While is an established fact that knowledge is playing a pivotal role in contemporary society, the changing nature of knowledge workers is related with the service improvements and customers expectations. The price ratio with the quality of goods has changed in comparison with the old system of economy. The dependence on physical premises in most of the commercial ventures is uncommon in current times due to technical support from information technology and emergence of information based services. The origin of innovative services has been found in the decentralized organizations with the changing responsibilities in the form of business leaders, service coordinators, innovative strategists, etc. The industries have witnessed and experienced the dissolving barriers with the interchanging roles and outputs due to data presence. The recent times in the information society have faced digital disruption and innovative service structure based on data, instead of physical possession of business. The examples are in the services such as Uber, Airbnb, Skype, etc.

As discussed by McKinsey about the impact of digitization in the US economy which occurred due to the ubiquitous nature of Internet and various digital devices. Since a decade the cloud computing along with the "big data analytics" has expressed ICTs providers' role in development. The statement relating to "new layers of specialists who are men of speculation and who made important contributions to the production of economically useful knowledge" (by Adam

Smith in Parry, 2016) relates to "knowledge" and "economy," provided the concerns for 'investment' of knowledge which is possessed by the people of society. As discussed in "Grundrisse" (1858), Marx mentioned the significance of knowledge as "direct force of production." People are using social media platform and information including product reviews for further planning and action, though the use of information was not precise at that time. During the mid last century, Joseph Schumpeter (1943) discussed about the innovation and its role as "the driver of the economy", which depends upon knowledge. The knowledge revolution is related with innovation as the sociological forces are associated in the context with the development of society, the roles of economic action are altered; and the knowledge is an essential component of economic growth as well as driver of change in development.

But there are few aspects on the contrary, such as differences in input and output in context with economic development are visible due to "free trade" agreements (Phillips, 2004; Phillips et. al., 2017) in economy of society, yet the applications of in artificial intelligence, etc., could not be foreseen. But the impacts of technology are visible and predictable in principle, refereeing to broader impacts. One pioneer discussion emerged about the challenges of contemporary society as following:

- The scope of digital economy is beyond the issues of digital commerce, as the communication methods are essential components of expression for the purpose of economic activities.
- The consideration of electronic communication in the commercial activities is related with growth and development of cyber-markets.
- The privacy issues, safeguards and encryption are related with production as the components such as demands of potential buyers.

- The technical Issues of open standards, universal access, legal and moral issues for competition rules in the context of customer data.
- The policy issues in the perspectives of quality of goods, customer data, purchase of goods, e-exchange, etc.

FRAMING PROCESSES IN INFORMATION SOCIETY

The flow of information in the information society is a deciding factor to frame the processes across networks due to new technologies. The propagation of such networks has been possible due to transformations created by ICTs in the shape of media skills and contemporary design of communication. New ICTs challengers related with mass-media filters are contributing as means of bypassing gatekeepers on the Web to frame as well as frame clouding. The ICT-mediated dissemination strategies have created information outlets on the globally connected Internet to provide access (Leizerov, 2000).

The prediction of Internet-enabled outsourcing and the digital revolution has been considered a tool for re-engineering processes as aspects of outsourcing, public-private partnerships, and provision of services beyond the geographical limits. The economic production, distribution, and the consumer satisfaction achievement are changed due to steps and levels of information exchange. The access to information and services has created growth and progress in the 21st century. During early new millennium, the learning society and knowledge economy have been working together as at different level the learning groups such as individuals, companies and organizations not only consume the information but also create and harvest the information assets. The innovation and learning are applied and these facets become the cause of the industrial framework transitions, and change in various components such as customers' choices, nations' policies, etc. The digital economy works in tandem with proliferating nature of innovation and learning. As discussed by Freeman and Perez (1986), "techno-economic paradigm" (TEPs) addresses the scope of conventional economic viewpoints. TEPs are the organized economic activity resultant of technologies. The old technologies seem to be exhausted and the "disruptive innovations" happen; the new technical and entrepreneurial advances come forward to create the "techno-economic paradigms". The role of existing market and available technologies is found in diffusion of innovative products and services. The major "techno-economic paradigms" with the early processes during 1700-mid-1800s have been followed by mass production during mid and later part of twentieth century and ICTs. The components of "digital economy" prevail in the layers of information society in the contemporary "techno-economic paradigm." The innovative approaches in industrial perspectives are dependent on ICTs. The TEP are responsible for changes to the modern companies by creating:

a. innovative business models
b. better mechanisms to achieve target
c. advanced modes of collaboration

The productivity is increased due to the positive changes. Digital economy has been an outcome of innovations in techno-economic paradigm. The unprecedented and unexpected results have brought a range of variations in the productivity. Various nations and geographical regions have indication of diverse capabilities for innovation due to the TEP. The concepts related with the neo-Schumpeterian and technological systems have given visuals of innovation drivers in the perspectives of organizations and regions. The technological trajectories are the images of evolutionary technological capabilities. In this context, the path-dependencies are carved due to the unique timeline of a nation while gaining knowledge and shaping the techno-economic paradigm. How a nation frames policies for technology innovation, generation and implementation is directly related with creating technological trajectories in order to pace up the economic progress. The need to focus on the growth and development of a learning society in context with facets such as economics and technology shifts the digital economy to learning economy, by knowledge accumulation at various levels; individual and collective. The implementing technology framework for the TEP must be related with "targeted growth" of industries inputting the information and knowledge into the system, development of ICT applications, commercializing scientific R&D outputs through innovations, and monitoring the innovation in learning society in suitable way. The formation of knowledge society and rising up to the global level happens when the learning organizations and institutions function at that level. In this context, the cluster theories share the idea of transfer of knowledge from and within the firm by the people (tacit knowledge) to create regional economic development. In the beginning of new millennium, the implemented technology processes and policies have been instrumental in sustaining the knowledge society as; proliferation of the innovative Internet startups. The coming augmented use of mobile phone technology and various other means of communication in context with macroeconomic impact; and indicated the economic impact through following:

a. Mobile based commerce
b. GPS based activities
c. proliferation of digital network
d. movement towards the tele-work

Till the early years of new millennium, the computers were mostly used in the e service sectors (Ayres and Williams, 2004); later the networked robots. The knowledge society began to witness changes in the convergence of computing and ICTs and the drops in bandwidth prices etc. bringing the "cloud" computing in scenario. The "Internet of Things" is another example of increased dependence in the information society. The formation, growth and development of digital society happened in phases due to the available and innovated technologies; the concepts such as "Internet domain name authority and net neutrality" are providing the live discussions. In the literature of "Technological Forecasting & Social Change", the observations emerged as the acknowledgements from OECD; considering the digital economy for global business processes and transactions to alter the conventional ways. The "digital economy" permits the possibilities to become global in nature due to decreased trade barriers and more liberal policies. During the end of last decade, various countries have become highly ICT oriented to function as stronger impacts in the contemporary knowledge-based global economy. For example, the manufacturing and design industry is dependent on the human capital and application of ICTs due to improvement in innovative product design through the learning capability.

The global industries have developed more networks during last two decades due to importance of knowledge. While discussing about Europe, Rodrigues (2002) stated about the altered European strategy relating to creating a knowledge-based economy. Such economies are functioning in highly competitive environment with augmented social factors. According to him, the challenges concentrate upon Europe-America relations as well as EU model, gaps and divide among the European regions etc. The "social and historical context" is playing supportive roles in context with "modification and more precise explanation." The EU's composing nations functioned as "living laboratories" as large information society for policy frames, and "open coordination."

LIBRARIANS IN A KNOWLEDGE SOCIETY

The shift from an industrial society to the knowledge-based economy has been discerned by many thinkers, organizations, nations and policy waves. The knowledge economy is based upon the knowledge of people within and outside the organizations. The intellectual capital assets become the basic cause of production and generation of development and wealth of all kinds. There is difference between the knowledge economy and other economies such as industrial and the agricultural economies. The role of libraries and information centers becomes crucial in the knowledge society. These are characterized by the concentrated focus on electronic resources along with the extensive use of digital channels for deliverance and dissemination of the information. In comparison with the digital environment, the knowledge society and economy expand more; as in a knowledge society, the knowledge transfer and transactions take place at individual and collective level. The areas of transaction are as following:

a. business environment,

b. social context and sphere,

c. the civic activities, and

d. the routine environmental actions.

The library professionals achieved a new height by providing information and services in the knowledge or information society. Their alignment due to the professional competencies and traditional functional competencies has been supportive with their expanded roles in the knowledge society.

TOWARDS A KNOWLEDGE SOCIETY

The developments in India have been reflective in the context of knowledge and information. Indian society is having only 1% of its population as computer literate among 64% of its people as minimum standard of literacy. The advantages of current educational measures are visible to make the population educated for the knowledgeable and competent society. The social productivity required efficient and innovative techniques as stated that "Knowledge is the key to realizing this vision of India in 2020". The human society is progressing due to the knowledge generation, exchange and transfer amongst the groups and individuals. This is essential so that formulation systematization, preservation of knowledge can be done. The revolutions in the technology and its implementation have shaped the "knowledge society". The methods of information collecting, transmission and application are changed when compared with the industrial society. The knowledge revolution and information society is the outcome of the confluence of technologies which are visible and experienced through computers, networking, Internet-based communications. There has been exponential growth of information and catalytically influenced acceleration in the knowledge society. The knowledge spread in information society has seen the changes in human development. The development which were limited by material processes have shifted towards the creative side of potential of human processes. The products created by human mind due to the values assigned are now changed in the knowledge Society as it is one kind of the learning society. The knowledge acquisition is different in knowledge society as the learning is available for entire range of population without any categorization to reach to the economic opportunities. This is possible due to various fast channels for information delivery. There are two aspects for adaptation of the challenges and opportunities:

a. The efforts to spread the Knowledge Society through the knowledge

b. Application of new strategies for knowledge revolution

The basic components of the knowledge revolution are as:

- technology,
- organization and

- information

In the information society, the entire spectrum of economic activities is becoming more knowledge-intensive. According to current scenario, the majority of industrial output is possible due to information and its application. The service sector is based on information. The information is vast source of occupations in the changing society. In the world economy, few of the significant service sectors are as following:

a. financial services
b. insurance
c. health
d. education

This shows the transition from "material to knowledge-based resources" provides new vistas for developments. The characteristics and differences between knowledge based resources and natural resources are:

- The context of conventional economic assumptions
- The factor of inherent limits of availability
- The aspects utilization and consumption
- The idea of sharing resources
- The transportability of knowledge

ROLE OF KNOWLEDGE IN DEVELOPMENT

The human process is determined by the exchange with the external environment. The development processes create awareness of opportunities and challenges involving the decision making process. The acquisition of knowledge in the human beings creates awareness of opportunities for finding solutions for the challenges met. The maturity of knowledge leads to acquisition of motivating factors and translation of knowledge into action. The adaptive response is outcome of knowledge application. Knowledge is an initial input in the development process for creating awareness of opportunities and challenges. This supports in assessing in alternatives and fining the solutions for the emerged challenges. The knowledge is helpful in planning and implementing the calculated and result-oriented initiatives. The speed and direction of development is determined by the following intangible factors:

- access to information
- acquired knowledge
- Induction of ICTs
- Levels in societal contexts

In the knowledge societies, knowledge contributes in several different ways:

- Functioning as a productive resource
- Contributing as an essential input in research and development
- Catalyzing the social transformation and economic development

Development throughout in knowledge societies depends on four knowledge processes:

- Knowledge generation through discovery
- Knowledge transfer through technology and innovation
- Knowledge dissemination through formal and informal channels
- Knowledge application through skilled action

The widespread of ICT facilities have created access to a greater range of knowledge. Even these efforts have taken place in a longer duration of time; a growing divide in the ratio of generation and dissemination of knowledge is witnessed. The quantification of knowledge gap can be done by measuring and examining a nation's progress on various aspects such as literacy, ICT application, and R&D.

RESEARCH AND DEVELOPMENT IN KNOWLEDGE SOCIETY

The rate of knowledge generation, expansion of S&T research, and permeation of global knowledge are increasing day by day. But the permeation of knowledge and capacity of a nation to adapt and harness the advances are at different level. The crude indices in the form of measurement of R&D activity are helpful to determine the knowledge gap, the knowledge generation pace should not be lagging behind the global knowledge revolution. The quantum of investment is related with research progress and determination of knowledge generation. To estimate knowledge gap, the technology application extent is measured. The informal channels and formal education system are based on media application for knowledge dissemination. The use and adaptations of mass - media is considered as "rough index" for information spread. The efficient information is essential along with infrastructure, industrial growth, technology application for building of knowledge society. The innovative initiatives are required for formulation of new models suitable for newly developed context. The current knowledge gaps in the societies indicate the underdevelopment and underutilization of resources. The education sector can upgrade and enhance in a knowledge society various facets:

- the extent of social inclusivity
- institutional and technological implementation and assessment
- quality of human and institutional resources

The current policies and trends evaluation of available resources and endeavors are directed improve the information use and application. The evaluation systems should be replaced by innovative mechanisms and accreditation processes. The demand of creating a self-sufficient information system's inclusion in each component of society is inevitable to spread the advantages in each layer and niche of information society.

REFERENCES

1. Alain, Ambrosi, Valérie, Peugeot and Daniel, Pimienta (2005). Multicultural perspectives on information societies. C & F Éditions.
2. Almudena, Moreno Mínguez and Ballesteros, Enrique Crespo. The Digital Divide in Education in the Knowledge Society. Encyclopedia of Networked and Virtual Organizations
3. Ambient Intelligence. https://www.igi-global.com/chapter/ambient-intelligence/13337
4. Arquilla, J. and Ronfeldt, D. (2001). "The advent of netwar (revisited)". In Networks and Netwars: The Future of Terror, Crime, and Militancy Edited by: Arquilla, J., Ronfeldt, D. and Rand, Santa Monica. 1–25.
5. Ayres, R.U., Williams, E. (2004). "The digital economy: Where do we stand?" Technological Forecasting and Social Change, 71 (4), pp. 315-339, 10.1016/j.techfore.2003.11.001
6. Bell, D. (1973). The coming of post-industrial society: A venture in social forecasting. New York: Basic Books.
7. Computer Communication and ICT Attitude and Anxiety Among Higher Education Students https://www.igi-global.com/chapter/computer-communication-ict-attitude-anxiety/13346
8. Cosmas L. Zavazava, Projects and Knowledge Management https://news.itu.int/#topicsscroll
9. Delanty, Gerard (2001). Challenging knowledge: the university in the knowledge society. Opèn University Press, Buckingham. ISBN 9780335205783
10. Denise, A. D. Bedford, Jennifer K. Donley, Nancy Lensenmayer, (2015). "The Role of Librarians in a Knowledge Society: Valuing Our Intellectual Capital Assets", in (ed.) Current Issues in Libraries, Information Science and Related Fields (Advances in Librarianship, Volume 39) Emerald Group Publishing Limited, pp.81 – 113.
11. Developed society based on the access to knowledge. Strategic Crowdsourcing as an Emerging Form of Global Entrepreneurship https://www.igi-global.com/chapter/strategic-crowdsourcing-as-an-emerging-form-of-global-entrepreneurship/139881
12. Diani, M. (2000). 'Social movement networks virtual and real'. Information, Communication & Society, 3(3), pp. 386–401.

13. Drucker, P. (1993). Post-capitalist society. HarperBusiness.

14. Etzkowitz, H., Webster, A., Gebhardt, C., and Cantisano Terra, B. R. (2000). The future of the university and the university of the future: Evolution of ivory tower to entrepreneurial paradigm. Research Policy, 29, 313–330.

15. Freeman, C., Perez, C. (1986). "The diffusion of technical innovations and changes in techno-economic paradigm." Science Policy Research Unit University of Sussex, Brighton.

16. Fuchs, C. (2016). "Reading Marx in the information age", Vol. 1, Routledge. http://fuchs.uti.at/wp-content/uploads/Grundrisse.pdf

17. Garrett, R. Kelly (2006). "Protest in an Information Society: a review of literature on social movements and new ICTs". Information, Communication & Society, 9:2, pp. 202-224.

18. Gates, B. (1999). Business @ the speed of Thought: Succeeding in the digital economy. Grand Central Publishing.

19. Grant, R.M. (1996). "Toward a knowledge-based theory of the firm." Strategic Management Journal, 17 (1996), pp. 109-122, 10.1002/smj.4250171110

20. Hofstadter, R. (1963). Anti-intellectualism in American life. Knopf.

21. Information, Knowledge, and Learning Society https://www.igi-global.com/chapter/information-knowledge-and-learning-society/112900

22. Kim, B., Barua, A., Whinston, A.B. (2002). "Virtual field experiments for a digital economy: A new research methodology for exploring an information economy." Decision Support Systems, 32 (2002), pp. 215-231.

23. Knowledge society definition - Library & Information Science Network http://www.lisbdnet.com/knowledge-society-definition/

24. Knowledge-Based Urban Development. https://www.igi-global.com/chapter/knowledge-based-urban-development/112448

25. Leizerov, S. (2000). "Privacy advocacy groups versus Intel: a case study of how social movements are tactically using the Internet to fight corporations". Social Science Computer Review, 18(4), pp. 461–483.

26. Magee, C.L., Devezas, T.C. (2017). "An extension of dematerialization theory: Incorporation of technical performance increases and the rebound effect." Technological Forecasting & Social

Change, 117, pp. 196-205

27. Manuel, Castells, Wallis, Annenberg and Barcelona, Gustavo Cardoso (2006). The Network Society From Knowledge to Policy, edited by Manuel Castells, Wallis Annenberg and Barcelona Gustavo Cardoso. https://www.dhi.ac.uk/san/waysofbeing/data/communication-zangana-castells-2006.pdf

28. Marginson, S. (2006). Putting 'public' back into the public universities. Thesis Eleven 84, 44–59. https://link.springer.com/article/10.1007/s10734-008-9123-7#ref-CR56

29. Marx, K. (1958). The fragment on machines. http://thenewobjectivity.com/pdf/marx.pdf

30. Masuda, Y. (1980). "The information society as post-industrial society". https://scholar.google.com/scholar_lookup?title=The%20information%20society%20as%20post-industrial%20society&publication_year=1980&author=Y.%20Masuda

31. Md. Ashikuzzaman. Types of knowledge. http://www.lisbdnet.com/types-of-knowledge/

32. Modeling Knowledge Society. https://www.igi-global.com/chapter/modeling-knowledge-society/112417

33. Naidoo, R., and Jamieson, I. (2005). Knowledge in the marketplace: The global commodification of teaching, learning in higher education. In P. Ninnes & M. Hellstén (Eds.), Internationalizing higher education: Critical explorations of pedagogy and policy (pp. 37–52). Dordrecht: Springer. https://link.springer.com/article/10.1007/s10734-008-9123-7#ref-CR50

34. Nelson, R. (1991). National innovation systems. Oxford: Oxford University Press.

35. OECD (2016). "New markets and new jobs. Background report for the OECD ministerial meeting on the digital economy", 21–23 June 2016, Cancún, Mexico

36. Parry, M. (2016). "Evolving business models to support the growth of technology-based start-up firms". World Technopolis Review, 5 (2), December

37. Phillips, F. (2004). "Trading Down: The intellectual poverty of the new FTAs." Technological Forecasting & Social Change (2004), pp. 71-78

38. Phillips, Fred, Yu, Ching-Ying, Tahir Hameed, Mahmoud Abdullah El, Akhdary (2017). "The knowledge society's origins and current trajectory." International Journal of Innovation Studies, Volume 1, Issue 3, pp. 175-191 https://doi.org/10.1016/j.ijis.2017.08.001

39. Planning Commission. 08-Feb-2014. http://planningcommission.gov.in

40. Reidenberg, JR (1997). Lex informatica: The formulation of information policy rules through technology. Tex. L. Rev., 1997 - HeinOnline. https://heinonline.org/hol-cgi-bin/get_pdf.cgi?handle=hein.journals/tlr76&section=24

41. Rodrigues, M.J (2002). "The new knowledge economy in Europe: A strategy for international competitiveness and social cohesion." UK: Edward Elgar.

42. Sally Burch. The Information Society / the Knowledge Society. https://vecam.org/archives/spip6232.html?page=auteur&id_auteur=220&lang=en&nemo=edm

43. Schumpeter, J.A. (1943). Capitalism, socialism & democracy. London: Routledge.

44. Tett, G. (2016). "The productivity Imperative: Advice for the president-elect." Foreign Policy (2016), pp. 98-99. December

45. The Information and Communication Technology (ICT) Competence of the Young. https://www.igi-global.com/chapter/information-communication-technology-ict-competence/35909

46. Udland, M. (2017). United Airlines loses $950 million in market value as shares tumble

47. UNESCO (2005). https://link.springer.com/article/10.1007/s10734-008-9123-7#ref-CR79

48. Use of E-Collaboration Technologies Among Students of Management https://www.igi-global.com/chapter/use-collaboration-technologies-among-students/12496

49. Välimaa, J., Hoffman, D. Knowledge society discourse and higher education. High Educ 56, 265–285 (2008). https://doi.org/10.1007/s10734-008-9123-7

50. "What Is An Information Society Media Essay." November 2018. Web. 26 April 2019. Source: Bureau of Labor Statistics, cited by Bell (1980: 521)

51. www.planningcommission.gov.in

52. www.newtimes.co.rw

Chapter Two

Library and Information Services in the Digital Age

SUMMARY : Library and information services have witnessed major developments, changes and improvements. The chapter aims to frame related concepts with a perspective of digital technologies application in libraries.

- Introduction
- The Perspectives from IFLA
- Information Services through WWW
- Various policies in the libraries:
- Libraries Use
- Collection Development
- Digital Libraries Policies
- Library Departments
- Reference and Information Service
- Whom the libraries serve!
- Service Limitations
- Licensing, Legal information and Commercial Products
- Provision of Services
- Professional Ethics and Information Services
- Services & Information for Students
- Various subject and research related Services
- Various Services and Tools
- Information Specialists
- Designing Innovative Information Services for Libraries
- Data Curation

INTRODUCTION

The advent of information and communication technologies has altered the mechanisms in providing routine functions and information services in the libraries across the globe. The digital technologies, media, applications and infrastructure are few of the major factors responsible for the dramatic changes and transformation inside the libraries. The process to organize information sources, facilitating access to information and changing users' behavior has created platforms for advances and adjustments in the library and information services scenario. The changing landscape of information services is the outcome of popularity of digital platforms, resources and methods for the users. The current visuals from the libraries reflect the combination of conventional as well as modern digital approaches in the entire range of services and phenomena.

The digital age has compelled the librarians to design the ambience and services in a manner that enhances the simplicity in a very intricate environment. The usual functions and services related with borrowing books, reference needs, free access to digital devices and internet, bringing own devices in libraries, framing and creating awareness of library policies, nurturing the collaborative nature, etc. have changed a lot. Moreover, a notable share of newly designed and emerged services is as following:

- Online research services
- Access to digital technology
- GPS-navigation apps support inside library
- Apps-based access to library materials
- Lending machines or kiosks
- Customized books/audio files/video programs
- Training programs
- Coordinating more closely with the communities

- Offering literacy programs
- Digital spaces and makers' spaces

Information is required for the users which include various guidelines, the standardized rules, their requirements, the best practices for information use, and some more information that help users to utilize the library services. In general, following routine facilities and services are available:

Perspectives from IFLA

The International Federation of Library Associations (IFLA) has always been active to shape the libraries and services. According to "The IFLA Internet Manifesto" the library and information services and "unhindered access to information" is related with the principles:

- The first, "Intellectual freedom is the right of every individual both to hold and express opinions and to seek and receive information; it is the basis of democracy; and it is at the core of library service".
- The second, "Freedom of access to information, regardless of medium and frontiers, is a central responsibility of the library and information profession".
- And leading to, "Barriers to the flow of information should be removed, especially those that promote in equality, poverty, and despair".

The emphasis on "Freedom of Access to Information, the Internet and Libraries and Information Services" has been given through various guidelines. It says that the role of information services as "vibrant institutions" is to connect human resources with "global information resources". This is applicable in the shape of digital libraries to nurture users' ideas.

It says that, "Libraries and information services make available the richness of human expression and cultural diversity in all media". The role of information services can be seen as "gateways to the Internet" due to offering the speedy information, relevant guidance, and academic assistance.

The idea of IFLA in the context of "Principles of Freedom of Access to Information via the Internet" is discernible in the context of access to resources and "the United Nations Universal Declaration of Human Rights and especially Article 19: Everyone has the right to freedom of opinion and expression; this right includes freedom to hold opinions without interference and to seek, receive and impart information and ideas through any media and regardless of frontiers." The responsibility of libraries while designing and delivering the information services in digital scenario is includes maintenance of privacy of users and recognizing the need to users' access and patterns of information behavior to remain confidential. To promote access to quality information, libraries are assisting the users with necessary skills, platforms and authentic information. The role of IFLA is not limited to providing guidelines or technical measures for enhanced library and information services, yet encouragement to governments "to support the unhindered flow of Internet accessible information via libraries and information services and to oppose any attempts to censor or inhibit access. IFLA urges the library community and decision makers at national and local levels to develop strategies, policies, and plans that implement the principles expressed in this Manifesto."

INFORMATION SERVICES THROUGH WWW

The role of World Wide Web (WWW) has been pervasive, including the designing of library services. The designing of library website and providing library and information services through the information and links displayed on the website became a common interface among libraries, worldwide. According to (Madhusudhan, 2012), the library services which are web-based in nature are provided through the platform of Internet and integrated library management system as gateway. Another aspect of such designing and maintain of services is that the information services would be provided by digital means, mechanisms. In this context, various forms and ways are also provided to users to reach to library resources and establish the interaction continuously 24 hours (Sangale, 2015), elaborating following the reasons as well as advantages:

- Matching users' needs with accessible information sources,
- Delivering the information sources in a timely and appropriate manner,
- Provision of high quality, accurate and appropriate information
- Promoting user awareness and research skills by training in fast implementation of digital technologies and tools.

Various routine functions and services are described as following:

Borrowing

Borrowing resources : Most of the collections and documents are considered as materials for borrowing unless noted and described as "not-for-issue" or "in-house use only" or placed on reservations. These materials may be checked out at service desks.

Borrowing Media : With the rules related with special loan periods, and renewal procedures, the library catalogues provide information of media such as "Music Audio/Video Items". Such materials can be borrowed unless there are other conditions or have been kept on reservations.

Need of library or institutional ID Cards : A valid ID card is required so that the users can check out materials using the issued library membership card. The visiting users also need to register in some ways as proscribed by the libraries to avail the Library Services.

Interlibrary Loan : The University libraries are determined to provide information access. The retrieval of items which are unavailable in library is done through the various other supplementary services, such as the interlibrary loan (ILL) and document delivery. For such services and facilities, certain time period and charges may be applicable.

Various Policies in the Libraries

Recall Policy : Information about recall policies for regular circulating items.

Returning Items : This kind of policy provide awareness returning the information material users have checked out.

Fines and Fees : Information about fine, ways of assessment and submitting in the libraries.

Damaged Item Charges : Various libraries have provisions for fines and fees related with damaged items.

Lost Item Charges : In general the lost item charges information include the knowledge about fines and fees related to lost items.

Overdue Items : This policy relates to "overdue items and fines rates" for various documents and materials.

Borrowing Reserves & Laptops : Rules and regulation for borrowing the laptops and reserves items. The users are guided for correct use and related procedure, such as time, borrowing conditions, usage rules, etc.

Media and Music Library Reserve Policy : This policy is helpful to understand the availability of Media Library items, to view in the library. This policy also encompasses the music items such as books, scores, and recordings, etc. with the perspective of their formats.

Libraries Use

Disability Accommodation : The Disability Accommodation Policy is related with the facilities provided to such kind of users with the flexibility in certain operations for them.

Library Use : Very basic yet significant policy includes information about library premises use, identification of authentic users, including other aspects such as animals, bicycles, noise, orientation, and reservations.

Special Collections Policies : The resource materials in collections are meant for research purposes according to the conditions and permissions allowed by the respective libraries.

Library Locker Service Policy and Procedures : Various rules about allocation, use and maintenance of library locker service policies and procedures are provided.

Collection Development

(a) Policy for Collection and Resource Development: This policy is concerned with the acquisition, disposition of reading materials. This policy supports the demands and development in the research and academic needs of students and faculty. This policy is framed and updated according to missions of the institution and the Library.

(b) Policy for Research Data : This policy relates to acquisition of research data resources required for inclusion in libraries' collections.

(c) Open Access resources and Digital collections Policies : The University libraries are providing the open access, as stated in the "IFLA Statement on Open Access to Scholarly Literature and Research Documentation". The digital resources are provided by the university libraries have included open access and born-digital products. These resources are supporting elements for the educational and research-related goals of the university.

(d) Collection Development Policy for Digital

Collections : The policy for digital collections is helpful in understanding various issues and aspects for building collections in digital materials across the subjects, distributed among faculties. The comparisons with print collections are made and rules for future-oriented research purposes are prepared.

(e) Disposition of Library Materials and Weeding Out Policy : This policy provides guidelines for the disposition of library materials within the general collection and weeding out the materials from the library collection.

(f) Government Documents Policy : This policy is related with the collection development of government documents, their acquisition, various copyright aspects, the issues related with reproduction and permissions, and appraisal, etc. This collection governs the legal materials, and maps.

(g) Media Collection Policy : To deal with non-conventional formats in the library, this policy addresses the various media and music related material collection development related aspects of the university libraries.

(h) Gift and Donations to Library Policy : This policy governs receiving gifts of books, various media documents and other resources for University students and faculty. These policies provide guidelines about their pertinence, coverage, relevance and physical status.

For example, "Applying Copyright Section 108(c) to the UNT Media Library Collection" is as following:

"The following are the UNT Media Library's policies and procedures for creating preservation copies of audiovisual materials from the UNT Libraries collections. These preservation copies will become part of the library collection and are not to be made for the purpose of supplying a patron with a personal copy of an item". These policies and procedures are based on "the Copyright Section 108(c) with guidance" from the 2012 report "Video At Risk: Strategies for Preserving Commercial Video Collections in Libraries" produced by the NYU Libraries".

These policies include information about the "Government Documents", their copyright aspects. These policies help in understanding the reproduction rules for such documents. The copyright and fair use policies are concerned with government documents and related digital collections. In this context, the media related copyright regulations are very much supporting the doubts and queries of using the Media Library. These policies include information about the various usage conditions, and exemptions for media materials, along with the policies related with the awareness of fair use guidelines.

Photocopy Policy : The policy related with photocopying of documents are related with general rules, "Coin-Operated Copying Machines", Interlibrary Loan services copying, unauthorized copying of content, reproduction and photocopy policy and library reservations, usage, etc.

Digital Libraries Policies

(a) Library Data Retention : The libraries make organizationally produced data broadly available in the respective Data Repository with the possible datasets according to "Creative Commons Public Domain Dedication (CC0) license."

(b) Open Source Software Policy : This policy is related to usage, contributing steps and permissions, creating and releasing of Open Source Software in the academic organizations in context with open source movement.

(c) Digital Preservation Policy : Very significant in the digital scenario, related with "preservation of digital collections" and various resources across the several platforms.

(d) Spaces : The guidelines related with use of "Study Spaces", and student room reservations for Faculty/Staff for events, training programs, etc.

LIBRARY DEPARTMENTS

There are various departments in a library, depending upon type and size of library. These are as follows:

Collection Management : The collection management section includes various sub-section and activities. These can be categorized as the Accessions Department, ISBN/ISSN provisions, Journals/periodical section etc. Few libraries have technical processing and Bibliographic Data Management Department

The Legal Deposit and Contribution department is also a significant component of collection management department which takes care of contribution in deposition and data submission. Framing of Policies is also required; subject to change in collection, organizational aims, and acquisition procedures, etc.

Bibliographic Data Management Department : This specific section in a library functions with different planning and responsibilities. The section staff analyzes the contents of books and journals, the supplemented DVDs, etc. Such documents are given the appropriate descriptions for understanding, providing the subject terms along with class numbers for records and resources. The Library catalogue are created and maintained. This process involves the addition and updating of MARC bibliographic records. The holdings information is also paid attention related to the library's collections. The quality of the data is maintained by authority control in the Library catalogue, this is followed by building user reference structures. Original bibliographical records are created so that the same can be contributed in bigger deposit and some Shared Cataloguing Programme. The examples of such submission and contributions are the Name Authority

Cooperative Program (NACO) and Subject Authority Cooperative Program (SACO). The section responsibilities completes by providing user education in order to create awareness of the resources as well as proper usage.

Digital Collections : Include the highlights of Digital Collections and Imaging Services, and other supports to students.

Guide to the Catalogues : The guides to catalogue helps in understanding and access the collection through "Named Collections", "Printed Catalogue Online" and reaching to the subject strength.

For example, the Scientific Library Services and Information Systems (LIS) related with German Research Foundation (German Research Foundation) have been effective. Various services and facilities are available for users in the forms as following:

- Forms and Guidelines Platforms and links to Open Access
- Information and provisions for National and international cooperation
- Interface and Information portal for research infrastructures
- Publications
- Committee on Scientific Library Services and Information Systems

Another component of Scientific Library Services and Information Systems programme include the funding, at libraries, archives etc. Such examples relate to research information systems at broader level. Various library services in routine are as following:

- Bibliographic Services
- Circulation
- Information and training

Services

- Borrow / Access / Request
- Print / Scan / Copy
- Research Assistance
- Scholarly Communication
- Copyright Guidelines
- Course Reserves
- Media Services

Library Classes

- Library Information Systems & Digital Applications
- Suggestions & comments

The services for People with Disabilities are also included in library planning. Various training sessions are also part of library services which include the training with variation at physical locations of library. The trainings can be about the learning software, and search strategies with the help of training videos. The trainings complete with the feedbacks, suggestions and comments. The information is provided about the services such as bibliographic services, general services etc. so that the users are aware of various steps, processes, rules etc. One example of such provisions is Nelson Mandela University library South Africa. In the similar ways, for example, Rutgers university library has services designed for the users. Services are designed for the various types of users. More or less, the users are categorized as:

- Students
- Faculty
- Researchers
- Visitors
- Alumni
- Persons with Disabilities

- International Students
- Off-Campus Users

PLACES & SPACES

To provide library services, different spaces in library are designated in libraries:

- Booking "Group Study Rooms" for collective academic efforts
- Maintaining "Quiet Spaces" in the busy libraries
- "Building Accessibility" for various kinds of users
- Providing "Digital Humanities Lab"

Various places may be identified as various libraries and centers; special subject libraries, few of them are:

- Reference and circulation desks
- Digital Maps and Directions

REFERENCE AND INFORMATION SERVICE

Information Service can be understood as general information that can be provided by library staff with the provisions such as in person service, or by telephone, and email etc. In this context, "Ask a Librarian" service comes into picture while providing information service by email. The other means in the library are also significant for providing information; the examples are: signage, printed/online locating aids, printed/digital guides. There are other intricate methods for reaching to real information, which include the Library Catalog, online indexes, reference tools, etc. The inclusivity of information services reflects the routine information requirements of users, which may be:

- Library collections/holdings
- Library Bibliographic Data
- Library policies
- Library timings/locations/directions

- Ready reference sources

Reference Service : Reference service is provided by all kinds of libraries, usually. There are degrees associated with the service experience of the users; such as in-depth reference service; and other levels of service as short information requirement of users. The place of reference service may differ according to the needs of users and provisions in libraries. These places may be designated as reference desk, or close consultations with reference specialists, may be provided by telephone, email. The alternate provisions are "Ask a Librarian", instant messaging/ text messaging, and any other kind of information delivery options. The development of location or finding aids and research guides is supporting for users. This includes automated reference systems and user interfaces for end-user searching in a library. In academic libraries, the reference service has instructional characteristics to foster the user's information demands.

The "instruction" like reference service helps in developing the tools of research (printed as well as digital), and assessing the quality of retrieved information. The inclusion of use of bibliographic sources; development of research strategies, finding the complex data, and finally the retrieval of data is included in reference services. The users with special needs are also served through reference assistance and provided the reference services by the following means:

- providing factual answers
- retrieving information
- packaging bibliographic and statistical data
- use of electronic resources

WHOM THE LIBRARIES SERVE!

Usually the patrons of library are served, including:

a. faculty members
b. faculty emeritus,

c. research scholars and students,

d. organizational staff, and

e. visitors

There are various ways though which the libraries are information and reference services are provided as following:

a. on-site services:

- by telephone, and correspondence,
- through online services

The online reference services include the following:

a. Ask a Librarian (email):

- Ask a Librarian Live (Instant Messaging),
- Text messaging, etc.

Reference service to outside users is provided as a professional courtesy. These users include independent researchers, post graduate students, senior fellows etc.

Service Limitations

(a) Electronic Service : Such services are provided through email or text messages when queries are received through options of "Ask a Librarian", to the user community. The users are provided information about the library collections, various information resources, and specific services.

(b) Telephone Service : Information and reference assistance is given by telephone which is usually short or brief in nature and content. For the deep level and specific information the users are advised to visit the subject specialist. Sometimes the instant responses are not feasible then the library staff calls back with the required information.

Licensing, Legal Information and Commercial Products

Sometimes, the licensing agreements restrict the usage

and services related to information products, the libraries refer the users to other information centers and sources. Also, the libraries do not recommend the commercial products or related services. The libraries do not support users by providing any legal or medical assistance. Only the reference services and sources are provided related to law or medical subject queries.

PROVISION OF SERVICES

Libraries take care of various aspects while providing services, as following:

(a) Code of Ethics : The information transactions between library staff and users are governed by code of ethics; sometimes formally written or framed and otherwise informally followed.

(b) Equity of Service and Professional Conduct : The equity of service means that provisions of information service will be made without discrimination to all users. No discrimination can be made on the basis of race, gender, disability, ethnicity, language or any other reason. The information services will be provided with professional courtesy, confidentiality, and users' needs.

(c) Instruction and Referral : Sometimes, the answer to the user's queries takes shape of "instruction" instead of routine information. In case of unavailability of information source, the user may be instructed to other institutions.

Library Staff Competencies : The reference service is provided with the adherence to the proficiency. The knowledge included at the level of staff includes following:

- Library collection and reference resources available in the library
- Library Catalog and networked electronic resources
- Local services and expertise available in the library
- Resources available in the areas of expertise at Regional

and national

- Various policies of library and organization
- Major bibliographic networks at Libraries' website

Development and Training: The library staff should be able to update and maintain skills and implement the library and information services in changing digital environment. The provisions of in-service training, encouragement for professional development are required for improved information services, to keep update of various technologies and advances, learning skills with the training by in-house and as well as external resource persons.

PROFESSIONAL ETHICS AND INFORMATION SERVICES

The libraries provide information services through organization and dissemination. Provisions of intellectual needs and access to information depend upon the free flow of information towards users. The libraries are responsible to ensure the information services for future generations.

(a) Equitable policy and access : The libraries provide information services based on efficient organization of resources, service policies related to equitable service, and access.

(b) Principle of intellectual freedom : Library staff should provide unbiased information and unrestricted access to library resources.

(c) Right to privacy : The provisions of information services should ensure the user's right to privacy. The aspects related with confidentiality of users and information sought etc.

(d) Copyright and user-information balance : Information services should be designed in such a way that users should be trained about the intellectual property rights, concept of fair use, digital rights managements etc.

(e) Human resource management : The library staff should be placed in appropriate positions to impart duties. The coordination among staff is essential to build a good team. Their professional development should also be given opportunities. To grow in profession and in organization are both required facets to have job satisfaction in library.

(f) The adherence to professional ethics : In the context of library staff, it is very significant to nurture a service-oriented library. To understand the difference between personal development and professional duties helps in fair exercise of duties.

(g) Excellence in information services : The library staff should strive for excellence in the library and information services. This excellence can be achieved by implementing and upgrading the skills and knowledge. The motivation and encouragement for the professional development foster the innovation and strength of library and services.

SERVICES & INFORMATION FOR STUDENTS

For the library usage : Few areas are specific according to needs of users, services designed and future requirements. The examples are as following:

Quiet Areas and spaces : The users require specific spaces and areas

Group Study Rooms : With a need to work on a group project or meet with the study group, users can reserve a group study room.

Wi-fi Access in the Libraries : Instructions and guidelines are provided for connecting to wi-fi internet connectivity for the students. Most of the academic organizations provide wi-fi facility in their campus for online access to digital resources.

Computer systems and other devices in the Libraries : The users are provided various computer systems and other facilities to use digital devices.

Peripheral facilities : The libraries provide facilities for printing, scanning and copying the documents/ information materials. These kinds of supports are additional services for the users, including poster printing and 3D printing.

Services for International Students : Few information counters and desks are designated for helping international scholars.

Facilities of Course Reserves : Students are supported by serving the information materials which are usually placed on reserve for their course.

Subject and Research Related Services

Provision and training of Citation Management Tools : The reference and citation management software are very much significant. Scholars are using such tools to organize, and apply the references in the research works.

Subject and Research Guides : The subject guides as well as research guides are specific sources of information to help the researchers. These sources help in finding the information related to topic.

Library Services and Tools

Research Assistance : The research assistance helps in getting in touch with the subject devoted librarian/ staff, shows the light on research support.

Scholarly Communication : The scholarly communication services help in finding information about institutional Open Access Policy, NIH compliance, digital humanities, and more. Such services include research data management also.

Media Services : The media services provide the available media, audio-visual facilities, facilitating the media on reserve for users, and streaming media.

Various Tools

BrowZine : It is a platform to discover, and monitor various journals.

EndNote : This is a citation management tool. It is used by researchers to collect and organize huge number of references which are collected from online and other sources.

RefWorks : It is a popular tool for bibliography management. It is a web-based bibliography as well as database manager.

Library Toolbar: It is an extension for Firefox or Chrome to connect with the respective library resources while user is browsing the web.

The example of Trinity College Dublin, the University of Dublin (https://www.tcd.ie/) has various Information Services (Fee-Based Account) which have certain features:

- Searching of Internet and other online information resources in all subject areas
- Searching of reference books, journals etc.
- Loan of books
- Use of the Library by a member of company staff
- Photocopies of relevant documents subject to the provisions of the Copyright Act

SPECIAL LIBRARY SERVICES

- Alumni Services
- Borrowing Policies
- Copyright Support
- Computing at the Libraries
- Interlibrary Loan
- Information Literacy
- ORCID iD
- Proxy Borrowing

- Spatial Literacy & GIS

DEPARTMENTS & SERVICES

- Collections
- Employment
- GIS and Spatial Literacy
- Information Literacy
- Interlibrary Loan
- Digital Solutions
- Staff Resources
- Technical Services

SERVICES IN ROUTINE

Library services to support users' needs are as following:

a. Borrowing
b. Printing
c. Book a study room
d. Library Search (Primo)
e. IT Services
f. Box of Broadcasts (BoB)
g. Equipment loans

For example, "BoB is an on demand TV and radio service" for education. University of Plymouth staff and students can record programmes from over "65 free-to-air channels, and search the archive of over 2 million broadcasts. Users do not need a TV license to access content" on BoB.

Additional services

- Distance, Placement and Part-time Students
- Disability Support
- Library Anxiety

INFORMATION SPECIALISTS

The "information specialist" supports and shows how to manage, access and use the information resources. The Library Subject Guide (for example at http://plymouth.libguides.com) is a collection of relevant resources plus help and support. It is observed that information specialists tend to function in collaboration with various other stakeholders such as faculties, instructors, authorities and programme teams in order to deliver learning oriented information services. Each information specialist need for establishing interactions and common platforms to work closely related with the concerned subject areas. This kind of approach supports in applying the expertise in wider academic scenario. The areas for interaction include selection, organization and access to information material with the help of tools, information literacy skills, etc. To add further, the example of IIITMK library has included facilities and services, such as:

- Circulation Service / Document Lending Service
- Collection Development with Participatory Role by Users
- WEBOPAC
- e-Access Stations
- Information Support Service for Assignments, Academic Projects, Externally Funded Projects & Research Programs
- Inter-Institutional Resource Sharing
- Photocopying, Printing & Document Scanning
- Reference & Referral Services
- Support Service for Academic Internship Programs
- User Education for effective e-Resource Database Searches
- Support Service for Scholarly Publishing & IPR Issues

DESIGNING INNOVATIVE INFORMATION SERVICES FOR LIBRARIES

The designing of innovative information services in libraries is not a task of short-term planning. It is outcome of observations from the past as well as the potential future projections of services. According to Wójcik (2019), entire process for innovation and adoption in information services is comprised of five main steps:

Diagnosis of the current state : The first stage dwells upon assessment of current level and quality of library services. The process for understanding research of users' needs to find out mechanism to step further. Understanding and defining the priorities is crucial to design the path of alterations to determine the levels of innovation and users' satisfaction.

Designing the direction of changes and choice innovation : The planning and decision related with the type of innovation to be introduced, and discovery of users' need by providing pragmatic solution and new approaches to fit in the contemporary environments can be several strategies.

Choosing sources of innovation : The need to identify an area to surface and implement the technological advances including the digital aspects, economic relations, service designing etc. is very significant. The choices may include more than one type of innovation and more than one option to proceed and progress.

Determining the structure of innovation : The measurements and determination of the structure of the innovation take place by observing the idea, direction of strategic changes and the estimated benefits for the library and users.

Designing desired user behavior : To understand the requirement of designing a custom-based service on the basis of users' experiences, it requires the close watch on the users' community. The users' behaviors, patterns and experiences are taken into consideration for eliminating the past decisions. To familiarize with the change related with designed service is the necessary action of library at this level.

The libraries discern the possibility of combining different technologies to serve the users. The transformation of static information interactive information through multimedia application is one example to introduce innovation in the information services. Various other examples include supplementing "analog (paper) information boards" with QR codes, along with elements such as "Internet of Things", 3D personalized map of access, user navigation and, options of "augmented reality". Academic libraries can explore many instances of innovation.

Data Curation

Data curation is an active service being provided at a big number of libraries. A designated team curates and manages the data which is produced by the respective organization's researchers. The facilities related with "Data Curation" service have been helpful in data management training and providing the consultation. The libraries provide high-powered systems which are helpful in various types of analysis such as statistical, spatial, and qualitative data analysis. The availability of professional staff functions as catalyst in using the tools and datasets. Various training programs and workshops provide opportunities to learn new digital scholarship methods.

Digital Scholarship and Scholarly Communication Program

Scholarly communication is an evolved system channelizing the research relating output and publications including curation, evaluation and dissemination. The libraries are committed to collaborate with technologies to seize the opportunities and bring the transformation in the scholarly communication. The unsustainable service models have been replaced by innovating strategies. The information services are being designed in a rapidly changing and expanding ICT influenced scenario. The new alternatives are being created for information services along with resources and tools are being provided to assist the users.

The scholar oriented environment in academic libraries is possible due to creation of scholarly communication program. The methods applied are facilitating outreach, exercising advocacy, and scholarly support. Such practices help in developing economically sustainable system. This innovative service functions as an instrument to improve the access to scholarship. Further enhancements are foreseen with the management of intellectual property and publication agreements, open access through attending workshops and consultation; and exercising users' rights under the institutional Open Access Policy. Consultations and presentations are available for users on demand in various libraries. Libraries arrange and provide a wide range of digital scholarship services. These services include online scholarly publishing, creation of datasets and navigation through the large amount of published data. The research scholars are supported by facilitating information spread across the disciplines.

Collections & Services

Library staff support in data usage and services by consultation and instructional services. The scholars are facilitated data access with the help of various programs such as "Qualtrics" and "Esri's suite of GIS software". Research scholars are supported in various areas, for example, interdisciplinary humanities. The use of analytical methodologies is becoming an integral component of research scenario. These techniques and methodologies include the creation and analysis of complex datasets, followed by visualization.

Software and Data Carpentry

This kind of new services includes various components such as studying and getting trained about "Bash", Pythos, etc. the Software Carpentry helps the scholars by enriching them in computing skills.

Quantitative Data

Various steps are required to help the researchers in dealing with the sources of quantitative and numeric data. These sources are found in many forms such as public databases, various subscribed sources. Few other examples include the limited access tools, also. Libraries provide consultation facilities for the specific sources, products and tools which are as following:

- Government data sources (including Census data)
- Datastream
- Twitter Public API using twarc
- Crimson Hexagon
- NCapture

REFERENCES

1. Borrowing. https://www.plymouth.ac.uk/student-life/your-studies/library/borrowing-from-the-library
2. Citation Management Tools https://www.libraries.rutgers.edu/researchers/citation_management_tools
3. COllaboratory. collaboratory@library.ucsb.edu
4. Collection Development Policy for the UNT Libraries' Digital Collections https://library.unt.edu/policies/collection-development-digital-collections/
5. Data Curation. https://www.library.ucsb.edu/data-curation
6. Digital Collections Highlights. https://www.tcd.ie/library/dris/projects.php
7. IIITMK library services. https://www.iiitmk.ac.in/
8. Information Literacy. https://www.smu.edu/libraries/services/information-literacy

9. International Federation of Library Associations and Institutions (IFLA). https://www.ifla.org/files/assets/wsis/Documents/wsis-lugano.pdf

10. Library Departments. https://www.tcd.ie/library/departments/

11. Madhusudhan, M., and Nagabushnam, V. (2012). "Use of web based library services in select university libraries in India: A study." International Journal of Library and Information Studies, 2 (1). Retrieved from http://ijlis.org/img/2012_2_issue_1/1_20.pdf.

12. Name Authority Cooperative Program (NACO). http://www.loc.gov/catdir/pcc/naco/

13. Qualtrics. https://www.library.ucsb.edu/qualtrics

14. Research Assistance. https://www.libraries.rutgers.edu/services_research_assistance

15. Rutgers university library services. https://www.libraries.rutgers.edu/about

16. Sangale, D.B. (2015). "ICT application and web based services in Library and Information Science". ASM's International E-Journal on ongoing research in Management and IT, 9-14

17. Scientific Library Services and Information Systems (LIS) (Research Infrastructure). DFG (German Research Foundation). https://www.dfg.de/en/research_funding/programmes/infrastructure/index.htmlLibrary Collections

18. Software and Data Carpentry https://www.library.ucsb.edu/software-carpentry

19. Subject Authority Cooperative Program (SACO). http://www.loc.gov/catdir/pcc/saco/

20. Trinity College Dublin, The University of Dublin. https://www.tcd.ie/

21. Wójcik, M. (2019). "How to design innovative information services at the library?", Library Hi Tech, 37(2), pp. 138-154. https://doi.org/10.1108/LHT-07-2018-0094

22. Welch, A.N. and Wyatt-Baxter, K. (2018). "Beyond metrics: connecting academic library Makerspace assessment practices with organizational values", Library Hi Tech, 36(2), pp. 306-318, available at: https://doi.org/10.1108/LHT-08-2017-0181

Chapter Three

Digital Libraries in Current Scenario

SUMMARY : The chapter has tried to encapsulate various components and approaches associated with the digital libraries in contemporary times with the following framework:

- Introduction
- Defining the Digital Library
- Background and Contemporary Times
- Understanding the Digital Library since the Past
- Characteristics of Digital Libraries
- Various Issues Related With Digital Libraries
- Digital Library and Community Perspective
- Challenges in creating Digital Libraries
- Digital Libraries and VLEs Integration
- Approaches to Digital Library Services
- Personal Digital Archiving Projects
- Types of Digital Libraries
- Digital Library Technical Issues
- Data Curation Issues and Big Data
- Data Standards
- Assessing the Impact of Digital Libraries
- Various approaches to searching in digital libraries
- Information Architecture for Digital Libraries
- Web-Scale Discovery Services
- Platforms for Digital Collections

INTRODUCTION

The digital libraries have faced many initiatives and revolutions due to changed behavior and needs of educational, scientific and other types of institutions. The example of transformations of "preprint services" is visible in "high energy physics". The focus on the growth and development of digital library collections to provide real time and archival data has been transitioned due to types of education. The rich array of innovative services is being created to enhance the learning practices and library services. The concept of digital library has gone beyond facilitating the information access. The inclusion of various services in digital scenario shows:

a. services for creating digital resources

b. supporting personalized content delivery

c. communication and collaboration services

The diverse approaches for digital library initiatives depend upon embracing compositions of technologies. There are many factors for the surprised change in selection and usage of digital libraries:

a. Large-scale social shaping processes

b. Upsurge in application of information technologies

c. Tradition and practices in various discipline

DEFINING THE DIGITAL LIBRARY

Digital Library Federation offered the following definition in 1998:

"Digital libraries are organizations that provide the resources, including the specialized staff, to select, structure, offer intellectual access to, interpret, distribute, preserve the integrity of, and ensure the persistence over time of collections of digital works so that they are readily and economically available for use by a defined community or set of communities" (DLF, 1998).

The digital library can be considered as electronic extension of functions. McLean and Lynch (2004) consider digital libraries as one of the components of the broader and so called "information environment" which also includes "records management, publishing, and scientific and scholarly data management". Sharifabadi (2006) presents what could be regarded as a visionary approach, by explaining that "in the e-learning environment, digital libraries are considered as a federation of library services and collections that function together to create a digital learning community" The various definitions explore numerous facets and aspects of digital libraries. These are from different authors, developers and experiences:

Digital Libraries, according to William Arms: "An informal definition of a digital library is a managed collection of information, with associated services, where the information is stored in digital formats and accessible over a network. A crucial part of this definition is that the information is managed. A stream of data sent to earth from a satellite is not a library. The same data, when organized systematically, becomes a digital library collection. Most people would not consider a database containing financial records of one company to be a digital library, but would accept a collection of such information from many companies as part of a library. Digital libraries contain diverse information for use by many different users. Digital libraries range in size from tiny to huge. They can use any type of computing equipment and any suitable software. The unifying theme is that information is organized on computers and available over a network, with procedures to select the material in the collections, to organize it, to make it available to users, and to archive it."

Berkeley Digital Library SunSITE explains: There are many definitions of a "digital library." Terms "electronic library" and "virtual library" are used for same purpose, in the context of technology, linking resources and information services to the users.

According to Digital Library Production Guide of the Kentuckiana Digital Library: It is "an organized collection of selected digital resources created to support scholarship, research and teaching. Through the use of appropriate technological standards, a Digital Library is created to facilitate permanent access to and resource discovery of selected digital resources".

The Project DL site explains as "Providing a definition of the term digital library is difficult; even a recently published dictionary may not give a good one-sentence definition. In part, this confusion comes from the fact that digital library can mean differently in different contexts, depending on the perception of the concept. For example, someone with a background in computer science may view a digital library as networked or distributed information system, while a librarian may define a digital library as a digital counterpart of the physical library. Actually, a digital library may encompass either of these concepts."

Few more definitions and understanding about the digital libraries:

According to the Digital Library Federation, "Digital libraries are organizations that provide the resources, including the specialized staff, to select, structure, offer intellectual access to, interpret, distribute, preserve the integrity of, and ensure the persistence over time of collections of digital works so that they are readily and economically available for use by a defined community or set of communities" (Digital Library Federation). In other words, "a library that maintains all, or a substantial part, of its collection in computer-accessible form as an alternative, supplement, or complement to the conventional printed and microfilm materials that currently dominate library collections. Used in this context, the term collection denotes the documents that a library acquires or maintains". In the contexts of digital and technological aspects, "Digital libraries are a set of electronic resources and associated technical capabilities for creating, searching, and using information. In this sense they are an extension of information storage and retrieval systems that manipulate digital data in any medium (text, images, sounds; static or dynamic images) and exist in distributed networks". From "Outline and Preliminary Evaluation of the Classical Digital Library Model", the working definition of digital library used by the CDLM is as follows: "A digital library is a collection of collections of electronic knowledge resources developed and maintained in order to meet the totality of information needs for a given user population."

The digital libraries are found within the traditional library types, such as: academic libraries, public libraries, school libraries, special libraries, and digital repositories, too.

Academic Digital Libraries

The academic digital libraries are the providers of digital information resources and services in the areas being taught and serves, as subjects and interdisciplinary research. The objectives are to support research, scholarly learning, along with the "knowledge-creation practices". Digital libraries reduce the interaction costs, support collaboration, and facilitate the shared research infrastructure. In the words of Dempsey (2015), "as more of the research and learning life cycle is carried out in a digital environment, the points of intersection with learners and researchers multiply, and the opportunities to provide support for creation and curation grow... As work is increasingly carried out in digital environments, activities leave a data trace, which can be aggregated and mined to provide analytics that may be used to support a variety of goals (student retention, resource usage metrics, and more)." Such patterns and trends reflect the responsibilities of libraries to consider the interconnection of communication channels and web-based scholarly publishing mechanisms in the perspectives of support resource creation and development.

BACKGROUND AND CONTEMPORARY TIMES

The image of digital libraries is related to designing generic, comprehensive ways of services, tailored services. The experiences from past include the following:

(a) Project ENVISION : during early 1990s, the project made efforts to build "a prototype digital library" in the field of computer science. The objective was based on the study of understanding of needs of computer science professionals, and this project was completed in a period of approximately four months.

(b) Project CORE : This project built the "task-oriented access" for digital library scenario (Fox et al. 1993). This task-oriented project emphasized on information discovery, browsing, searching. Project CORE was known as "Chemistry Online Retrieval Experiment.", a number of organizations, such as the "American Chemical Society", "Chemical Abstracts Service", Bellcore, Cornell University and OCLC tried to build "the chemist's workstation" providing a "single, seamless, unified interface".

(c) Community-based digital libraries : Various examples such as "K-12 mathematics" (Math Forum), "Earth system science" (Marlino *et al.* 2001), and higher education have been showing the community-based digital libraries.

The community based digital scenario brings few challenges as well; diverse subject areas, plans and strategies, fast pacing technologies implementation along with demand-based services. Without print equivalent, more digital information is being produced or generated. The usage statistics of produced and consumed information are evidences of widening gaps (Lyman and Varian, 2003). There are various approaches to understand user needs, bridging the organizational capabilities and the needs by involving the users of diverse backgrounds in designing and governance as following:

User-centric design : The focal points of user-centered design are related with quick and continuous involvement in the design process. The library users' needs understanding and process of "iterative design" leads towards task-centered design, objective-oriented and "scenario-based" design. The standard design and evaluation techniques related with digital libraries in the form of hypertext/hypermedia have been continuous process.

The objective of this "user-centered design process" is emphasis upon thorough understanding and comprehension of user requirements. These requirements include the technology design and planning.

(a) Participatory design : Participatory design method is related with the "co-designers" users. The users' participation is needed in proposing and generating the design alternatives. The participatory design is found in industrial democracy involving the empowered users who perform:

- Participation and co-designing though the technology for innovation,
- Responsible roles by co-determining the nature, process and outcomes of the design process, and
- Actively understanding the situations and scenario of technology use related to practices, structures and organizational responsibilities.

The participatory design includes "contextual inquiry". The contextual enquiry provides a platform "where the designer works/interacts with the user in the work environment, is a particular technique and is intended to support the development of products that support, extend and transform user work". The requirements of "participatory design" are collaboration between designers and users, bringing the users "organizationally, logistically, and financially" together. The examples include in-house software development showing the users participating in design process as being co-located. In the past, digital library project (MatDL) was involving few geographically distributed institutions, open source tools to complete the task.

The consideration of World Wide Web as a platform for the technical mechanism is to enable participation of users in the design process. Collaboration systems provide a virtual commons where distributed stakeholders engage in collaborative design regularly. Such arrangement is beyond geographical factors; including in distributed nature of digital libraries, its users, and the participation in the design and planning. Another example was the DWEL WorkHub (an online communication tool) which utilized the knowledge of the developers and the users. Participatory design projects focused on technology innovations, co-designing, capacity building transformational needs, instead of social change (Bishop et al. 2003).

The "Inquiry Labs" (iLabs) has been an example of stimulating, improving, integrating learning by infusing library technologies. The iLabs suite was considered as "simultaneously a Web site, a community of learners, and a locus for knowledge construction".

b. Shared governance models : The shared governance models had its emergence from educational administration as well as organizational development (Shafritz and Ott, 1992). Very early, John J. Corson in 1941 talked about "The process of consultation strengthens the allegiance to the institution and their individual zeal and satisfaction" (in Douglass 1998). The shared governance model is about:

i. Understating the different roles played by user community members

ii. Ensuring that each component shares the responsibility for the organization.

iii. Straitening the significance of shared governance into academic governance (Sachs, 2004).

The social and educational changes have been affected and the impacts have been visible. The creation of Connecticut History Online (CHO) supported the cross-institution collaboration facilitated by different advisory groups. Related to this entity, it was observed that there are relations of partnership as having core value, and the concept of ownership brings the integral approach. McMartin focused on the shared governance while considering its significance as integral component of "MERLOT's business model"; sustainability and partnership among a large and distributed group. The digital libraries involve users who are distributed, and sometimes the "semi-virtual communities". These communities are composed of:

- **traditional users :** related with research work, academics and education.
- **general public :** the stakeholders including the funding institutions, policy framing organizations, etc.
- **contributors and developers :** software developers, library and archive staff, and museum curators.

The output of their collaborative work is explained as following:

a. creation and sharing data/content,

b. conducting scientific research,

d. developing metadata schemas,

e. management

The early digital library development efforts were based on "system-oriented" or followed "structured development design". Later the mix and match approaches emphasized upon the involvement of users as integral component in the digital library life cycle: design, use and sustainability. The hybrid approaches included while integrating digital library users for the purpose of designing the digital libraries may appear as potential methods for improvements in development of digital information platforms.

UNDERSTANDING THE DIGITAL LIBRARY SINCE THE PAST

The digital library has always been considered a research in progress as the new technologies and innovations are arriving and affecting the contemporary system of digital libraries. Sometimes the digital library is observed as a threat or replacement of the conventional printed book; and at the other times it is seen as modernity and salvation arrived in library culture. The growth of digital libraries has witnessed phenomenal changes. There have been initial efforts such as the first UK digital library project, ELINOR, during 1991 though World Wide Web facilitated much technological support. It has been observed that the terms electronic library and digital library are synonymous during 1984, author Kenneth Dowlin's book "The Electronic Library" with the characteristics of the electronic library as given:

- Use of computer for managing resources
- Linking the e-resources with user through
- electronic channels
- Trained library staff to support users
- Electronic storage, organization and transmission of information

During 1991, in the project "ELINOR" at De Montfort, the following working definition was found more suitable:

- A teaching, learning and study environment in which learning resources are held primarily in electronic form

The inferences emerged that a library is considered digital when its resources are digital, by format and service. The term hybrid library shows that printed books and digital resources co-exist in library. Another term virtual library is the extension of the digital library. The virtual library is a state which is beyond the single physical access locale. It also reflects that absence of single point of digital storage. The virtual library can be explained as an electronic library which supports the distributed nature of resources and users at different geographical locations yet the management of both is coherent in nature and practice.

The digital library development in the shape of various projects happened at various places. For example, in the United Kingdom, the "eLib programme" funded many projects leading to have major impact on digital library development. The initiation of digital library took place simultaneously at various geographical locations though it was considered a complex entity involving high risks related to investment and implementation. The global market invited co-operation among the libraries and other sectors. The primary emphasis was on technology which later shifted towards the content and access. All this invited attention towards copyright issues and the economics of the digital library; along with jobs, skills and infrastructure. The advent of digital spaces in academic libraries brought many changes and development whereas the public libraries have also been enthusiastic to articulate the altered mechanisms of rendering services in the current scenario. The academic libraries tend to serve the organization staff and user community in the form of faculty members, research scholars and students; the public libraries enhance the citizenship by the combination of access to vast amount of information, and culture, strengthening the social fabric.

Characteristics of Digital Libraries

Long ago, almost three decades before, Cleveland (1998) described few characteristics of digital libraries, as follows:

- Digital face of traditional libraries composed of digital collections, and fixed media collections.
- Beyond the one physical and administrative permits.

- Inclusion of technological infrastructure and services, to update as the new technologies arrive.
- Provision of information without boundaries and limitations of physical nature of library and resources.
- Requirement of the skills of library professional and a computer professional
- Expansive and accurate searching system as a network of multimedia system.

Digital libraries are the extension of traditional libraries, not the replacement. The resources, services, support and technological enhancements provided by the digital libraries, are complementing the traditional libraries. Thus the characteristics of the digital library must be observed in the context of following:

Beyond space and time : the access to the digital library is beyond the physical boundaries and library timings. The access is provided from anywhere at any time.

Enhanced content : the content in digital form has continuously enriched the users' experiences. The inclination of users towards the digital content has declined the demand of printed books in myriad libraries. The usages of digital resources are increasing in comparison with the printer information sources.

Variety in content : the content is found and facilitated in textual, visual/ image, and the sound form also. The features of navigation along with the colored visualization have supported readers' experiences with many subjects such as medical sciences, etc.

Increasing expenditures on digital environment : the expenditure on digital libraries development and maintenance has been increasing over the years. The expenditures on digital resources and maintenance of them have been shifted from the concept of ownership to the mechanism of subscription and licensing. This expenditure includes the equipments and development and upgrading of infrastructure.

The issues related to recruitment and training of the staff is also significant in the digital library contexts.

VARIOUS ISSUES RELATED WITH DIGITAL LIBRARIES

(a) Funding : Funding for new technology and infrastructure is always demanding the adjustment in changing circumstances. The less leeway has been available due to the digital thinking. Usually the libraries do not observe much improvement in financial positions in order to augment digital infrastructure and services. The expansion of digital information has happened at the expense of printed resources at many libraries due to shrinking budgets. It has been the exacerbation of the polarization of printed sources against the digital electronic materials. There may be operational savings yet not sufficient for the content acquisition. The development of user-centric, resources on financial grounds requires the restructuring of pedagogical as well as learning methods. The movement towards the becoming of "learning organizations" or "knowledge-based organizations" has been possible due to enterprising nature of digital libraries. The expensive nature of digital information argues the measurement of relative cost benefits. The calculation of benefits of digital resources should be based on:

- Licensing versus ownership
- Pay per user versus subscription
- Physical and digital space requirements
- Infrastructure, equipments and communication expenses Human resource, skills, training
- Co-operation with other sectors

(b) Free or fee : The provision of services based on some fee or without any charge is always a matter of debate. The free services based on digital resources are the usual mechanism of academic libraries. The scenario may be different in public libraries. The constrained budgets compel libraries to rethink about the planning and implementation of digital libraries; including negotiations of digital acquisitions/subscription and yearly increased high pricing. The principle of "free at point of use" is very much relevant in order to facilitate the maximum use of library digital resources.

(c) Authority : The quality of digital library depends upon the authority. The document authority was earlier supplied by the publishers, later supported by the librarian due to subject knowledge. The authority is affected as in the contexts of "proliferation of unvalidated documents" with the possibility of changing of sources. The risks of incorrect material, copyright or paternity rights related issues are authority driven aspects.

(d) Censorship : The freedom of information and issues of censorship are among the basic principles of librarianship. The availability of information which may be illegal or undesirable content demands the policy framework in digital library. The digital environment provides easy access to information yet requires proactive and preventative approaches. The definitions and framework of the digital library can be explained as following:

- Electronic storage and access of digital library
- Quality assurance in the perspectives of "authority, stability, and legality" of content
- Access management and ownership
- Users-friendly interfaces and internal structures
- Financially manageable including the predictable, and sustainable costing
- Sophisticated navigation and effective searching
- Assurance to copyright holders and protection from infringement

- Tracking, and controlling for usage at point of use

DIGITAL LIBRARY AND COMMUNITY PERSPECTIVE

For different communities of users, the digital libraries are providing varied sense; the computer science community considers the digital library as distributed database services, which is based on management of the unstructured multimedia data. It becomes "a new marketplace" for the business and political communities. The information science tradition has been instrumental in shaping the views about digital libraries. The digital libraries can be considered as the logical extensions and manifestations of conventional libraries based on amplification of resources and services. Another dimension of digital libraries is related with facilitating the users in fast and speedy manner. Creation of different levels of access and opportunities for the users has emerged in the advanced manner. The initiation of digital library development has been fuelled by the following two factors:

a. by finding mechanisms for application of innovative technologies developed during the late 1980s.

b. by innovations for creating methods based on technologies to manage the distributed information resources.

The digital libraries were technology-centered and content-centered whereas later on these were community centered. The extended access was focused through digitization work and networking approaches in the digital libraries. Availability of digital collections offering services was dependent upon voluminous homogeneous digital data. Creation of digital objects and related services become remotely accessible due to network based services. These digital objects and services are, sometimes, distributed from a number of machines at different locations. The mutually dependent attributes such as content, technology, and services define and frame the digital library.

Content Significance

The digital libraries have contents which are posing technical, and some other specific challenges related with "authority, surrogate creation, formats, intellectual property rights and costs of acquisition and maintenance." The digital libraries have been providing renderings for textual objects as digitally coded (e.g., ASCII, Unicode) renderings. The OCR accuracy, scanning resolution have been affected by costs and human validation; and at the same time very high resolution bitmaps were expensive for storing and transmitting purposes, to be retrieved later on in the form of ASCII/ Unicode.

The texts were marked up by the "Standard Generalized Markup Language" (SGML) to provide the structural content. Various surrogates in the form of bibliographic records, keywords/ phrases, or abstracts are required to facilitate users. The single medium objects and formats, for example, images, statistical data, different media files and sound recordings, etc. are provided through specialized digital libraries and collections. The indexing for non-textual objects is not an easy task due to the dependence upon on the textual captions meant for retrieval. As per structure, the different "textual objects" are placed and located in different files. The provision of interactive multimedia content is dependent upon the following technologies:

a. Computer simulations,

b. Video games, and virtual worlds

c. Surrogates mechanisms such as document vectors and color histograms

d. Keyframe video extracts

Standardizing metadata to insure interoperability

The use of metadata for intermediating steps towards content and information retrieval. The creation of surrogate facilities to quick preview and browse is much needed. The retrieval through the words, such as titles, manually created various descriptions, automatic keywords, etc. is in vogue. The current attention related to non-textual surrogates (color and shape characterizations) is significant. This goes further for "speaker identification schemes" in the audio recordings. The creation of user profiles and customized, original information objects are provided by the modern digital libraries. The limitation of physical libraries is observed while the digital libraries save and index the results. Digital libraries have a responsibility and target to characterizing the possible content instead of existing content.

Managing Content

Most of the planning and resources are invested in the content management. Various management functions in a digital library are as: selection of resources, acquisition and subscription; indexing, storage, and access, etc.

Selection and Acquisition

The collection development policy is the guiding force behind the selection of information sources. The expended budgets, digitization, IPRs, are few of the significant components among the policies. The aspects such as new translations, images and original photography, spatial information, combining digital representations for visual objects, text-based attributes of names are always demanding attention for better selection and information retrieval. The cost and quality are the two basic factors which pose challenges before the library. There are few facets such as the costs of acquisition, and IPRs in context of digitization. The quality of the content is related with issues of authenticity and the veracity of content. The selection of content is followed by acquisition by file transfer, subscription, or mass storage. In case of digitization, there are few challenges such as quality of original documents, policy documents, resolutions, formats, etc. to define.

Indexing, Storage, and Access

After acquisition and subscription, the content is added to the collection. This addition to collection is to reach at the level where it is retrievable. The steps of indexing, storage and access are the areas which have been demanding the curiosity and research as always. The concepts such as automatic indexing, manual indexing vector-space indexing and probabilistic information retrieval models have been associated with information retrieval. For example, the Inquiry system (the retrieval engine) was an approach for retrieval at the Library of Congress. The earlier traditional approach of manually assigning objects was related to the manually constructed concept classes as dealt in a controlled vocabulary. Later the automatic techniques were indexing the objects to "mathematically abstract concept classes". This includes the "latent semantic indexing where the documents are assigned to concepts, comprised of "term-vector document singular vectors".

These indexing systems were followed by the hybrid approach with the combination of manual classification and automatic assignments of objects. During late 90s, the application of highly sophisticated digital technologies was initiated in indexing to overcome the subject and language related problems. The application of text retrieval methods and approaches towards the "cross-language retrieval problem" supported the users. The role of text items in searching the various kinds of texts, images, video, audio recordings and other non-textual objects etc. is dominant. The terms such as title, creator and subject headings are significant for retrieval. The dependence on text representations is an area of indexing techniques in digital libraries. Adaptation of the statistical techniques for text retrieval made its place in relation to characterize objects by feature vectors. The example is color for which color histograms are applied. The other areas of applications are robotics (including the vision systems) and signal processing. These techniques are used to extract various unique attributes (shapes, optical flow, and pitch). For example, the image segmentation has been used in image processing; few feature analysis techniques are applied to identify images in the past. These techniques provided few factors for queries; including "edge and corner detection", foreground/background separation, texture analysis. The feature analyses were supported estimating the optical flow in moving images. Researches and experiences from the earlier times expressed the developments taken place in automatic indexing of "non-textual objects" with the "non-textual attributes". The following aspects reflect the advantage in digital environment:

- Many index terms are assigned and various levels of representation can be created and generated in a digital environment.
- The digital objects can exist and be accessed at many locations.

Storage is an essential component, no matter the data is in the form of streaming video or audio or placed in library as discrete files, such provisions require alternative technologies. In the past multiple levels of storage media and mechanical robots have been applied to access the large amount of data.

Maintenance

The maintenance of digital libraries is quite different from the conventional physical libraries. Up gradation of the system hardware and software, alternative network infrastructure, training of personnel and preservation are few of the areas which are continuous in nature for survival of a digital library. The change in the digital content, having many versions, the maintenance of most recent and essential need updating and linking the component objects, are few aspects. Hypertext links also need a policy guideline for management and proper navigation to locate the information. Creation and development of digital libraries can be supported by various composition of tools, meant for selection and acquisition of documents, indexing and maintenance of the digital content. These tools are corresponding to:

- library building tools and converting formats
- visualizing the objects, and encryption of data
- application of interface simulators on multiple platforms
- file naming histories, links, and metadata definitions
- tools for updating versions
- security and future backing up the digital system

Services

The library designs and provides services to the range and depth which are formulated by keeping the mission and policies in mind. The determination of types of content and its availability according to allocation depend upon the users as well. The potential and user demands play a great role in deciding the digital content and services generation. Mixed kinds of users depend upon the nature and scope of organization. The physical location, timings and few specific services are the routine conventional aspects of libraries which do not matter in digital scenario. The nature of library may affect the decisions about the selected contents such as academic libraries will consider the interdisciplinary nature of research; and a public library may decide about the popular literature and community building resources. It also leads towards the maintaining the community user policies, authentication and provisions of universal access to local bibliographic holding data. Apart from the digital access to library data and information, some arrangements such as facilitating access ramps, Braille books to the users with special needs. The challenges to provide digital information services and choices to offer diverse services are as follows:

- reference and referral services

- instructional services
- added value services
- promotional services

Digital libraries bring people closer and collaboration is possible due to communication channels at various levels. The ready reference services, exhaustive searching, bibliographic instruction, preparation, the facility of language translation are provided. The another challenge before the libraries is to keep revising the policies due to changing nature of technologies, organizational policies and users' demand.

Search Services

The digital libraries provide a comprehensive search service to users. In the past where the OPACs have been instrumental in providing the results based on the searches by author, title, along with the some subject access to library holdings, later to the union holdings across a number of libraries. The seamless linking and access has always been the dream of libraries which could have been achieved by the arrival of digital technologies. The access, display of bibliographic information, and primary information objects are expected in the digital libraries. Differentiating the metadata with the primary data is found as a problem in homogeneous collections as well as heterogeneous collections. To access the aids and various types of formats such as manuscript bit maps, hypertexts, image and video files require the mechanisms within the digital libraries based on levels of representation. The available search form, query line/phrase are related with the type of indexing in use; the results take shape of the "ranked lists or exact-matched sets". There are few limitations in the format and structure of the World Wide Web that affected the digital libraries in the past. But the recent times have visualized few options which supported the searching. These supports have been in the form of "server-side caches, client side caches (e.g., cookies)". In this context, the development of "Java" has helped in improving the search capabilities including relevance feedback and user profiles. The later web-based designs have been providing solutions for intricate search options such as proximity-based searching, and scope limits.

The current digital libraries provide many features such as control over the results; instead of simple lists, now the collection, item, type of resources, and media with the features of sorting etc. The browsing has been observed as a general manner of searching information. The navigational mechanisms in WWW environment have influenced the digital libraries. These mechanisms are based on high-level hierarchical classification to facilitate to the selection of categories related with the various levels of granularity to access the specific information objects. The hybrid solutions in digital libraries provide formulation of search strategies. The facility to manipulate visualizations of collections is possible due to dynamic query interfaces. Merging of clustering techniques (scatter gather) is significant in searching with visualization of desired results. Creation of semantic maps helps in depicting the "two-dimensional maps for high-dimensional concept spaces" that are related with the users' points of interest. The combination of "dynamic query interface style" along with visually enhanced preview methods has been fetching the results in digital library. Few tools in digital interfaces have been the spoken queries, video walls and video skims which are based on pattern recognition systems.

Reference Services

The digital yet informal communication channels (e.g., chat rooms services, etc.) are also popular along with the individual query to the library. There are few methods being used in digital libraries for reference services.

- Provision of FAQs based on anticipated questions and

readymade answers before human assistance. The FAQs provide answers to system-related questions. The electronic assistance in the form of pathfinders are highlighted at the interface point.

- The asynchronous exchange also happen users and library/ content experts. The email facility permits users to avail reference services. Though digital solutions provide services yet human intervention is often required.
- Another type of approach is the combination of automated and human services, given the earlier options does not suffice. This combined approach facilitates sharing the queries and related responses by taking benefits from both human and machine capabilities.
- The real time dialog with the reference expert is supported by technology. The use of databases and telephone management software could be helpful in reference service.
- Such aspects help in remote reference service along with the internet chat or video links.
- Moving towards the sophisticated support system based on natural language understanding, the user's contexts are comprehended with the help of "human surrogates".

The digital libraries have been advancing to offer various opportunities to go beyond classroom walls. The digital library experiences often provide scholars the rich and interactive resource and multimedia materials. The digital resources have the capacity to drive both classrooms inducted and self-directed learning due to high quality resources navigation facilities are available for the user community. The roles of digital libraries are expanded and extended to information-seeking skills, rich bibliographic instructions, collaboration on information literacy, and distance learning.

Technology Requisites

The extended roles of digital libraries are possible due to various features such as strong infrastructure, networking facilities and interoperability. The continuous development of digital libraries is based upon creation of standards for the storing data and further dissemination and distribution. This also depends upon query representation with the support and application of vocabulary control. The adoption of standards, content and related services favor shared interests and innovation to map local content and queries with other digital libraries with the help of Z39.50 protocol. The organizational impacts of digital libraries are being addressed as it has been observed that the "digit centered" genesis is now becoming communities of practice.

CHALLENGES IN CREATING DIGITAL LIBRARIES

The development and growth of digital libraries have been a long-term effort of planning, technological implementations, up gradations, keeping the librarianship in strategies as well. Creation of effective digital libraries is full of problems and challenges. Beginning with the integration of digital media, running parallel with print collections could have been possible due to uniqueness of digital resources and contained information being flexible and remotely accessible. Cleveland (1998) and IFLA identified few issues as intrinsic challenges as following:

- **Technical architectures :** their ever changing and advancing nature; required to progress and implemented in library.
- **Building of digital collections :** the identification and selection of resources for subject as well as interdisciplinary academic requirements.
- **Digitization and born-digital documents :** the choice and decisions about the inclusion and process of digitization along with the born-digital resources for the

library.

- **Metadata :** the aspects, tools and items related with information display, identification and retrieval; the metadata helps in searching, approaching and finding the documents.
- **Naming, identifiers, and persistence:** the facets related with naming, digital identifiers and the persistent availability of digital documents are very significant.
- **Copyright/rights management :** apart from the technical aspects and maintenance, the issues related with IPRs are very much crucial, bringing the challenges of digital rights management, authenticity of users and concepts of fair use in routine digital library services.
- **Preservation :** the preservation of digital information requires technological updating and implementing the advanced techniques to preserve and access to the information.

DIGITAL LIBRARIES AND VLES INTEGRATION

The digital libraries have been instrumental in supporting the learning environment. There have been few factors for the integration of digital libraries and virtual learning environments (VLEs), as following:

- Positioning and creating niche for VLE;
- Supporting the traditional teaching and quality of learning;
- Increasing the use of digital resources by linking them with the learning modules and creating awareness among the academic community;
- Following and maintaining standards for quality resources and services;
- Augmenting the creation, and using the reading lists for scholars.

The integration of digital libraries and VLEs is helpful due to the following perspectives:

- Firstly, a content delivery approach, or information resource oriented, which regards the library as information resource provider.
- Secondly, there is an approach of content plus service supplying and interaction (McLean and Lynch, 2004). Those services include virtual or online reference, bibliographies and "webliographies", online library instruction, and access to third party commercial information services.
- And, thirdly, an organizational view, which includes the library as a whole (collections, services, and educational and managerial perspective) merged with processes and human resources into the academic community and its activities.

Various online resources are available as features and highlights on the library website. The users are facilitated by navigating through the variety of digital resources. The examples are literature, history, topics of citizenship, religion, topics for teaching etc.

APPROACHES TO DIGITAL LIBRARY SERVICES

The approaches to digital library services have been based upon the implementation of technologies, users' demand and expectations, usage and access. The tools for accessing the digital resources, facilitating reference queries and rich platforms of online information are the outcomes of digital library revolutions and services; strengthening the library staff to serve the users in innovative ways. It has been observed that the last two decades have witnessed the widespread adoption of the World Wide Web for information access and exchange. The methods for communication and researching area are quite different from the conventional print information environment. The digitization of print and other forms of information sources in libraries has paved way for wider access. The born-digital materials, later, enhanced the user experience in highly developed scene. The support of discovery tools, facilitating the text and image search has been revolutionizing. The aspects of "data visualization, document clustering, and topic modeling; self-archiving and long-term preservation of digital assets; and digital humanities research support" have provided fast and quality data access for researchers (Kirchner and others, 2015).

- Digital Library Service: the libraries provide not only the access to information in digital format but also specific needs of users.
- Transforming the library Services: The shift towards online nature of services has been the focus point of libraries. The use of various online services by users in the form of e-resources access, digital reference services, online communication s are few of the examples in digital library scenario. The example of massive digital library "Hathitrust" gives the glimpses of digital services.

Service Areas

The digital libraries are providing various services other than information access and downloading (Kirchner, 2015) :

Digital archiving : Technical platforms and tools are needed to support preservation.

Data management : To manage data in all formats, including both structured data and unstructured data, this facility is supporting users.

Multimedia resources : The integration of multimedia resources and the adoption of new information delivery.

Discovery of information : Tools and techniques for information discovery by browse strategies, data/ text mining, etc.

Scholarly communications : Publishing approaches in current times, keeping open access and collaborations in mind.

Digital humanities : Digital humanities help scholars by assisting scholars through digital tools.

The needs of libraries is observed in continuous coping with increased needs of resources and services and highly innovative areas such as identification of areas and times to understand the "networks of expertise"; creation of environments to augment the collaboration and mechanisms to assess the services and deliverables; developing the community-building services and strategies, and taxonomy for collaborative activities.

Digital Collection, contents and connections : The users are provided subject and topic- specific digital information including the high quality digital objects and supplemental materials.

Digital Literacy : The digitally literate users explore and utilize the digital libraries at maximum; this includes the searching resources, understanding copyright, etc.

Digital Library Programming : Digital library programming includes:

- online reading programs
- Self-paced Learning
- Special Needs Services (such as audio Reading Services)
- Online Exhibits

To help the users various kinds of reference Services are provided. The digital environment reference services are different in their format, deliverance and time spent. In this context, assumption of longer hours of operation with the help of supporting technologies related with reference provisions can be indicating the improved services and frequent interactions due to remote/VR (Yang and Dalal, 2015) through digital library reference services.

User Assistance : The assistance to users while using an online database, e-book or platform, the role of digital devices is also significant. Due to lack of basic technology skill, sometimes, users need library staff assistance which should be taken care by carefully designed library website, FAQs, video tutorial, creating "help sheets" for using an equipment or resource. The following example shows the efforts of libraries:

- **Library Spotlight :** "The Columbia River Basin Ethnic History Archive includes digital objects from a dozen different ethnic groups who have lived in the Columbia River Basin. In addition, the project includes a tutorial to help users find, interpret, and teach about the primary source materials" in the collection.

Anywhere, Anytime Access: with the advent of mobile apps and various other features, the digital library services are accessible from anywhere and anytime.

Enhanced Digital Collections : The searchable collections are not enough the attention has been paid towards the enhanced digital collection with the quality services. For example, to have "Digital Library Spotlight", the "Allen County Public Library Genealogy Center" (http://www.genealogycenter.org/) has been providing access to discovery tools, as well as online assistance to community users. The creation of digital resources by libraries for the users has been observed at a big number of libraries. For instance, Louisiana Purchase: A Heritage Explored has been facilitating the teacher guides and American Journeys. The highlight of digital objects is an example of enhanced digital collections. Various examples of "enhanced digital collections" are given as:

- *The Library of Congress*: "Teacher section".
- *The National Archives*: "DocsTeach resources".
- *The Southern Nevada*: "The BoomTown Years project", meant for high school students and through the website

along with teaching activities, to support learning.

- *The Hudson River Valley Heritage project*: creation of exhibits for the educator section.

For example, American Centuries provides many methods to access digital collection by focusing on "digital objects from New Collection Tools". The provision of digital tools to assist users in various activities related to digital collections, such as "recalling standard searches, or sharing results with their collaborators. In this context, the Bracero History Archive provides the facility to users on login basis "My Archive" to let them prepare notes etc.

Digital Object Pathfinders : The users have myriad information needs and that may also be vague in expression. The intuitive nature of digital libraries helps in providing the information to users. The digital pathfinders *help* to find digital objects across the digital collections. The pathfinder projects support in locating the digital objects, by providing access to resources stored in various collections.

Digital Scholarship : While helping the scholars with their research projects at different levels, the libraries play a participatory and significant role working while with students. Also the libraries are supporting research digital research services to users for completing and sharing their research.

PERSONAL DIGITAL ARCHIVING PROJECTS

In the context of digital information and human dependence on the same, the development of personal archiving workshops have been able to train and assist people to archive the collections of their choice (Brown (2015). The role and efforts of Library of Congress have been encouraging people and libraries for mutual benefits in archiving the collections (Ashenfelder, 2013). Hawkins (2013) in his book "**Personal Archiving: Preserving Our Digital Heritage"** has observed the "growing interest in preserving digital heritage".

"Traditionally, libraries and other cultural institutions have played major roles in preservation, but individuals have now become interested in preserving their digital heritage". Witten, Bainbridge, Nicholas (2010) discussed few methods that users can apply and supply their contribution to digital libraries:

- *Annotations* : Adding notes to documents.
- *Keywords* : Adding tags to assist others in searching.
- *New additions*: Uploading the images, audio, or videos.
- *Partial and Fluid Documents* : Making additions to collaborative projects and documents.

There are many experiences and stories shared by libraries such as:

- In the Europeana (1914-1918) project, the contribution and sharing of stories by users were encouraged.
- The "Papers of the War Department" facilitated the users for "transcribing the documents by allowing them to play role as "transcription associates". This could be possible with the help of an open source tool "Scripto for transcriptions".
- Another example of the Bracero History Archive facilitated the users adding items by providing short video tutorials for collecting objects and conducting oral history interviews.

Social Media and User Participation

The researchers are approaching the social media services for various sharing and communicating the research. In this context, the visibility through culture of participation related with the digital collections and services is associated with knowledge, ability and skills of users and communities. These kinds of digital activities are facilitating the increasing demands of creative expression and cultural preservation among communities, thus helping "the exploration of identity and for cultural participation" (Liew, 2014). The skills related with creation and sharing the digital content are supportive to demonstrate their contributions in enhancing the culture of specific geographic locations.

DIGITAL LIBRARY TECHNICAL ISSUES

There are various issues associated with digital libraries. The issues are categorized as:

Accessibility Issues : The accessibility issues are often related with the digital divide and understood as the library to act as an intermediary between community and resources. Libraries provide equitable access to digital content with the support of technologies. The digital resources and availability of such supports help communities irrespective of geographic location.

Legal Issues and Copyright Issues : The informed users are the vehicles of rightly used information. Libraries can provide awareness by workshops, training programs, and "rights management" information on the website. The scholarly communication practices are developing, evolving and providing platforms for authors to publish and share the content. There is also need to review and alter the existing copyright law in context with the new paradigm. Awareness of fair use guidelines is crucial for the users. The rights management is the area where again the library has to play a significant role by advocating and advising the best practices.

Mass Digitization and Copyright : There are policies and frameworks for the mass digitization in the libraries. Mass digitization and copyright problems arise while building collections and archives in the libraries.

Ethical Issues : Along with the IPR related issues, the ethical issues and considerations related to usage and collection building.

DATA CURATION ISSUES AND BIG DATA

The concept of Big Data and data curation aspects has been recent yet significant issues in libraries. Data management services with the aims to serve the discovery, archiving of data have been initiated in libraries since last decade. The ALA also expressed concerns as "Academic researchers are users of big data, extremely large data sets that are beyond the capability of most software tools to process and analyze. Academic librarians traditionally assess the research needs of academics, but big data poses new challenges. The sheer quantity and rate of accumulation of data require new skills and resources to enable researchers to share, analyze, and reuse it" (ALA, 2015). Libraries are emphasizing on various components of data management, such as understanding and implementing the research data lifecycles, followed by use and application of data tools. Data sharing, collaboration and maintenance of various subject devoted repositories are also facets of such planning.

DISASTER PLANNING ISSUES

Libraries have faced many disasters in the form of natural disasters, electrical storms etc. which caused to the physical resources as well as digital data. Few examples are shared as following to reflect the planning and preparations of libraries:

Examples of Library Disaster Plans

- Disaster Response and Recovery Planning has been initiative of Penn State University Libraries
- Disaster Response Manual is prepared by Columbia University Libraries
- Emergency Preparedness has been the outcome of efforts of Harvard University Libraries
- HathiTrust Disaster Recovery Plan is well known plan
- University Library Emergency Response is the outcome

of initiatives of University of Michigan Libraries

Privacy Issues : The users have been concerned about their behavior and patterns of usage of library resources; relating to the privacy issues.

The need to have users' data and usage statistics for improvement of library services based on resources and library collection are routine practices in libraries. Such aspects require attention from library to respect the users' privacy. Libraries have been instrumental in developing a big number of policies which are very significant to guide, practice and protect the privacy of users". ALA's website supports users by providing resources for "Developing a Library Privacy Policy". In this context, the NISO was tasked with developing a "Consensus Framework to Support Patron Privacy in Digital Library and Information Systems". The specific thoughts and concerns are continuously evolving in this context due to changing digital landscapes.

Security Issues

The authenticity of users and Digital Rights Management are few of the facets related with the security issues in the library, while saving the digital content from the professional hackers.

Collaboration

Collaboration is required among the fellow workers related to one task; similarly in there are territorial issues while building a digital collection. Collaboration within various agencies contributing in the creation of a digital library or project is seen in the form of expertise and contributions.

Sustainability Issues

The fear of losing data or resources is much common among the scholars and libraries, too. The provision to increasing number of users as well as funding the digital libraries are few of the concerns of libraries related to the sustainability in context with the digital presence.

DIGITAL LIBRARY MANAGEMENT

Digital library management is beyond the acquiring and subscribing the resources. In this context, digital preservation is not only a technical problem, but also there are more aspects related with backup maintenance and turnkey repository. The requirement of technical infrastructure and the skilled staff is observed as to operate and ensure the access to digital content (Corrado and Moulaison, 2014). The budgeting for digital library and digitization is the most important administrative component. Distribution and division of costs related to tasks and time are very tedious aims to achieve. Next, the finding partners, collaborators and guides for creation of digital libraries and digitization process including technological and contributing partners.

While organizing the finance and collaborators, the assessment of digital library is an essential step to estimate the strength and weaknesses. The assessment is necessary in the context of quantitative and qualitative measure. These measurements are made in context with library's collections, digital library services to serve the demands of users to improve the digital library performance. The assessment leads towards creation and improvements of high quality digital library. In this context, DeRidder and Chapman (2015) have provided the information about the development of best practices and guidelines by the Digital Library Federation (DLF):

- Determination of measuring the impact of digital collections
- Development of areas of commonality and benchmarking
- Understanding cost and benefit of digital collections

- Exploration of methods of collections, management and analysis in the digital libraries

DATA STANDARDS

There are many standards which are guiding force for the digital libraries. Few years ago, there has been visible developments and progress for developing tools and concerned standards for growth and preservation digital media and institutional repositories. The standards provide guidelines for uniformity and interoperability. Houghton (2015) mentioned the significance of "the Trustworthy Repositories Audit and Certification: Criteria and Checklist (TRAC)", later on it was developed into ISO 16363-2012.

DIGITAL LIBRARY EVALUATION

The digital library evaluation is based on judgments about quality towards the determination of meeting goals. In this context, Fox and others (2011) defined quality as "the parameters that can be used to characterize and evaluate the content and behavior of a Digital Library. Quality can be associated not only with each class of content or functionality but also with specific information objects or services. Some of these parameters are objective in nature and can be measured automatically, whereas others are subjective in nature and can only be measured through user evaluations (e.g. focus groups)", also, there are "quality dimensions" for digital libraries.

ASSESSING THE IMPACT OF DIGITAL LIBRARIES

Kostkova and Madle (2013) studied the digital libraries in terms of "impact on their community, technology, services, and content". The observations made upon the National Resource of Infection Control NRIC digital library have been in context with positive impact, and the evaluation framework "Impact-ED criteria" is based upon the following tools include (Kostkova and Madle, 2013):

1. Community
    1. Use of digital library in the work setting
    2. Understanding work environment for integration of digital library
    3. Acceptability of the digital library in the workplace
    4. Awareness creation in the target community
2. Services
    1. Understanding of user needs and satisfaction with the digital library
    2. Preferred digital resources/services
    3. Awareness of current digital library services
3. Technology
    1. Digital library access log statistics
    2. Usability of the digital library
    3. Search query analysis
    4. Navigation pathway analysis
4. Content
    1. User perception change
    2. The impact of digital library on work
    3. The dissemination of digital information

The inclusivity of digital libraries is visible in many contexts. Fox and others (2011) define functionality as "the services that a Digital Library offers to its different users, whether classes of users or individual users. While the general expectation is that digital libraries will be rich in capabilities and services, the bare minimum of functions would include such aspects as new information object registration, search and browse. Beyond that, the system seeks to manage the functions of the Digital Library to ensure that the functions reflect the particular needs of the Digital Library's community of users and/or the specific requirements relating to the Content it contains." The user interaction and feedback is significant.

Further it is described that "specific problems he encountered in using this digital collection of eighteenth-century texts". The efforts have been contributing in the digital library service improvements.

Various approaches to searching in digital libraries

- Multi-faceted Interfaces: ranging from maps, timelines to "word clouds and games" and facilitating interactive experience.
- Theme-based Approaches: Online exhibits with the "browseable interface" based on interactive themes.
- Timeline Interfaces: A timeline for locating digital objects from particular points in time.
- Image-based Interfaces: Engaging image serving at a focal point for exploration.
- Game Interfaces: Engaging users with digital objects.
- Map-based Interfaces: Maps as tool to explore place-based digital objects.
- Reference Book Interfaces: Embedding digital objects into a reference book environment
- Teaching Interfaces: Building in learning resources for theme

INFORMATION ARCHITECTURE FOR DIGITAL LIBRARIES

The information architecture for digital libraries focuses upon the evaluation and selection of software including the open sources and commercial software; data and "digital object interoperability", and finally developing a prototype digital library collection. The understating of key concepts related to digital library technologies are must. Sometimes it requires technical skills in building the basic infrastructure, preparing the code and setting up digital library websites, too. It is defined as "a software system that is based on a defined (possibly distributed) architecture and provides all functionality required by a particular Digital Library. Users interact with a Digital Library through the corresponding Digital Library System." The preparation and maintenance of user-friendly library website or portal along with a "discovery interface" is very significant. In this context, further, Fox and others (2011) define a "digital library management system (DLMS)" as "a generic software system that provides the appropriate software infrastructure both:

(i) to produce and administer a Digital Library System incorporating the suite of functionality considered fundamental for Digital Libraries and

(ii) to integrate additional software offering more refined, specialized or advanced functionality."

Easy navigation and access to electronic databases, downloading ebooks and other materials are needed along with searching the digital collections.

Web-Scale Discovery Services

The web scale discovery services help users searching, browsing, selecting, and accessing the digital content. The users may desire to seek any kind of document from diverse formats e.g. an ebook, or some historical images. The intuitive nature of discovery services interface assist the users in locating information. There are various Web-scale Discovery Services which function as tools facilitating the seamless search across local and remote content. Few examples of such tools and services are OCLC, EBSCO, ProQuest, Ex Libris, etc. According to Reitz (2014), discovery of resources in the library service is "a single interface, providing integrated access to the multiple information resources (catalogs, publishers' e-book and e-journal collections, subscription databases, archival collections) to which a library has rights. Discovery systems use consolidated subject indexing and metadata. Search results are generally deduced and relevance ranked." The discovery interfaces are available in both kinds of platforms, commercial and open source. Commercial examples include:

- Innovative Interfaces Encore
- ProQuest AquaBrowser Library
- BiblioCommons
- Ex Libris Primo
- SirsiDynix Enterprise

Commercial resource management systems with discovery services include:

- EBSCO Discovery Service
- OCLC WorldCat Discovery Service
- ProQuest Summon

For example, "Sowiport" uses the discovery power of Vufind. Open source options include:

- Blacklight
- eXtensible Catalog
- VuFind

PLATFORMS FOR DIGITAL COLLECTIONS

To create digital collections with specific purposes and intended users, various software or suites are available. Some software have been available as technical support in keeping digital collections, according to their format or type of services. Few examples are in the form of "Digital Assessment Management (DAM)", "Collection Management Software (CMS)", "Content Management System (CMS)" and library Repository Solutions. According to the shared experiences (Reitz, 2014), **digital asset management** (DAM) have placed themselves at a significant place in libraries. These are "systems designed to organize and display digital content produced in a variety of media types. The content is usually locally owned and controlled, rather than licensed from a third party. Most of the DAM systems offered by the leading library automation vendors use standards other than the MARC record, such as XML, the Open Archives Initiative Protocol for Metadata Harvesting (OAI-PMH), Metadata Encoding and Transmission Standards (METS), and JPEG2000. The rapid pace of archival and special collections digitization projects has created the need for DAM systems. This is synonymous with digital object management."

Few more examples are BePress, Digital Commons, and ContentDM. And other resources include "CARLI, Fedora, and Omeka. Few (open-source as well as, for example, commercial) solutions are as following:

Annotum : an open source scholarly publishing platform.

DigiTool : This is a commercial tool developed by Ex Libris.

Drupal : A content management system.

EPrints : An open-source "institutional repository solution".

Hydra : This is a "free and open source repository solution" for digital content.

Islandora : This is open-source software to discover digital assets.

Greenstone : An open source option for digital library collections.

Open Repository : Commercial software to maintain institutional repositories.

VIVO : This is a "semantic web platform enabling research discovery".

OPEN SOURCE TOOLS

Anthologize : open-source software to convert online content into digital book.

PressForward : for content curating and sharing.

Scripto : To enable "community transcriptions" of document and multimedia files.

Complex objects are significant components in a digital scenario, according to Kozievitch and Torres (2014), "complex objects consist of multiple digital objects. In other words, a complex object is an aggregation of objects that can be grouped together and manipulated as a single object." A number of technologies are used to handle complex objects. Earlier "Digital Content Component (DCC)" was introduced as a "generalization format for representing complex objects". A DDC contains few components, such as content, structure, interface and metadata. The buckets provide an "archive-independent container construct that allows data types and objects to be grouped together into a single object". The following aspects show the advanced features of digital libraries:

Content-Based Image Retrieval : Content-Based Image Retrieval (CBIR) systems are responsible for performing queries on visual properties for creating significant descriptors for images.

Annotation : Annotation is another example of a digital tool involves working with "subdocuments within original digital objects".

Geospatial Information : When the connection of digital objects to geospatial information in the form of images or videos are needed.

Thus various tools and services are available from various digital library platforms to enrich user experiences.

REFERENCES

1. ACRL (March 2015). Environmental Scan 2015. http://www.ala.org/acrl/sites/ala.org.acrl/files/content/publications/whitepapers/EnvironmentalScan15.pdf
2. ALA (April 2015). The State of America's Libraries: A Report from the American Library Association 2015. American Libraries. Special Issue.

3. Allen County Public Library Genealogy Center. http://www.genealogycenter.org/)

4. American Centuries. http://www.memorialhall.mass.edu/

5. Arms, William Y. (2000). Digital Libraries. MIT Press in January 2000..

6. Ashenfelder, Mike (2013). "The Library of Congress and personal digital archiving." In D. Hawkins (ed.), Personal Archiving: Preserving Our Digital Heritage. Medford, NJ, USA: Information Today, Inc. Available as an ebook through IUPUI.

7. Bartolo.https://journals.tdl.org/jodi/index.php/jodi/article/view/119/hdl.handle.net/2249.2/jodi-151

8. Berkeley Digital Library SunSITE. http://sunsite.berkeley.edu/ARL/definition.html

9. Bracero History Archive. http://braceroarchive.org/

10. Bishop, A. P., Mehra, B., et al. (2003). "Participatory Action Research and Digital Libraries: Reframing Evaluation". Digital Library Use: Social Practice in Design and Evaluation, edited by A. P. Bishop, N. A. Van House and B. Buttenfield (Cambridge, MA: MIT Press), 161-189

11. Brown, Nathan (May/June 2015). "Helping members of the community manage their digital lives: developing a personal digital archiving workshop." D-Lib Magazine, 21(5/6). Available online.

12. Douglass, J. A. (1998). "Shared Governance at UC: An Historical Review", Center for Studies in Higher Education, University of California, Berkeley http://ishi.lib.berkeley.edu/cshe/jdouglass/gov.html

13. Chen, H., Ng, T., Martinez, J., and Schatz, B. (1997). "A concept space approach to addressing the vocabulary problem in scientific information retrieval: An experiment on the Worm Community System". Journal of the American Society for Information Science, 48(1), 17-31.

14. Cleveland (1998). "Characteristics of digital libraries." (In) Integration of digital libraries in e-learning. https://www.tlu.ee/~sirvir/Information%20and%20Knowledge%20Management/Integration%20of%20digital%20libraries%20in%20e-learning/characteristics_of_digital_libraries.html

15. Corrado, Edward M. and Moulaison, Healther Lea (2014). Digital Preservation for Libraries, Archives, and Museums. Rowman & Littlefield.

16. Costantino, G., Crowley, B., Morin, R., and Thomas, E. (2011). "Heeding the Call: User Feedback Management and the Digital

Library". Microform & Digitization Review, 40(4), 146-157.

17. Croft, B., Cook, R. and Wilder, D., (1995). "Providing Government Information on the Internet: Experiences with THOMAS," in Proceedings of the Digital Libraries Conference DL'95, Austin, TX. June 10-12, pp. 19-24.

18. Dempsey, Lorcan (2015). Introduction: rules and roles. In N. Allen (ed.), New Roles for the Road Ahead: Essays Commissioned for ARCL's 75th Anniversary. ACRL.

19. Digital Library Production Guide of the Kentuckiana Digital Library. http://www.kyvl.org/kentuckiana/bpguide/about.shtml#two

20. Development and Characteristic of Digital Library as a Library. https://core.ac.uk/download/pdf/82300967.pdf

21. DeRidder, Jody L. and Matheny, Kathryn (July/August 2014). What do researchers need? feedback on use of online primary source materials. D-Lib Magazine, 20(7/8).

22. Dowlin, K.E. (1984). The electronic library. Neal-Schuman.

23. Fox, Edward A. (2011). Guidelines and Resources for Teaching Digital Libraries. JCDL 2011 Tutorial. PowerPoint Presentation.

24. Fox, Edward A., Yang, Seungwon, Ewers, John, Wildemuth, Barbara, Pomerantz, Jeffrey P., Oh, Sanghee (2011). 1-a (10-c): Digital Library Curriculum Development Module. Collaborative Research: Curriculum Development: Digital Libraries. Available: http://curric.dlib.vt.edu/modDev/modules/DL_1-a_2011-05-11.pdf

25. Fox, E. A., et al. (1993). "Users, user interfaces, and objects: Envision, a digital library". Journal of the American Society for Information Science, 44(8), September: 480-491

26. Hathitrust. https://www.hathitrust.org/

27. Hawkins, Donald T., (ed.) (2013). Personal Archiving: Preserving Our Digital Heritage. Medford, NJ, USA: Information Today, Inc.. Available as an ebook through IUPUI. http://site.ebrary.com.proxy.ulib.uits.iu.edu/lib/iupui/detail.action?docID=10778521&p00=digital+preservation

28. Houghton, Bernadette (March/April 2015). Trustworthiness: self-assessment of an institutional repository against ISO 16363-2012. D-Lib Magazine, 21(3/4).

29. http://ils.unc.edu

30. https://journals.tdl.org/jodi/index.php/jodi/article/view/119/123

31. IFLA. http://archive.ifla.org/VI/5/op/udtop8/udtop8.htm

32. Kirchner, Joy, Diaz, José, Henry, Geneva, Fliss, Susan, Culshaw, John, Gendron, Heather & Cawthorne, Jon E. (February 2015). The center of excellent model for information services. Council on Library and Information Resources. http://www.clir.org/pubs/reports/pub163/pub163.pdf

33. Kostkova, P., and Madle, G. (2013). "What impact do healthcare digital libraries have? An evaluation of national resource of infection control at the point of care using the Impact-ED framework." International Journal On Digital Libraries, 13 (2), 77-90.

34. Kozievitch, Nadia P. and Torres, Richardo da Silva (2014). Complex Objects. In E. Fox, R. Torres, Digital Library Technologies: Complex Objects, Annotation, Ontologies, Classification, Extraction, and Security. Synthesis Lectures on Information Concepts, Retrieval, and Services. Morgan & Claypool Publishers. Available as an ebook through IUPUI. http://site.ebrary.com.proxy.ulib.uits.iu.edu/lib/iupui/detail.action?adv.x=1&docID=10857385&f00=all&f01=subject&p00=digital+library&p01= %22Digital+Libraries%22

35. Lyman, P., Varian, H., et al. (2003). How much information? http://www.sims.berkeley.edu/research/projects/how-much-info-2003/

36. Overview: Digital Libraries: By Library Type. https://www.eduscapes.com/digital/1c.htm

37. McLean and Lynch (2004). Reasons to integrate digital libraries and VLEs. in Integration of digital libraries in e-learning. https://www.tlu.ee/~sirvir/Information%20and%20Knowledge%20Management/Integration%20of%20digital%20libraries%20in%20e-learning/index.html

38. McMartin. https://journals.tdl.org/jodi/index.php/jodi/article/view/119/hdl.handle.net/2249.2/jodi-148

39. Marlino, M., Sumner, T. R., et al. (2001) "The Digital Library for Earth System Education: Building Community, Building the Library". Communications of the ACM, special issue on Digital Libraries, May, 80-81

40. Outline and Preliminary Evaluation of the Classical Digital Library Mode, Steven L. MacCall, Ana D. Cleveland, Ian E. Gibson (1999). Proceedings of the Fall 1999 Annual Meeting of the American Society for Information Science

41. Project DL Site. http://www.coe.missouri.edu/~is334/projects/Project_DL/overview.html

42. Reitz, Joan M. (2014). Online Dictionary for Library and Information

Science. Libraries Unlimited. Available: http://www.abc-clio.com/ODLIS/odlis_a.aspx.

43. Sachs, J. D. (2004). "Sustainable Development: Editorial". Science, 304 (5671): 649

44. Shafritz, Jay M. and Ott, J. S. (1992). Classics of Organization Theory, third edition (Pacific Grove, CA: Brooks/Cole Publishing)

45. Sharifabadi (2006). Reasons to integrate digital libraries and VLEs. In Integration of digital libraries in e-learning. https://www.tlu.ee/~sirvir/Information%20and%20Knowledge%20Management/Integration% 20of%20digital%20libraries%20in%20e-learning/index.html

46. Schatz, B., Mischo, W., Cole, T., Hardin, J., Bishop, A., and Chen, H. (1996). Federating diverse collections of scientific literature, Computer, May, 28-35.

47. Sheridan, P. and Ballerini, J. (1996). "Experiments in multilingual information retrieval using the SPIDER system". Proceedings of ACM SIGIR Conference on Research and Development in Information Retrieval, 58-65.

48. Witten, Ian H., Bainbridge, David, and Nicholas, David (2010). How to Build a Digital Library. Morgan Kaufmann: Elsevier. Google Preview Available: https://books.google.com/books?id=HiJNbEy5f70C. Available as an ebook through IUPUI. http://site.ebrary.com.proxy. ulib.uits.iu.edu/lib/iupui/detail.action?docID=10344401

49. www.eduscapes.com

50. www.home.wlu.com

51. Yang, Sharon Q and Dalal, Heather A. (2015). Virtual reference: where do academic librarians stand? Computers in Libraries, 35(5), 4-10.

CHAPTER FOUR
Information Management

SUMMARY: The concepts of information management have been significant in library and information management, thus the following approach has been followed to explore the chapter:

- Introduction
- Exploring Information Management
- Principles of Information Management
- Librarianship and Information Management
- Information management challenges
- Basic Understanding for Information Management
- Access to Information
- Digital Transformation and Information Management
- Information and Data Management
- Management Information System
- Designing of data/information management system
- Information Management and Library Operations
- Information Management Architecture and Components
- Perform Information Management
- Fostering Facets in Information Management
- Strategies for Information Management
- Benefits of Information Management

INTRODUCTION

The libraries have been designing services with the continuous understanding of users' needs. The factors such as the technological, economical and social changes have been contributory in compelling the libraries to play transformational roles. The recent past has witnessed the impact on the sustainability of the library and information centers. The challenges before the libraries have been accompanied by various opportunities and venues regarding the management of information services. The innovation and need to update the information services are the components of changing contexts. Information managements been linked to data computing skills. Improvements in professional capabilities of library staff leads towards the better information management in digital age. Upgrading information management skills is instrumental in effective information services in the perspectives of present and anticipated needs of users. The challenges in developing information management skills revolve around the steps such as resource sharing/ collaboration, flexible approaches, social networking, ICT infrastructure developments. These steps transforms into the strategies to deal with the broader issues of information management. IM is not same as content management or knowledge management. There are overlapping processes in these three ideas though technical differences are there such as content management is related with data and display (e.g. HTML coding); while knowledge management deals with information for various purposes such as training of people, transfer of knowledge, and empowering the shared wisdom in any area; academic or industrial.

EXPLORING INFORMATION MANAGEMENT

"Information management" is a term which has comprehensive in nature and includes various kinds of information managing systems and processes which are meant in an organization. Information management is popularly, in context with technology, known as:

- web content management (CM)
- digital asset management (DAM)
- document management (DM)
- learning management systems (LMS)
- records management Systems (RMS)

Understanding the deeper and comprehensive meaning of information management relates to implementation of technology in the business processes related with creation, storage and use of information. Information management is composed of the element information, structure, i.e., "information architecture", including metadata, and other elements to manage and retrieve. These facets are categorized as content, technology, process and the human resource.

PRINCIPLES OF INFORMATION MANAGEMENT

Information management is based on various processes and principles. Various attempts and efforts have been made to formulize the principles applicable by keeping various strategies and objectives in mind. The information management principles are mentioned as the "Information Management Body of Knowledge (IMBOK), it provides a framework that breaks down management skills into six knowledge areas and four process areas.

Knowledge areas : The knowledge areas include the following:

- **Information Technology (IT) :** Hardware and software
- **Information Systems :** IT built into a system that meets business needs and policies
- **Business Information :** Created by analyzing and contextualizing data using tools such as the information system

- **Business Processes :** How to evaluate and use the business information to make decisions
- **Business Benefit :** The desired advantage the business information will provide
- **Business Strategy :** The master plan that gives a company a direction. Ideally, decisions made through the business processes, which are based on business information, will guide the strategy and lead to the realization of the business benefits.

Process areas : The IMBOK process areas are:

- **Projects :** Adding new capacity, software, and hardware to information systems
- **Business Change :** Evaluating information to drive improvements in processes
- **Business Operations :** The day-to-day of a business. These will guide improvements based on updates to processes, and will hopefully increase benefits.
- **Performance Management :** Trying to ensure operations are running at peak capacity

LIBRARIANSHIP AND INFORMATION MANAGEMENT

Role of librarian encompasses the management of information and services towards users. The responsibility of librarian involves the creating provisions of access to information. Duties and functions in routine begin with the acquisition of information, organizing in a manner that the information is accessible, and dissemination of the information. Later stages include "weeding out", archiving and deletion as the requirement is posed before library. Contributions of librarians are related with the research support, too with the efficient information management. The dedication and commitment to the information management helps the library to achieve an ideal status.

Information management and related practices are

driven by a range of factors which include the continuous improvement in the efficiency of information services, compliance regulations and the keenness to managing information. Information management has been deploying and implementation the technology based solutions in library related with print and digital information management. Without information management, the libraries struggle to create an information efficient environment and deliver an integrated information management scenario. Information management deals with the organizational targets and the cultural issues which may create a complex picture to comprehend. The critical success factors for information management in libraries can be considered as guiding principles. Information management is organizational context, rather than the technology perspective. The challenges in information management are more contextual and organizational strategies in nature, less technological implications.

Methods to Understand

Identification of most valuable asset: The information is the most valuable asset of library which requires the forward approach. This involves the understanding of distinguished and unique features of resources and services of the library. The developments in infrastructure and facilities are supporting the access to information. The advent of cloud computing is the example from last decade yet the volumes of data, and its transmission across the people is at greatest pace. The data zipping from library server to users' smart phone and other digital devices is travelling all over the globe. Information management transforms the organization into an agile platform for improved versions of information products and services.

Measuring the colossal benefit: The role of information is found in many directions. The information stored in databases or with the human resources, is never entirely utilized. Efforts to unlock the full potential of the information are yet need exploration. The use of information also varies from person to person. Capabilities of users are different in their groups. Sometimes the same information may give greater results, and other times it does not prove fruitful more than very minor usage and impact. Unlocking the information, getting it out of silos and creation of a robust information system in library would be able to fill the gaps in information services.

Unlocking the information assets of Library: The road map for unlocking the information assets of libraries may be diverse yet including few of the following aspects:

1. Setting up an organization level information management system, giving responsibility to a senior library staff and creation of risk controls for the information.
2. Conducting an audit of library' information to identify the costs and bottlenecks, applying the digital approaches and leading towards new information management insights.
3. Managing the physical and digital storage to the optimal combination of physical and digital library
4. Using content management or data management system the management of unstructured data of library.
5. Applying data management and analytics to the enormous amount of data available in the library.

The information has power and the information management provides the opportunity to unleash the strength of library with improved efficiency and insights.

INFORMATION MANAGEMENT CHALLENGES

The libraries are confronted with myriad management challenges and issues where the explosion of information has also augmented the responsibilities of libraries. The usual problems and issues in the information management are as following :

- Scattered and unaccounted number of platforms and strategies for information management systems.
- Diverse range of components needing the upgrade
- Need of long-term strategic direction relating to Information management.
- Updating the knowledge, adaptation of working practices and processes by the staff
- Aspects related with the quality, consistency, duplication of information.
- Administrative and technical support for of information management.
- Availability of resources for information management.
- Understanding the "enterprise-wide definitions" for information.
- Challenges relating with types of information management and values of data.
- Addressing various users' needs and issues.

BASIC UNDERSTANDING FOR INFORMATION MANAGEMENT

The basic concepts of information management include the understanding of the complex nature of information, its storage in the organization and how to disseminate. Identification of technology and its adoption requires much expertise which may not be available in the library. In that situation, the library may discuss with other departments and outside the organizations, if the previous efforts do not cater the need. Information management should be able to deliver tangible & visible benefits. The library should prioritize according to the aims of parent organization and users' needs. Information management demands strong leadership and the abilities to mitigate risks. Since it is a team work, the extensive communication is applicable at each level. The information management in library aims to provide seamless user experience.

Information management begins with focusing on implementing the single technology in isolation. The choice of software, open source or from a commercial vendor may be a decision taken after much research. The standardized solutions may be answers to information management while the needs of each section should be taken into consideration. The consideration, controlling and centralization of every single activity are required in the information management. Conversion of complex set of needs into the simple solutions is possible by planning. Information management is successfully implemented with the strong leadership, clear direction and addressing the issues at right time. Information management success also depends upon the use and involvement of library staff. Their involvement is beyond the installing the software and input the data. Few aspects such as the saving significant a files into the system; regular update by the decentralized contributors, learning the routine activities and their troubleshooting are the staff duties. The adoption of information management system by the staff requires the communication of purposes, targets, understanding the change management, and wide implications. The information management strives on continuous improvements in the storage and services. Information management systems are comprehended to produce "*tangible* and *visible* benefits". The main objective is to achieve the users' satisfaction by meeting their needs.

Instead of the technology-driven approach, the planning for information management should be able to drive the process and meet targets by addressing the library needs. Overall strategy and direction bring the urgent library goals before information management system. It is difficult to find an information management without being considered by "analysis paralysis." It is also problematic to find a perfectly planned approach, but the strategy of small components. Replacing a single large (centralized) target to be achieved, the multiple teams and small projects may be better planning options. It may be a composition of small projects run by number of inter-related groups. The inherent complexity of the niche within organizations; there are many risks which are as following:

- Selecting unsuitable technology
- Wrong estimation of time and finances
- The staff, preparedness and will to accommodate new approaches
- User needs and expectations
- Technical issues and fragile solutions

The identification of risks and application of an approach is needed to understand the gaps. "Risk management approaches" are applied to budgets, planning, steps taken and the technological aspects. Extensive communication brings the clear understanding, increased level of adoption and guidelines for "command-and-control approach". Such practices help in reaching to the eventual goal. To provide a good users' experience, the information management should be able to deliver on a single intranet for access and ensuring the standard navigation and "single sign-in" to the users to easy access to information.

ACCESS TO INFORMATION

The retrieval-based information service is found in the form of libraries, museums, archives and records managements. Each of these centers has distinct nature of collection and services. Users with specific needs reach to these information centers to access the information. The nature of each individual information service can be identified in their specific element in the shape of organization's mission, user groups, collection of information which is to be catered, sources of information and various techniques associated to facilitate the access to information. The ultimate goal of each information center and service is the access to information. To understand the term access, it needs attention to the activities in libraries. It is observed that "Indexes" facilitate the subject access while the "censorship" discourages the access to information materials. Few more examples explain more about the "access" in routine information services:

- ICTs in libraries have facilitated the remote access
- Chargeable and fee-based information services are less accessed due to cost factors
- The "open access" has been a parallel approach to reach to the information
- In the information centers like museums, it is the "closed access" is the usual practice.

The access is simple yet reflecting the various connotations in the information service scenario. The "retrieval-based information services" are having the "access" in the core of various provisions and categories.

Various Facets of Access

The "access" is defined as the ways to enable an inquirer to learn from a source pertinent. The source of information should be able to serve the information related to an inquiry. The access provides the evidence that proceeds in the acquisition of desired knowledge. The provisions of access are difficult once there are no pertinent sources, or the inquiries are vague in nature, absence of expertise, etc. There are few aspects and barriers related with the information access. Understanding of these aspects helps in retrieving the information through the access:

1. Identification : Identification of suitable sources is relative to the access. The sources of information and process of access may be hidden in the form of bibliography of materials, documentation process, classification of such resources, indexing tools for information retrieval.

2. Availability : The availability of information sources ascertains the user's satisfaction as the document and information delivery related with technology, sometimes. In case of unavailable document or source of information, there arises need of identification and availability of another source of information.

3. Price to the User : The price of information costing to users or otherwise can be understood as the price for acquisition of the same. The inclusion of time, efforts, and any unpleasant experiences completes the "real price" along with the monetary terms. The price includes the endeavors to learn, and use difficult and "user-unfriendly systems".

4. Cost to the service provider : The libraries also have to face the expenditures and prices in the form of efforts. The organization of information is the outcome of many efforts of library which may be freely available to users. There may be few instances where the access to information is not allowed due to national security, or any other factors.

5. Cognitive Access : The cognitive access is related with the inquirer's own abilities and expertise to understand the information provide in the form of source. Failing to understand, the user may take help of explanation (additional interpretation of the source) and education (needing more subject expertise). The explanation and education are helpful when the source of information is in other language and there are other sources to supplement the reading and enquiry.

6. Acceptability : The acceptability of information is related with the reluctance to rely on the credibility of source due to "cognitive authority". The unacceptability is also related to the "conflicts with other beliefs, a matter of cognitive dissonance". This kind of problem arises due to the previous possessed knowledge and arrival of new opposite knowledge revealed though an information source.

The *information system* denotes the systems in which various forms and elements such as data, objects, and documents are retrieved. The phrase *information-supplying system* provides more awareness of few facets such as identification, availability, and cost involved with the provider. The access in the information system should lead to "information-as-knowledge" not as "information-as-thing". The knowledge management should frame a *system which supports the access to information with* cognitive access and acceptability. Various remedies for information access are in the form of:

- technical nature related with the better retrieval systems including authenticity for identification, information delivery
- required time, and costs involved
- instructional issues and assessment of expertise and acceptability

DIGITAL TRANSFORMATION AND INFORMATION MANAGEMENT

Digital transformation is the streamlining of the organization's information scenario. The integration of digital technology into the routine functioning, operations has been instrumental in augmenting the quality of deliverance towards the library users. The optimization of existing technology infrastructure, observing the complex digital scenarios, is difficult toward reaching an agile and scalable structure. The solutions are available in the form of following components:

- Storage of data in the huge clouds,
- Automation of routine workflow,
- Preservation, imaging and restoration,

- migration services

Digital transformation integrated with the information management help the libraries to:

- Improve service structure with improved access and usage of information
- Augmented functional and operational efficiency along with processes involving assessing the information growth
- Focus on the goals of library with core strategy and optimization

The further elaboration of digital transformation and Information Management as follows:

Cloud Data Management : Leveraging a secure, "purpose-built cloud" to keep the data accessible and protected.

Data Centers : Collaboration in establishing, upgrading and migrating, the data to keep in secure ways.

Digital preservation : To keep the "analog information and assets" for better accessibility by converting into digital format.

Media Restoration and Migration : Very significant step to preserve archived data for future needs, followed by migration.

Workflow Automation : To support the routine tasks through digital workflows, and enabling faster processing.

The Road to Digital Transformation is mapping the survival in the fast paced ICT influenced environment by planning a journey towards the complete digital change. The digital transformation involves the solving the problems and evolving above them. The information converted into graphics with the help of digital tools is one facet among the many. Libraries should address the changing user demands by optimizing the existing IT infrastructure.

In the libraries where problems are found with the collection and management of information, the "information management" helps in improving the effectiveness of organizations. The information management supports resource-providing access in a timely fashion with cost-effective processes. Effective information management catalyzes the flow of reliable and usable information for the organizational goals and users in the library. It ensures accountability and risk management by solving the problems such as handling inadequate storage and flow of information for decision-making. The identification of information needs by the libraries is followed by engaging qualified staff, training, and automation of library routine processes and adoption of information management strategies to lead the information management.

The globalization became the reason for the large scale interaction and integration at various levels including people, organizations and governments. Challenges, due to globalization, before library, have compelled to brace up and deliver effective services the "global user'. Globalization is observed in the form of information, itself and providing knowledge access. Identification and determination of the services which are influenced by globalization has become must.

INFORMATION AND DATA MANAGEMENT

Significance of data in an organization is found in flow its systems, databases, processes, and sections. The organizations consider the data asset very significant, in context with searching and retrieval. The importance of data is visualized in making well-informed decisions. These decisions are related to measuring the achievement of the strategy. The process to find out any fraudulent activities is possible if historical risk-related data is included. The methods related with the data management are as significant as the mechanisms to create the same. The availability of right data supports the organization to perform processes and measurement of their impact. Accessibility of data assets should be maintained for the processes and human resources in case of need. Other attributes are quality and timeliness provisions of data. The data life cycle: the life cycle of data begins with effective data management for the reliable information. Different uses and management handling takes place at different stages in the life-cycle phases. The example of such scenario is the discovery of data at the initiation of some task, not later on at the completion of task.

Usually the lifespan of data is more than the task or project that was the reason of creation of it. The availability of resultant data is useful for the organizations whenever required. The investment into the data creation, generation and preservation is fruitful when in future it brings the desired result many years afterwards. With the right techniques applied for data preservation, the problems for future access are taken care. The investments, in the form of technology, time finances, made are directly related to the access, visibility, and relevance of data.

Types of Data and Environment

The value of data is determined by the context it relates to. The data which is not used by anyone is also worthless. The information contained and carried on by the data makes it worth. Extraction and delivery of information can be done as summary through data analysis and compilation of report. Many subjects/disciplines involve statistical analysis for research, data mining in information retrieval, predictive analysis in futuristic approaches and business intelligence. Good and systematic use of data is the common feature of various disciplines.

Big data : The expression "Big data" informs about exponential growth and availability of data. This availability of data is found in both structured and unstructured manner while the main characteristics of big data are volume, velocity, and variety.

Operational data : The operational data is outcome of the processes of environments that provide "core transactional capabilities" including the processing applications, as in DBMS.

Data exchange : The use of data exchanges and related standards for sharing the information. Exchange formats and metadata are useful for reducing cost and delivery time.

Knowledge discovery : The hidden patterns within data are very useful for predictive models and the use of specific software perform advanced statistics, graphical visualization, etc.

The focus of the invested time and energy by the organizations is observed in application development and developing the technical infrastructure. This approach is often responsible for delays in implementation, and system failure. The coordination of data and library staff with the IT experts is required to place the system. The libraries should interweave the core aspects in information management as follows:

- Collection of data/information in timely and cost-effective.
- Cost-efficient and purposeful data/information with minimum redundancy.
- Use of data/information for monitoring and improving policies and programs.
- Coordination for standardization of data and sharing.
- Cultivation of mechanisms to support data/information activities.
- Following the certain principles such as related with confidentiality, privacy, and organizational rules etc. related with the creation and sharing of data.

Information management supports the framework to manage the coordination among the library staff, administration, academic communities, etc. Technical architecture implementation is helped by the planning and coordination among the stakeholders of the library.

MANAGEMENT INFORMATION SYSTEM

The purpose of a management information system is to support the human resources of an organization in decision making towards achievement of the goals. An effective MIS assembles data generated in the organizational operations, received from the external inputs, etc. The features of good information system are as following:

Relevance of Information : The information from an MIS is that data was output of various activities. The organization needs the information in a form that is useful for decision making.

Accuracy and Reliability of Information : The accuracy and reliability of the data is related to determination of the effectiveness of the information.

Usefulness of Information : The relevance of information may not be the factor for being ultimate in nature; it is the usefulness of the information that is related with the decisions.

Timeliness of Information : The timeliness and current provisions of information are very significant in anticipation of the trend. The potential inaccuracies may arise due to untimely provided information. Data given in timely fashioned as real-time information serves the purpose of information management.

Completeness of Information : The missing data, the gaps and other discrepancies become factors for improper decisions leading to undesired effects.

DESIGNING OF DATA/INFORMATION MANAGEMENT SYSTEM

Like in physical library, the acquisition, organization and making available the books, the data or information is managed. In the data/ information management at a deep and intricate level few steps such as acquiring, managing, and extracting information are taken. The complexity of the tasks in information management grows due to certain factors such as library needs, number of users, and various new services. The information management depends on following facets into considerations:

- Library requirements
- Operational requirements of library services
- Library access and resource usage requirements
- Data-sharing and other technical requirements
- analytical requirements (various types of library reports)
- Privacy and security

The complexity data and quality of data is significant in library operations, the "Federal Data Architecture Subcommittee" (DAS) Data Quality Framework defines data quality as "the state of excellence that exists when data is relevant to its intended uses, and is of sufficient detail and quantity, with a high degree of accuracy and completeness, consistent with other sources, and presented in appropriate ways." Various characteristics of data can be found as accessibility, completeness, consistency, accuracy, relevancy, timeliness, and validity. The following environments introduce key considerations:

Standalone : This kind of system is related with access of data from a single application. This single application is considered with limited or not many interfaces.

Enterprise-wide : This enterprise wide system expresses relevance of data for enterprise level without any interface for external areas.

Multi-enterprise : In this system, data is shared and available among more than one enterprise with multiple interfaces.

Applications of data stewardships and data governance can facilitate mediation and conflict management in the organization. Data governance relates to accountability, and policy enforcement. This entire range of tasks is based on the component processes considering "data value and standard definitions". It also entails the entire ranges of processes such as "the availability, accessibility, and integrity of the data. An effective administering includes an accountability structure, a defined set of procedures, and a plan to execute those procedures. The Data Governance Framework is related with responsibilities, and authorities for the strategic and operational levels. Data security encompasses the policies related with data protection from unauthorized access, disclosure, etc. This also concerns the integrity of data. The data security is ensured by having physical security, equipment/ devices security, and network security.

INFORMATION MANAGEMENT AND LIBRARY OPERATIONS

The definition of information management during early development is as "Information management is a cycle of processes that support the organization's learning activities: identifying information needs, acquiring information, organizing and storing information, developing information products and services, distributing information, and using information" (Choo, 1995). Therefore, the information management is related with the managing organizational processes and systems which are based on acquisition, creation, organization, distribution and using the information. The process view is composed of various activities:

- identification of information needs;
- acquisition and creation of information;

- analysis and interpretation of information;
- organization and storage of information;
- information access and dissemination;
- information use.

Various assumptions related with term 'information management' show its usage in many fields such as in computer science as "information technology management" or "data management", though related with database design; in business or management studies; it is associated with business performance; and in the field of librarianship and information science, information is related with external information resources and the associated technology; user and information retrieval issues. Library services provide various information management services to all staff and projects.

Information Management Practices in Libraries

An information management process is the method an organization uses to:

- Acquire or retrieve information
- Organize information
- Maintain information

The recent professional roles are reflecting the practices of knowledge management in library and information management. The knowledge management practices are closely related and share resemblance with librarianship and information management. The emphasis by knowledge management practitioners on the significance of knowledge elicitation and knowledge creation, imbibes the values of team work. This also recalls the deeper relation with organizational strategy development.

INFORMATION MANAGEMENT ARCHITECTURE AND COMPONENTS

While understanding information, it is "an ordered

sequence of symbols that record or transmit a message." The collection of facts in the information has additional value. Relating to IM process, it is "a set of activities associated with the collection and management of information from one or more sources and the distribution of that information to one or more audiences." Existence of information in any organization or library may be found in different assets and levels. There are interrelated steps which are known as information systems, system of systems (SoS), technical architectures, hardware/ platforms, and human resources. The purpose of information management is to find out services and solutions in organizations. Set of activities are composing a process for improving system. These processes include designing, use of technologically-based systems and processes in operational contexts. Information management refers to the structure, processing, and delivery of information. Information management is beyond source or format for delivery through multiple channels. The "computer-based" system is an organized information management system of various components functioning together. These components are hardware//software, networks, data resources and human resources. An IM system depends upon "rate-limiting architecture" and design variables. These variables are in the form of intangible aspects such as information quality, network security, etc.

The variables are further may be categorized as architecture aspects, design issues and considerations in the context with "system-of-interest" (SoI). In this context, the attribute "quality" can be observed in the perspectives of "data validity, and consistency". Effective IM systems have aims to solve business and organizational needs. The development of IM systems supports in strategic planning for the concerned organization, intricate understanding of technology trends, various applications' development, and analyses of operational components. This entire range of process takes involves various techniques for resource control. The last step for the IM system development includes evaluation of organization structures. The target of IM process is: creation, storage, security, and made easy access for use in problem-solving, solution finding and decision making process.

The Information Management Process can be explained as the quote from ISO/IEC/IEEE 15288 (2015):

"The purpose of the Information Management Process is to generate, obtain, confirm, transform, retain, retrieve, disseminate and dispose of information, to designated stakeholders. *Information management plans, executes, and controls the provision of information to designated stakeholders that is unambiguous, complete, verifiable, consistent, modifiable, traceable, and presentable"*. The "Plan Information Management" is the first step. There are various components and issues related with IM such as:

Scope : The scope of IM plan includes the identification of information to be managed. The extent of time period for the retention of that information along with the understating the need of system data dictionary. The requirement of such dictionary is to "tag" information retrieval. The choice of media (physical, electronic, or both?) and "work in progress" (WIP) should also be considered at initial level for establishing data repositories.

Constraints : The level of configuration control to the information is associated with regulatory requirements. Consideration of users' requirements and agreements, industry standards, and organizational directives is essential.

Control/Security : The permissions granted to the persons, authenticity of users and protection of information from unauthorized users, are few facets of IM control and security mechanisms. Unauthorized access and protecting the intellectual property (IP) rights are also extended responsibilities related to IM security.

Use and choice of data repository: The technical aspects and specifications are to be decided; volume of information to be stored, speed of access, search facilities, formats of files, etc. Validity of information, correct disposal of information, defined review period for each piece of information is few of significant areas.

Life Cycle: The storage of information relates to the extent of period, being "future-proofed" availability of neutral file formats, etc. are considered. The disaster recovery requirements (including back-up copies, regular access of back-up copies to check flawless information recovery) are the formal requirements to retain the information for future use. The availability of archiving facilities with the legal (including regulatory), and audit process, are responsible planning. Defining the archive and archiving method is essential in such environment. Cost-benefit analysis for retention or regeneration of information is must in order to save time and money.

Perform Information Management

While performing information management, there are certain issues as follows:

- Validity of information
- Workflow, timely review and steps to check the progress
- such as "work in progress" to "released"
- Configuration management and its application to the information
- Application of correct "tags" for search, access and retrieval
- Access rules, permissions, and selection of information
- translation of information, a neutral file format consideration before storing it
- Assessment and review date related to continued validity of the information

- workflow for review and removal of unwanted, invalid, or unverifiable information
- Backup recovery system and archiving the information in compliance with legal aspects.

Challenges and Problems

The following technical aspects require attention, without which there may be severe problems, while planning, implementing and working upon the IM:

Data Dictionary : Defining a data dictionary is needed for consistencies in naming conventions for information. This is required for accurate and complete searches.

Metadata : "Tagging" information with metadata provides effective search results.

Back-Up Verification : It is significant to ensure that back-up information is secure and accessible

Access Obsolescence : Related with maintain the currency of format and retaining of working copy of software for the accessible information.

Long-Term Retention : This refers to archiving information with required durability on the digital medium.

Validity Maintenance : Checking the validity of information for the "correct information" being retained and used.

FOSTERING FACETS IN INFORMATION MANAGEMENT

The following facets are significant for consideration in IM:

Guidance and planning : The guidance, planning and strategy for IM at both the task and organization level should be availed to avoid pitfalls.

Value of information : Recognition of information as a strategic asset.

Storage Capacity : Planning to have storage capacity to hold on and need to double yearly basis

Information Access : Sitting information has no value; the use makes it valuable, therefore access is very significant.

Data Modeling : Designing consistent data models according to needs (along with the underlying structure)

Quality Management of information : The quality of information is contextual with cost-effectiveness.

Repository Design : The information management includes following IPRs and "export control rules"

Information Management Strategies

Information management strategies the planning guides to maintain the flow of IM steps, improvements and preparations for future with the following processes:

- Present status and planning
- Setting objective
- Planned steps to meet the objectives
- Strategies to focus on information generation, acquisition and management
- Inter-departmental processes and policies for interaction
- Clear responsibility and reporting

TYPES OF INFORMATION MANAGEMENT SYSTEM

There are various kinds of IMs with the specific and distinct functions:

Business Intelligence System (BIS) : BIS uses "business intelligence system" for decisions making.

Customer Relationship Management System (CRMS) : This kind of information management system related to the storing data about customers, sales, and sales opportunities, meant for business development.

Sales Force Automation System (SFAS) : This system is related with automation of tasks, contact management, and order management.

Transaction Processing System (TPS) : This is functional in the areas of sale and functions as a point-of-sale (POS) system (such as searching and booking a hotel through web site).

Knowledge Management System (KMS) : KMS helps in training and services area by providing answers and troubleshooting the problems.

Data analysis seeks improvement opportunities for driving the methods to achieve the organizational goals.

STRATEGIES FOR INFORMATION MANAGEMENT

The discussion on i-SCOOP states, "By being strategic about it all and looking at the business reality and priorities, we can make sure that we don't belong to the two-thirds of enterprises that fail to meet best practice standards for data control." There are few steps which can be considered as features and good starting points:

Ease of Use: Easy to use is an important point as, the third edition of "Strategic Information Management: Challenges and Strategies in Managing Information Systems", (Robert D. Galliers and Dorothy E. Leidner), states that "the notion that systems should be made to appeal to their users in every stage of development and in their final form encouraged the development of 'user friendly' systems, in the hope that early usability would reduce the requests for subsequent maintenance."

Planning and Designing : This should happen at the organizational level keeping all the stake-holders in planning, while maintaining the sharing and interoperability.

Data Management : Creation of policies to frame the inclusion, archiving, and removal of information.

Centralized Data Management and Governance : This is related with the governing body, defined procedures, and plans discussed in "Globalization and Information Management Strategies", which emphasized upon "Lack of a centralized information management strategy often causes corporate entities (e.g., customers and products) to have multiple attributes and values across databases. This makes linkages or data sharing among value activities difficult at best. These factors make important performance and correlation data unavailable for decision making, thereby creating important obstacles to the firm's competitive advantages."

Metadata and Quality Management : Categorization, tracking, and quality of data are very significant in order to make it accessible and usable.

Creation of Taxonomy : The nomenclature and structure of data make efforts to connect different terms and searching possible, due to classification of terms (through taxonomy).

Rules and Accountability : These facets relate to training, following rules and fixing accountability for the maintenance of present status and planning for future. The room for continuous improvement is always there; hence collaborations and future prospects are foreseen.

Audit, Apps and Interoperability : The assessment of security aspects along with sharing information with interoperability among the systems is also needed. The progress in the contexts of access and technology is always welcome as everything is now on figure tips in the form of apps.

Benefits of Information Management

The information management has reached the levels which have entered into many areas of human life. According to Venkatraman, who developed DIKAR (Data, Information, Knowledge, Action, Results), following aspects have been instrumental in describing the hidden purposes of IM:

Role of Data : to be interpreted to provide information

Transformation of Information : to be change and emerge as knowledge

Effects of Knowledge : helping in effective decisions

Conversion of e decisions : implementing decisions towards appropriate actions

Meaning of Appropriate actions : receiving the meaningful results

The future trends can be guessed with the recent developments before us and their application in routine human life. The examples are the dreams coming though little induction and promise of artificial intelligence (AI) as; "Analytics Augmentation" for more automation, data preparation and pattern matching. The advent of intelligent devices (e.g. auto-piloted drones) and intelligent agents (i.e. Siri and Alexa) are here to process large amount of data, provide information and answer the human queries.

REFERENCES

1. Bert, Markgraf (2019). Characteristics of a Good Management Information System. Rev. by Michelle Seidel.
2. Bowen, P., J. Hash, and M. Wilson (2007). Information Security Handbook: A Guide for Managers: Information Security, National Institute of Standards and Technology (NIST) Special Publication (SP) 800-100, Rev. 3.
3. Brendan, Loughridge. Knowledge management, librarians and information managers: fad or future? https://www.emeraldinsight.com/author/Loughridge%2C+Brendan
4. Culnan, M. J. (1984). The dimensions of perceived accessibility to information. Journal of the American Society for Information 36, pp. 302-308.
5. https://www.mitre.org/
6. INCOSE. (2012). Systems Engineering Handbook: A Guide for System Life Cycle Processes and Activities, version 3.2.1. San Diego, CA, USA: International Council on Systems Engineering (INCOSE), INCOSE-TP-2003-002-03.2.2.

7. Information Management Strategies: From Punch Cards to Data Warehouses, and Looking to the Future with Big Data and AI. https://www.smartsheet.com/enterprise

8. ISO/IEC/IEEE. (2008). Systems and Software Engineering - System Life Cycle Processes. Geneva, Switzerland: International Organisation for Standardisation/International Electrotechnical Commissions. ISO/IEC/IEEE 15288, 2008.

9. ISO/IEC/IEEE. (2015). Systems and Software Engineering – System Life Cycle Processes. Geneva, Switzerland: International Organisation for Standardisation / International Electrotechnical Commissions. ISO/IEC/IEEE 15288.

10. Library Trends (1986). Issue on Privacy, Secrecy, and National Information Policy. 35, no. 1: 3-183.

11. Machlup, Fritz. (1980). Knowledge and Knowledge Production. Princeton, NJ: Princeton University Press. Martin White. Information Management. What is Information Management? http://www.tlu.ee/~sirvir/Information%20and%20Knowledge%20Management/Key_Concepts_of_IKM/information_management.html

12. Michael Buckland (1986). Chapter 8 of Information and Information Systems, by. (Westport, CT: Hardback: Greenwood Press; Paperback: Praeger; 1991. 1-800-225-5800) American Library Association. Committee on Freedom and Equality of Access to Information. 1986. Freedom and Equality of Access to Information. ("Lacy" Report"). Chicago: American Library Association

13. Michael Buckland's Design of library services. http://people.ischool.berkeley.edu/~buckland/library.html

14. Mosley, M. (2008). September 10, 2008, DAMA-DMBOK Functional Framework, Ver. 3.02, Data Management Association (DAMA). http://www.dama.org/sites/default/files/download/DAMA-DMBOK_Functional_Framework_v3_02_20080910.pdf

15. Mosley, M. (ed.) (2009). The DAMA Guide to the Data Management Body of Knowledge (DAMA-DMBOK Guide). Bradley Beach, NJ, USA: Technics Publications.

16. Principle of Information Management. Information Management Body of Knowledge (IMBOK) http://www.imbok.info/

17. Project Open Data. http://project-open-data.github.io/

18. Redman, T. (2008). Data Driven: Profiting from Your Most Important Business Asset. Cambridge, MA, USA: Harvard Business Press.

19. An Inquiry into the Wealth of Nations. The Data Warehousing Institute (TDWI), http://www.tdwi.org/

20. U.S. Federal Data Architecture Subcommittee (2008). October 2008, Federal DAS Data Quality Framework, v1.0. http://semanticommunity.info/@api/deki/files/2388/=Fed_DAS_DQ_FINAL_Release_v1.doc

21. Venkatraman, N. Benefits of Information Management. https://www.smartsheet.com/enterprise

22. Wilson, Patrick G. (1983). Second-hand Knowledge: An Inquiry into Cognitive Authority. Westport, CT: Greenwood Press.

CHAPTER FIVE

Library and Research Support

SUMMARY : The recent trends have reflected the increasing role of libraries in research support system and research data management in universities and research institutions around the globe. The efforts to comprise the entire range of related components of research support and data management system are as following:

- Introduction
- Research Collections and Support
- Emerging library role in research information management
- Research support systems
- Copyright and Research
- Managing the Information in Research
- Scholarly Publishing
- Scholarly Identity
- Digital Conservancy
- Research impact measures
- Reproducibility
- Library Research Support Strategy
- Research Ethics and Integrity
- Research Support Strength
- Research Data Management
- Platforms for Research Data Management
- Research Data Repository
- Various Tools and Mechanisms
- Research Support Service and Research Life Cycle
- Research Support Open Science Services

INTRODUCTION

The role of libraries in research information management is found at academic and research organizations worldwide. The libraries are offering the information and data harvesting, support for researchers. While understating the "Research information management" (RIM), it is conveyed that the aggregation, and curation, of metadata is done for the research activities. The RIM is also understood as Current Research Information Systems (CRISs). Libraries are helping in connecting various stakeholders and intricate components in research environment, a full range of datasets, funding grants, research projects, and their persistent identifiers. There have been tremendous efforts of OCLC in understanding the roles of libraries and research needs of the organizations they serve. It is worth comprehending the difference of RIM with RDM (Research Data Management) which is about the organization, and exchange of research data throughout the research lifecycle.

Related to RIM practices, the study and its output (by OCLC and euroCRIS) have shown the global nature of research information management activities. Apart from library and teaching departments, various commercial and open-source platforms are coexisting and providing two types of solutions, based on nature and demand of problem; the region-specific solutions and locally developed systems. These systems are the outcome of sincere planning including the factors such as system-to-system interoperability, use of identifiers, standards, and protocols metadata. It addresses two-fold goals: defining the RIM and related models; articulation of specific value proposition of libraries. The efforts of OCLC Research in collaboration with "LIBER (Ligue des Bibliothèques Européennes de Recherche - Association of European Research Libraries)" during 2017 have been associated with examination of RIM practices (Finland, Germany and the Netherlands)—such as integration of persistent identifiers (PIDs). These PIDs have been instrumental with activities such as helping disambiguation, interoperability, and scaling.

RESEARCH COLLECTIONS AND SUPPORT

Libraries are active in identifying the basic materials for academic pursuits and knowledge formation, with the recent emphasis upon curation of research assets, and organizational outputs. The steps taken in the shape of digitization of special collections, data, and other significant materials are the building blocks of research support systems in library. Libraries are supporting contemporary modes of scholarship. The roles and steps, libraries are taking to support the research process, are implementing the research tracking systems (researcher identifiers, etc.), data curation and evaluation exercises.

Libraries are outreaching the researchers in many ways and addressing the issues: digitization, curation of born digital documents, creation of discoverability and accessibility of less used information materials. These types of materials include documents which are distinctive, or rare in nature. Adaptations are the best strategies. The transition phase libraries faced are involving the curation of data, resources and maintaining long-term accessibility to retain evolving scholarly record a digital, networked environment. The approach of from the hidden sides of collections to the deliberate services and coordination is significant. University libraries are associated with various research related support activities as making efforts for understanding of ethics and governance, research data management, research impact, providing multidisciplinary research themes, and digital living.

EMERGING LIBRARY ROLE IN RESEARCH INFORMATION MANAGEMENT

The areas covered by research services include formal internships, speculative applications and networking. Research information management (RIM) in libraries involves the collection and curation of metadata from the entire life cycle of a research project, from "grant application metadata to impact metrics" for the research results. In this context, a comprehensive RIM program can be facilitated with "research information management system". Technically speaking, RIMS is an enterprise software solution meant for researcher profiles management, showcasing the research assets, reports generation, and encouraging the research collaboration. The RIMS makes supports research management due to having centrally located and interrelated data, saving time through the speedy searching. The streamlining of steps and formalities by the RIMS, the policy compliance easy,

RIMS is useful in various organizations where the research activities and reporting is carried on. It takes shape of comprehensive database having research related entire information (scholar, topic, process, etc.). Various departments such as the research sections, academic departments, library and the research grant section are interrelated and function accordingly. The research output and quality can be measured through both grant success rates and altmetrics. Though this system is commonly known as RIMS, but in Europe, it is called as current research information system (CRIS) and "faculty activity reporting" (FAR) is found in US. Various features of RIMS are:

Central data usage across campus : The RIMS supports data stewardship, helping saving time by permitting data input into the system once for using across the organization. The presence of validated data maintains accuracy.

RIMS support the library scratch from the acquisition in the library to research data curation. These RIMs may be home-grown systems or the commercial products based on institutional needs. It may be the decision of library to handle and maintain it or by the research section. The libraries play a role of "administration information partner" as the data can be pulled together and researchers are supported in different ways. It helps in managing the collection of primary sources, report generation, creation of metrics by curating metadata. In general understanding, RIM is the platform for consolidation, curation, and dissemination of information about institutional research activities as well as analysis of scholarly activities. For example, the information services at Rutgers University include services for researchers and resources for scholarly communication. The research data services are provided through the following methods and design of services:

- Research Data Services
- Citation management tools and research impact
- Digital Humanities
- Digitization Projects
- Open Access Policy
- Author identification
- Institutional repository and scholarly networking tools
- Copyright and Licensing

RESEARCH SUPPORT SYSTEMS

Library offers various service and tools as research support systems, for example, at Imperial College London for the management of research project activities comprising:

- Proposals
- Grants
- Publication portfolios
- Professional Web pages

- Archive

The provision of information for the staff related with research support system includes:

- Manage publications portfolio
- Using the digital archive for research outputs
- Manage funding proposals
- Using the online Research Facilities Directory
- Manage research grants
- Access management information using by Analytics, and
- Management of the research data and software code

Research Computing Service : The Research Computing Service provides access to powerful computing resources, expert consultancy and training for all researchers.

An example of Digital archive for research documents (Spiral) : The Spiral Digital Repository is open access repository for the scholars. This the Imperial College London institutional system allows the scholars to make the research material, documents and output as open access without incurring additional publication costs. The process of self-archiving a research document in this system "Spiral" makes it free for reader. The copies can be uploaded in the Spiral by using "Symplectic Elements". The role of library encompasses the technical support, user guidance, access mechanism and management of publications.

Organization of Research Workshops by Libraries : The Library offers training through workshops which are designed to induce relevant skills. These workshops encourage analytical thinking required in the research process. The training areas include the conceptual information about the research process. The popularity of reference/ citation management tools has compelled the library to include such software in the training schedules. The examples of citation management software are Mendeley, Zotero, and EndNote. The use and application of mapping and visualization tools in research is very significant. The organization of data with software such as spreadsheets and in specific databases has been in practice. The usual support for scholars include the identification of places for reading and collaborating with other researchers, reflecting their research outputs and helping with the research projects. The library supports instructors by helping them in assignment designing, teaching consultations, paying attention in instruction session. Library provides "library teaching toolkit" and organizes various workshops, etc. to equip the teachers and instructors.

The provision of variety of services assists them in inspiring the student learning, research. Library helps in the selection of research materials, assignments, and the use of new technologies. The guidance of scholars through all stages of the research process, in the instruction design, is provided by libraries. The toolkits are comprised of variety of handouts, interactive online modules, etc. The provisions of "Affordable Course Materials Initiative" are emerging to support researchers.

Various workshops are related with the following topics, issues and learning areas:

- Digital Tools and Methods for the Humanities and Social Sciences
- Data Manipulation with Python
- Scripting, Looping, and Automation In Unix
- Introduction to High Performance Computing
- Open Access resources and publishing
- Social Science Data
- OpenRefine
- Python
- Text Analysis in social sciences and humanities

- Intrinio training for Financial Data Intelligence

Copyright and Research : IPR issues are intricately woven with research and scholarly communications. The understanding and knowledge of copyright law can be done with "Copyright Reminders" to create awareness about copyright concerns. Copyright awareness can be created as following:

- The information and resources for day- today situations
- Recommended best practices for greater concerns
- Copyright law overview and specific information related with copyright

MANAGING THE INFORMATION IN RESEARCH

The researchers can extend their search in archival and special collections, in unique collection of library resources (books, manuscripts, and artifacts), university digital repositories. The archival collection and resources guides are helpful in searching archival records, manuscripts, etc. the inter library loan and digital delivery of information are also mechanisms for extended information supply. Researchers' support is available in the form of citation tools, and Data services. The researchers are supported in the areas of getting published (author workshops, IPR information awareness, writing styles etc.). The users can retrieve resources and research materials by format and subject, facilitating peer research consultants Researcher support services include services related with "managing your information", the research reproducibility, steps related with research impact measures, identification of scholars, etc. These services are equipped with the provisions to facilitate access to information and supportive tools for research plan and management:

Managing information : The research information management is done with the help of citation managers, and various data services.

Publishing and sharing: The research publications are significant and required in many contexts other than sharing the results. University libraries are providing platforms and management systems for publishing and sharing. The preservation component is also associated with the research publishing and sharing. The example of "universal digital conservancy" and research repositories are showing the efforts by the major libraries. The support in scholarly communication is instrumental in creating presence and preservation.

Maximizing impact of research : Identities and visibilities of scholars and research outputs are possible due to few major platforms. It is supporting the availability of research; their impact in subject can be correlated and measured. Few specific databases are creating the scholarly identity. The possibility of research impact metrics, and Altmetrics has supported the research output and its application in future research. Organizational research output is measured and compared in national and regional contexts.

Reproducibility : This concept has created its niche in research area. The libraries are supporting in "Reproducibility bibliography", and much talked "Software Carpentry".

Systematic reviews : The roles of libraries are encompassing the provisions of systematic reviews in various disciplines such as Arts and Humanities, social science, and science.

Finding data : The researchers' needs related with data are solved by the subscription and services of libraries. The provisions for accessing Government data & statistics and Business & economics statistics are made for research scholars. The increased needs related with the specific and highly indicative "GIS data and Spatial data" are also being listened by the libraries and information centers. Another emerged field is the Health data and statistics.

Citation management tools : The significance of citation managers is due to the creation of personalized databases of references, cited information. These citation managers allow importing and organizing the reference/ citation information. This information is collected from article indexes and other related sources. The researchers using these citation tools can save pdfs of article and other documents. With the help of citation managers and tools, the users format citations easily according to required citation style. These tools support inclusion of own notes.

SCHOLARLY PUBLISHING

Scholarly publishing requires various components and demands to be addressed and understood. These components and issues are related with:

- Impact measures
- Managing the rights
- Open access and Open science
- Scholarly identity
- Sharing and preserving of research

Scholarly publications are based on informed decisions related to ways of communication. The choice of publishing affects the impact of research due to accessibility of article/ research publication. The scholars needs to know about the diversity in published content, choice of subscription and open access journals, are few of the factors before deciding for publishing.

Transforming scholarly communication

The creation, sharing, and publishing of research make it widely available for other researchers through scholarly communication. Publishing is one of the ways to share the research work; through journals, books and other platforms.

Managing researchers" rights: the copyrights and other IPRs should be explored by the researchers. The issues of ownership can be understood so that rights can be retained.

Open access : Open access (OA) publications make research and data freely available for reading/using for academic purposes. The knowledge and awareness of OA publishing can make the research work available at wide level

Scholarly identity : a researcher's scholarly identity is instrumental for scholarly reputation.

Sharing and preserving : the preservation is the step toward making research available for future. Sharing research through the institutional repositories makes it discoverable.

Impact measures : to understand the impact of research, various platforms, and ways are available.

Open science : for accountable and reproducible research, "Open science" practices can be supportive for researchers.

SCHOLARLY IDENTITY

The scholarly identity is related with the researcher's information and portrayal on web. The kind of information may be related with :

- Presentations and publications
- Fellowships and grants
- Courses taught
- Research interests

Managing the Scholarly Identity

By searching about a researcher brings out few aspects at the surface such as time taken, kinds of research details, etc. The digital narrative of a researcher requires review. Managing the research identity can:

- Augmenting the discoverability of research work
- Enabling the research relationships among researchers across institutions

Researchers can initiate the research and scholarly identity management by

- Organizing publications, datasets, and grey literature
- Having access to online services such as ORCiD, Google Scholar, etc.
- Using proper settings for visibility of research output
- Protection of research profile and feeds
- Hiding these profiles from search engines

ORCiD ID and ORCiD Profile

An ORCiD ID is a lifelong digital name for an individual researcher that consists of a persistent, unique, numeric identifier. Every scholar should have an ORCiD ID. An ORCiD ID is unique id. The ORCiD ID number is used consistently while publishing process. This id helps in pulling together all of the research without losing identity even after changing the workplace or name. For example at University of Minnesota, the facility of "Experts@Minnesota" helps researchers in various activities such as placing altogether the research work, supporting the collaboration by creating awareness about each other, storage of research output, analysis and report generation for academic purposes. Though the ORCiD ID the users get ORCiD profile page. This profile page showcases the researcher's information and associated research output. The users can add other names they have used for publishing. Apart from names, the previous organizational affiliations, and identifiers can also be added from other databases. Users can also be granted permissions to databases such as Experts@Minnesota, Web of Science, or Scopus. This permission helps to automatically update ORCID when a new publication is observed in user's record. ORCiD IDs are an important tool for researchers as they:

- Distinguish user from other researchers with the same or similar names.

- Helping in creation of a profile for research activities, regardless of whether a researcher with changed names, or multiple variations of name, changed switched institutions.
- Needed by major publishers (PLoS and IEEE).
- Required by funding agencies.

ORCiD ID Supports in many ways:

Increase the visibility of research : Inclusion of ORCiD ID on researcher's webpage, at the time of submitting publications, application for grants, and research workflow for credit.

Automate the process : Using ORCiD ID to link accounts and automatically import content from Web of Science, Scopus, and CrossRef, etc.

There are few another platforms being used as scholarly identity purposes, such as:

ResearchGate : This "for-profit social networking site" used in the sciences subjects. The researchers set up an account for free to follow researchers and research interests. They can add a list of publications and adding PDFs. The users should follow the guidelines of the publisher.

Academia.edu : This is also a "for-profit social networking site" with wider range of disciplines. The basic version of this platform may be used free but the advanced services are paid related with features of advanced search and data analytics. The researchers are followed own publications can be added (with or without PDF) with the agreement with the publisher.

Google Scholar : The creation of Google Scholar profile brings all existing publications together. The users are notified when new publications are observed by Google Scholar. Google scholar profile helps in inclusion of links to co-authors as well as citation information.

Microsoft Academic : Microsoft Academic also creates user profile with an image of user, affiliation and research area/interests. The user's page shows their publications in terms of papers and related number of citations, links to co-authors, etc.

DIGITAL CONSERVANCY

The digital conservation is instrumental in sharing and preserving the research output. The "Digital Conservancy" at University of Minnesota, for example, is facilitating users in the following ways:

- Free & Open Access
- Increase Visibility
- Data Repository
- Full-text Search
- Persistent Access
- Long-term Preservation

RESEARCH IMPACT MEASURES

The significance of research impact and measuring the same has been observed in academic scenario. Citations are significant in understanding the measures by collecting and the objective data reflecting the publication's contribution in research area. Calculations of these measures are complex comparing across disciplines. There are few commonly-accepted measures, such as:

h-index : for individual impact measures.

Essential Science Indicators : for the research group or a particular department impact measures.

Impact Factor and Eigenfactor score : for the individual journal impact measures

Altmetrics : significant for measuring impact outside of academia and citation counts

Citations are significant in understanding the measures by collecting and the objective data reflecting the publication's contribution in research area. Calculation of these measures is complex comparing across disciplines.

REPRODUCIBILITY

In the current scenario, the science research fields the "reproducibility" is about the subject related progress. The feature of "replicability" is observed in scientific research. The Open Science Collaboration talks about the claims and supporting evidences of reproducibility. Few definitions given by experts are as following:

"The ability of a researcher to duplicate the results of a prior study using the same materials and procedures as were used by the original investigator" (Bollen et al., 2015)

"In this replication crisis era, reproducibility is the only thing that can be effectively guaranteed in a published study. Whether any claimed findings are indeed true or false can only be confirmed via additional studies, but reproducibility can be confirmed immediately." (Broman et al., 2017)

"The ability of a researcher to duplicate the results of a prior study if the same procedures are followed but new data are collected." (Bollen et al., 2015)

There are few guidelines and resources for reproducibility, as follows:

Reproducibility Bibliography: Guidelines and Examples: This is a compiled resource for various stakeholders such as researchers, research support staff, related to reproducibility for their disciplines.

Transparency and Openness Promotion (TOP) Guidelines : These guidelines (2014) provide a set of 8 standards for adoption by academic journals.

National Institute of Health (NIH) : Rigor and Reproducibility: these guidelines are a set of 5 guidelines for reporting "preclinical research".

National Science Foundation (NSF) : This provides Framework for "National Science Foundation Activities" to improve three significant aspects of research such as "Reproducibility, Replicability, and Robustness".

Services for Reproducible Research Libraries

Support research reproducibility by the support provided by subject librarians to researchers for reporting guidelines, managing and sharing data. The libraries are creating repositories for sharing and preserving research.

Consultation Services : The researchers can seek support from the subject librarians for advice on reproducibility. The guidelines for reporting the methodology are helpful in evaluating and reproducing the research work. Research Data Management: Data Management is helpful in improving the consistency and rigor of data for understanding and interpretation..

Systematic Review Support : To conduct systematic reviews for research, the role of librarians has been associated for reproducibility in research.

Tools for pre-registration : The steps such as pre-registering the studies and analysis plans are supportive in finding the research with specific differences.

Data Curation and Sharing : The data curation and sharing of research code, etc. are helpful in reproducing the research result.

Some specific tools and services are useful for reproducibility:

Documentation : Documentation work is important while organizing the research workflow. Few tools for document and organize the research work are Markdown/ LaTeX, some other tools are:

- Qualitative Analysis Tools: NVivo, and Atlas.TI,

- Quantitative Analysis Tools: R, SPSS, and Stata

Open Science : There are significant steps for preparation for data and code for sharing. The Open Science has been instrumental to:

- Review datasets for potential privacy/identification issues
- Extract metadata
- determine the appropriate ways for data availability

Version Control : Related with integration of version control systems in the research workflows (for example, github).

Automation : Research automation tools for research workflow (initiating from data collection to data "wrangling"). For example, the tools are R and Python.

LIBRARY RESEARCH SUPPORT STRATEGY

Research priorities : Research priorities at universities are guided aims to augment research productivity and impact. Focus on research quality and evaluation compels the research institutions to support and promote quality research. The libraries are strategic partners in the research initiatives by providing resources, and management of research output. The determination of library's engagement is supporting the competitive research environment. Additional roles are played by availability of online content and tools. The observations related to ensure the libraries continued relevance to research priorities are intricate and compelling.

Library staff : Library staff serving as the intermediaries between research resources/services and users are usually known as "Liaison Librarians", "Research Coordinator," etc. The representation of library is found in various committees such as Research Committee, Research ethics and tools committee, etc. Through the roles in such committees, the library plays a crucial role in providing research and training assistance. Various training and support programs are provided to specific the needs of diverse users. The researchers are provided individual consultations on demand.

Content management and analysis tools : A good selection of research specific databases and content management/ analysis tools are significant. Many supports such as document delivery and interlibrary loan are also playing crucial roles, along with indexing and abstracting databases contributing for development of research strategies.

Library manages the institutional repository, to showcase the research output, provides the avenue for worldwide exposure through open access and increase the visibility. Library is also responsible for the digitization and developing new research collections to attract international collaborations. The library leadership emerged in the form of various initiatives, such as training and promotion or digital resources, and open access research data with the help of library staff. Their involvement with the research and data services supports the scholars. The libraries contribute in the research support and direction through:

Collaboration and Team-building

The research staff and students collaboration is significant to create awareness among the scholars about the availability of various information services and resources. The mechanisms to know the scholars' research needs, is the basic step to help the researchers. Libraries work in collaboration with key stakeholders, who are the research sections authorities, library chairperson, research committees, etc. The planning and initiation of collaboration and support, related with research activities, contributions such as and initiatives such as provisions for appropriate skills training, information literacy programs et.

Providing Support for Researchers

Researchers 'training and skill development programs can be challenging and complex due to their different disciplines, research needs and level of knowledge. The subject and liaison librarians help the research scholars to access resources. They support the users for training on information literacy and skills, bibliometric tools, reference management tools, and other skills development. Library's role begins with identification of appropriates research skills, creating awareness about the research training. The use of analytic tools is significant for reporting and analyzing the research output and quality. Few other aspects such as strategic planning with research funding, publishing research output, and research management also invite attention where the libraries help by providing access and training of bibliometric analysis tools.

Building Relevant Library Collection

The collection management and resources development strategies are few of the major steps a library takes for providing access to useful information. Mapping of organizational research strengths, reviewing collection planning, intuit potential growth areas and enabling open access. The tools such as "Blackboard", "PebblePad" are few good examples.

- Finding innovative solutions to real world problems
- Joining the research community supports research work by funding and fellowships.
- Integrating research, library services and teaching
- The researchers' collaboration with state, national and global government systems and other organizations supports the delivery of innovative research output.

RESEARCH ETHICS AND INTEGRITY

Every researcher and collaborative research teams have responsibility towards research ethics. The researchers should be aware ways to conduct the research meeting standards and organizational policy. Research is an integral component of academic and research landscape with identification of emerging research concentrations. Various committees related with framing policies, guidelines have commitment to ensure adherence to academic codes of practice in context with standards of ethics and welfare. Various factors are taken into consideration for research integrity awareness, which are integrity of researcher, compliance with the organizational rules, and respect for fellow human research participants, including the animals and the environment. For example, the University of the Sunshine Coast (USC) policy and procedural framework resources are as following:

- Authorship and Dissemination of Research Findings - Procedures
- Responsible Research Conduct - Governing Policy
- Managing and Investigating Breaches of Responsible Research Conduct - Procedures
- Animal Ethics - Governing Policy
- Human Research Ethics - Governing Policy
- Student Academic Integrity - Governing Policy
- Higher Degree by Research Supervision – Procedures

EXCELLENCE IN RESEARCH

The research support section and activities helps the scholars in data collection and analysis including research performance measures. Relating the various steps of research such as "statistical quantitative and qualitative analysis, performance benchmarking" are supportive in identification and management of research strengths, capabilities and opportunities. Research performance data is utilized for funding schemes, and assessment of organization's research excellence.

Utilization of Internal Reports

The research supporting sections in the organization prepare research performance data for the organizational reports, for example, may include research performance reports, etc.

Role of Research Repository and Other Platforms

The institutional research repository (IR) with vast technical features and aspects of IR such as being indexed by search engines and facilitates retrieval and collaboration among the researchers. Implementing the research information system is a complex task, yet for example "Research Master" is a kind of "corporate information system" for research related activity. For the purpose of "statutory research reporting", this facility of research master is very helpful, preparing data reports to monitor research performance. Such reports are useful to plan the organization research targets.

Enhancing Research Experience

- Research scholars' orientation and induction
- Academic writing, critical and creative thinking
- Literature reviews, research methods, research presentation skills
- Research ethics, publishing and authorship
- Research project management
- Statistical software and packages

RESEARCH SUPPORT STRENGTH

The universities' research output is related with academic strength and libraries'' roles in supporting the researchers. The current scenario has witnessed advent of ICTs to transform the conventional research practices. The concept of "*e-research*" has provided an entire spectrum of ICT based research processes by embracing the combination of research methodologies implemented through technological advances. The arrival of "data-intensive research" has altered the contexts and interpretation of data towards the unconventional discoveries. The research transformation has been instrumental in understanding researchers' demands. The contemporary academic libraries have experimented to reform the research oriented services. The current status of research support service in academic libraries is generating the transformative nature of libraries.

CATEGORIZING RESEARCH SUPPORT SERVICES

Academic libraries in the perspectives of data-intensive research are providing research support services; a few observations are as follows:

- Many academic libraries are framing RDM policies as a central guiding force for researchers.
- The steps such as introducing research data, guidelines for data management and curation, including specific training for researchers are taken worldwide.
- The pressures to produce quality research and wide dissemination have been instrumental in excessive use of ICT based research data management systems.
- Recently, the roles of academic libraries have included as facilitators in awareness and training for publishing and scholarly communication.
- The roles and responsibilities of library staff have expanded with the objective to serve researchers including updated skills in tools, publishing modes, etc.
- In addition, the significance of knowledge of highly dynamic scholarly publishing has emerged as a necessary area of research support. Libraries are providing innovative platforms for awareness and training for researchers to understand the complex nature of publishing research data and output.

Academic libraries are compelled and focused to evaluate the research support and research impact measurement. Bibliometrics has emerged as a comprehensive mechanism to assess the research. The bibliometrics has been prevalent as well as comprehensive area regarding bibliometrics training for researchers, awareness and designing programs for research impact calculations, comprehensive citation reports, including subject research trend reports. To support researchers, libraries are informing them about h-index calculations. The research organizations and academic libraries are paying attention towards altmetrics.

IMPLEMENTATION MODES

The changes and diversity in the research environment and researchers' needs have motivated the libraries to frame services such as subject and research consultation, provision of research guides, creating awareness of research tools, etc. The objective of research support services is to address information needs of researchers. The sequence of specific steps and services shape it in the form of research life cycle. In other words, research lifecycle indicates about the stages of research, beginning from idea to generation of data after application of research process and returning to emergence of new idea. In general, researchers have a routine of using, creating, exchanging and managing information during their research process. According to the academic library practices, few of the common tailored services at different research stages being provided, are identification of research problems and formation of new research ideas, appropriate research outline, implementation of research processes, reaching to the publication of research output, followed by evaluation. The library research services can be identifies and categorized on the basis of the aims and targets to achieve. Few library research support services are designed to facilitate the researcher during the entire research process. These services may include facilitating subject guides, research consultation, training for literature search, reference management, etc. Some other services are provided at different research stages such as facilitating the funding process, training for research data management, report writing, and sharing the research output. The knowledge of research data software and publication channels is provided in this category of library research support services.

The research support services in academic libraries are comprised of the following steps:

- Conceptualization of research
- Data collection, processing and analysis
- Publication and sharing
- Preservation and curation

Usually, academic libraries frame components and navigation systems to integrate research. The level and extent of research support services in libraries may differ according to the needs and types of users being served. Various kinds of service provisions can be made, such as research guides access, research consultation and facilitating research tools. This can be accompanied later on with access to OA, understanding the research impact and modes of scholarly publications. The separate supports can be provided for research data management.

RESEARCH DATA MANAGEMENT

It is about planning, organizing, sharing, and preserving the data. It also deals with documentation related to generation of published research output. The aim of research data management is to facilitate the data sharing and making the funded research publicly available for reuse. The libraries help the scholars in following ways:

Plan: providing advice on preparing Data Management Plans for grant proposals and on best practices for handling data.

Organize : advising on preparation of structure and documentation of data. This structure and documenting the data augment the data usability.

Share and Preserve : identification of the repository for sharing and preservation of data.

Various platforms are available for access to Government documents, research guides, popular resources, and WorldCat. The scholars are provided Research Assistance, facilities for Scholarly Communication, and Course Reserves. To create awareness about IPRs, the Copyright Guidelines are provided to students. Various tools are available in the form of BrowZine, EndNote, RefWorks, and RefWorks. The availability of Guides & Tutorials, and options like "How Do I...?" are helpful or the researchers. The facilities such as "Building Accessibility", Digital Humanities Lab, are very useful. To manage the research data and find best practices to plan ahead for data management and sharing. Various guides are available for research data management. The topics for guidelines are:

- Storage and preservation of research data
- Data sharing processes
- Data and information privacy
- Discovery of data

Policies for research data management are available in context with:

- Policies related with research funding
- Application for research grant
- Data Management Plans

Resources and Services can be provided in the areas:

- Research Data Storage
- Research Data Repository
- Subject-specific research support

- Data Management Planning tool

There are queries and answers related with research data management which are:

- Preservation and sharing research software
- FAIR data
- Data Protection legislation
- transferring data and the new Privacy Shield agreement
- Digital Object Identifier (DOI)
- Use of cloud services to store and share data
- Sharing personal or sensitive data, and related legislation
- Writing Data Management Plans
- Understanding policies on information and research data

PLATFORMS FOR RESEARCH DATA MANAGEMENT

Research Data Repository

Institutional Research Data Repository enables researchers to preserve research data of value long-term and make it available to others. The advantages are as following:

Long term data preservation : With the support of data repository, the data is preserved for more than ten years. The data curation is also supported.

Storage: The large storage facilitates access and sharing of data. The availability of data supports worldwide access and sharing.

Multiple formats: The data repository supports storage and access to most of the file types.

Visibility and citations : The availability, access and sharing enhances the chances of visibility, use and credits to the published research data.

Discoverability : The technical aids present in data

repositories supports discovery of research data.

Defines reuse : The reuse of data is possible with the application of Creative Commons and other appropriate licences.

Institutional Embargo : The research outputs are embargoed where the organizational policies find it necessary.

Selection of data : The various factors for selection and retaining the data depends upon funding agencies data policy, organizational research data guidelines, legal and ethical requirements; and future needs.

Prepare data : Data preparation involves organization of data, naming files, choosing the file formats, anonymity of e personal data, and more. Preparation of research data upload is composed of few steps, which may be as following:

1. Identification and naming of research dataset. The size may differ according to technical permissions.
2. Authenticating and checking the data publication permission
3. Ensuring the correct names and ORCIDs of ALL authors and collaborators
4. Categorization and setting keywords for data, for description and discovery
5. Metadata preparation for the data
6. Providing funding agencies related information such as title, grant name/number, date etc.
7. Knowledge of type of intellectual property and copyright licence to be use
8. Preparation of suitable links, DOIs and references to related research outputs/data
9. Taking care of personal data to be anonymous as per organizational guidelines

The academic libraries are the central force for research data management by designing a wide range of specific services. It is observed that the services offered by libraries include data management practices, sharing and best practices. The peripheral services include the preservation and storage aspects, research data backup, etc. The library staff plays supportive role by providing consultation services, training facilities, and assisting users with the answers to subject or technical tool related queries. The designing of research data services takes place to support the researchers during the research lifecycle. Further adding the more understanding the research data services are as following:

Research planning : supporting users by meticulously designed training workshops and online guides

Data management : helping researchers in research data collection, management and analysis.

Research publication : creating awareness for sharing research data and output.

Policies and procedures : providing guidelines for research ethics, and integrity.

Research Output and Data Management

The libraries populate and promote the research data bank by working in collaboration with research sections towards the expansion of research data bank, and building additional research collections in different fields.

VARIOUS TOOLS AND MECHANISMS

Research guides : To enhance researchers' efficiency, the research guides help users. The research guides promote the specific collections which are meant for disciplines specific services with emphasis on disciplinary context, The examples are include research guides, specific course guides, and "help guides."

Research consultation : By consulting the librarian, the researchers can obtain correct information and guidance in context of research grant, thesis report writing, data management, etc. In general the roles of reference librarians are expanded from routine services to discipline specific intricate information provisions. The libraries aim to offer:

- Supporting the users in identification of specific information needs
- Providing research topics consultation, and access to resources
- Facilitating consultation services for research data, patent filing, intellectual property awareness, etc.

Research tools : With the development and impacts of exponential growth of data and presence of "big data", students and research scholars from various disciplines such as natural sciences, social sciences and humanities are compelled to perform high quality data analysis, and other related steps. With the help of various tools, such as data analysis tools, research management tools and citation management tools, libraries have been able to cope with the demands of researchers. Few examples of these tools are:

- EndNote, RefWorks (reference managers),
- Library Bookmarklet, and DMP Tool (for data management),
- platform Data Lab (working with data),
- Stata, SPSS and SAS (few statistics analysis software).

The citation management tools or reference managers, as popularly called, are divided according to their technical functionalities and platforms. For example, Endnote and Papers function as "desktop software". Few others are web-based tools and provide extensive coverage of features, such as Mendeley. In this series, Zotero is a "browser-based" reference management tool.

Scholarly publishing : As expressed, scholarly publishing has been considered the scholarly communication since a long time. The observations and practices state that it is composed of organized production, information retrieval and dissemination, showcasing, display and preservation in the form of documents and in IRs. In this context, for example the Purdue library services supports at various steps of scholarly publishing tasks, as follows:

- Publishing and authoring
- Research output production
- Dissemination and distribution
- Preservation and archiving

The libraries have been concentrating on the evolution and evolvement of scholarly communication practices in the perspectives of copyright laws, thus providing support for copyright services.

Research impact : Measuring research impact in the academic libraries is possible by providing researchers with tools. The expansion of academic impact is related with research impact which is measured with the help of various tools and techniques. Few libraries focus on much intricate "bibliometrics services", further divided as follows:

- *Research output metrics* : to estimate the overall research output.
- *Author metrics* : related with understanding the author's contributions in research arena.
- *Journal metrics* : to focus upon the journal research measurements.
- *Altmetrics* : to provide a clear visual of research output.

For example, Chalmers University of Technology, Sweden library follows the principle that "bibliometrics analysts carry out quantitative analysis of scientific publications and supply bibliometric indicators for management's operational planning discussions with departments and Areas of Advance. We measure productivity in terms of the number of publications, the impact of publications in the form of citations, and co-authorship and citations to visualize collaboration patterns and subject structures." There are few citation analysis tools which are highly impressive and supportive to analyze the researchers' output and produce report. Few tools and techniques are including h-index, and Google Scholar. Few data bases and platforms such as Web of Science, and Scopus help to understand the citations received by a publication and author. The altmetrics tools are supporting the research impact measurement. Libraries also provide "name disambiguation" and "journal-level metrics". It is significant to understand that the author disambiguation is possible by tools such as "ORCID, Scopus Author Identifier and Researcher ID"; but the "journal impact factor measurement can be done through sources such as the Scopus Journal Analyzer, SCImago Journal Rank, Eigenfactor.org, *Journal Citation Reports*, Google Scholar Metrics, etc. The Altmetrics tools include, tools and platforms such as "ImpactStory, Scholarometer and Mendeley".

RESEARCH SUPPORT SERVICE AND RESEARCH LIFE CYCLE

Wide range of library research related services are required by academic organizations. Libraries are striving hard to fulfill such goals which aim to provide strength during the entire cycle of research and publishing. The cycle of research may require a number of steps, spread across many stages to be completed by the support of tools, techniques and platforms. The areas which are instrumental, as follows:

- Identification of stages of the research process specific to researchers;
- Consulting services, support through specialized tools;
- Scholarly communication;
- Data creation, reuse and curation
- Content management in context with visual resources and matters of primary research

The optimization of library services for scholars in research institutions has taken place. The research and publication areas are being transformed with the help of tools and techniques. The innovative and practical approaches for research related library services are instrumental in helping the researchers at various stages of research life cycle. Research activities having own lifecycle are linked with specific supports and tools meant for particular stage; such as segmentation into following stages:

- Identification and access to resources
- Collection of related literature, writing and referencing
- Research data publishing, sharing and reusing
- Research Data Management
- IPRs related measures

For example, the following structure for research support system life cycle reflects the steps as following:

1. Design to discover : Various research and discipline consultation processes, research design and planning to complete the task in timely fashion, funding procedures, guidelines etc.

2. Research and financial Plan : Aspects related with research impact, data management planning, literature bibliographies, and research funding procedures are covered.

3. Research and experiment : Exposure of scholars towards rare books, special collections, digital resources, e-books, and awareness of research ethics and integrity are provided.

4. Curate and preserve : This stage includes various activities such as IPRs awareness, open access publishing, promotion including measurement of research impact; implementation of repository and preservation.

RESEARCH SUPPORT OPEN SCIENCE SERVICES

Earlier most of the libraries were lacking the systematic structure of research support services. The use of e-resources, databases, etc. was not determining the maximum support to researchers. Though the libraries have been careful in designing the research support services, yet the challenges are always unknown. The research support services and libraries' association with open sciences services are significant for the users. The initial stage is the benchmarking the library against other libraries. Study and review of websites and online resources of various libraries give a glimpse of comparative nature of available resources and services. Building a sustainable service structure is a basic component for setting up a research support and open science services. The services can be categorized as following:

- Open research data
- Library resources and information literacy
- Open access publishing
- Research assessment
- Research visibility

Simultaneously, for example the SURIMA project was funded by Finland's Ministry of Education and Culture. Our library and Jyväskylä University Library were chosen to plan and implement the project. The model process for "green open access publishing" is found in a national project called SURIMA. SURIMA is an acronym for a Finnish sentence meaning "Finland – a Country for Green Open Access"). The project completed in the shape of a repository for green open access publication during 2016 which is called as "eRepo". This e-repository has been able to provide basic infrastructure and services with the purpose of self-archiving full-text articles. The "eRepo" repository has also been used as a metadata repository. The setting up of team for research support services require knowledge of library and information science, open access publishing, and scholarly communication. The inclusion of research support services in the job descriptions is another parameter. The open science challenges in library require coordination among the administration, ICT department, faculty members, and other segments of organization.

Role of Library as Promoter of Open Science

The libraries which observed the significance of Open Science have been actively promoting at their organization. The academic libraries are providing relevant tools, required infrastructure, and training for the research scholars. These tools include research data management tool known as "DMP Tuuli", "SciVal" research assessment tool, and the "RefWorks" citation manager. The library's research support services related with open science include compilation of open science web pages, use of social media such as facebook and Yammer (locally grown), and newsletter, etc. for awareness. The university's newsletters, other strategic publications may also include information that emphasizes the significance of open science in education and research. University's cultural change of open science is foreseen and it requires changes in leadership styles and management facets to support the transition. Formal discussions, meetings and plans are needed for careful handling the open science problems in the library. The everyday interactions between the staff and research scholars are learning lessons. Systematic work, strategic roles, and determination for open science are essential for multi-professional working communities.

Expanding the Impact of Research

Many academic libraries are emphasizing upon open access journals in open science arena due to reduced budgets as well as rising costs for journal subscriptions. As possible publication outlets, open access journals are suggested by creating awareness maintaining open access publishing funds, to help defray the costs of publishing. The open science encompasses open textbooks, open access journals, and open data etc. The aspects such as open systems and standards are supporting the interoperability; such as Open Science Framework, GitHub and Mendeley are examples. In the open science movement, "Open science also can mitigate the reproducibility problem plaguing several research fields" (Nosek, 2017).

Individual and research group consultations

Libraries provide advice for the advantageous activities:

- Conducting a literature search
- Creation and maintenance of an ORCID iD
- Adding research outputs to the researchers' profiles and designated research repository.
- Managing research data.
- Measuring the research performance, including finding citation of the work, evidence of journal quality, the H-index and evidence of engagement with the research beyond academia.
- Citations, Altmetrics and Researcher Profiles
- Keeping Research Current
- Library Research Support Program
- Access training
- Deposit research work

To support at ground level, the offers to researchers by libraries include as following:

- Open Access publishing support, "REF compliance" etc.
- Open Access research funder policy, data management, and data sharing.
- Guidance on copyright and licencing regarding publishing and making publications and data openly available.

- Researcher profile management, (ORCID and PPPs).
- Researchers' Support with bibliometrics, (Scopus and SciVal).
- Statistics, and reports generation.

REFERENCES

1. ACRL (2015). "Environmental scan 2015." www.ala.org/acrl/sites/ala.org.acrl/files/content/publications/whitepapers/EnvironmentalScan15.pdf.
2. Blackboard. http://online.usc.edu.au/
3. Broman, K., Cetinkaya-Rundel, M., Nussbaum, A., Paciorek, C., Peng, R., Turek, D. and Wickham, H. (2017). Recommendations to Funding Agencies for Supporting Reproducible Research. American Statistical Association.
4. Bollen, K., Cacioppo, J., Kaplan, R., Krosnick, J. A. and Olds, J. L. (2015). Social , Behavioral , and Economic Sciences Perspectives on Robust and Reliable Science. Report of the Subcommittee on Replicability in Science Advisory Committee to the National Science Foundation Directorate for Social, Behavioral, and Economic Sciences.
5. Brown, R.A., Wolski, M. and Richardson, J. (2015). "Developing new skills for research support librarians", The Australian Library Journal, 64 (3), pp. 224-234.
6. Budapest Open Access Initiative (BOAI) (2002). www.budapestopen accessinitiative.org/read
7. Butler, K. and Byrd, J. (2016). "Research consultation assessment: perceptions of students and librarians", Journal of Academic Librarianship, 42(1), pp. 83-86.
8. Cornell University Library (2011). "Toward 2015: Cornell University Library Strategic Plan, 2011-2015", available at: www.library.cornell.edu/sites/default/files/CUL_Strategic_ Plan_2011-2015%28re-numbered%29_1.pdf (accessed 11 January 2018).
9. Cox, A.M. and Pinfield, S. (2014). "Research data management and libraries: Current activities and future priorities", Journal of Librarianship and Information Science, 46 (4), pp. 299-316.
10. Eurocris. http://www.eurocris.org/
11. Gessner, G.G., Eldermire, E., Tang, N. and Tancheva, K. (2017). "The research lifecycle and the future of research libraries: a library of apps", Proceedings of the ACRL 2017, pp. 533-543.

12. GitHub/other code repository. https://www.software.ac.uk/choosing-repository-your-software-project

13. Haddow, G. and Mamtora, J. (2017). "Research support in australian academic libraries: services, resources, and relationships", New Review of Academic Librarianship, 23 (6), pp. 1-21.

14. Hensley, M.K., Shreeves, S.L. and Davis-Kahl, S. (2013). "A survey of library support for formal undergraduate research programs", College and Research Libraries, 75(4), pp. 422-441.

15. Harrington, E. G. (2019). Academic libraries and public engagement with science and technology. Cambridge, MA: Chandos Publishing.

16. Harrington, Eileen (2019). Expanding the impact of research. https://libraryconnect.elsevier.com/print/

17. https://www.usc.edu.au/library/about-the-library/library-research-support-strategy

18. https://libanswers.ioe.ac.uk/faq/179235

19. https://www.chalmers.se/en/departments/CLS/divisions/research-support-bibliometrics-and-ranking/Pages/default.aspx

20. http://www.library.ucla.edu/support/support-instructors

21. https://www.oclc.org/research/themes/research-collections/rim.html

22. https://www.libraries.rutgers.edu/services-for-researchers/research-impact

23. http://thompsoninstitute.usc.edu.au/research-and-innovation/research-ethics-and-integrity

24. http://thompsoninstitute.usc.edu.au/research-and-innovation/research-performance

25. https://thompsoninstitute.usc.edu.au/research-and-innovation/research-students/research-training

26. https://www.ucl.ac.uk/library/research-support/research-data-management/ucl-research-data-repository

27. https://www.ucl.ac.uk/library/research-support/research-data-management/best-practices

28. https://www.uwa.edu.au/library/help-and-support/support-for-uwa-researchers/

29. Imperial College London. https://www.imperial.ac.uk/admin-services/ict/self-service/research-support/

30. Jaguszewski, J.M. and Williams, K. (2013). "New roles for new times: transforming liaison roles in research libraries", available at: www.arl.org/storage/documents/publications/nrnt-liaison-

roles-revised.pdf

31. Jia, D., Wang, M. and Sun, Q. (2017). "Study on the research support services in American University Libraries: based on an analysis on strategic plans texts of libraries", Library Development, 281(5), pp. 59-65.
32. Krishnamurthy, M. (2008). "Open access, open source and digital libraries: a current trend in university libraries around the world", Program, Vol. 42 No. 1, pp. 48-55.
33. LIBER (Ligue des Bibliothèques Européennes de Recherche – Association of European Research Libraries). http://libereurope.eu/
34. Library survival guides. http://guides.library.uwa.edu.au/sb.php?subject_id=146380
35. Li Si, Yueliang Zeng, Sicheng Guo, Xiaozhe Zhuang, (2019). "Investigation and analysis of research support services in academic libraries", The Electronic Library.
36. Nosek, B. A. (2017). Opening science. In R.S. Jhangiani & R. Biswas-Diener (Eds.), "Open: The philosophy and practices that are revolutionizing education and science" http://www.ubiquitypress.com/site/books/10.5334/bbc/download/1451
37. OCLC Research. http://www.oclc.org/research.html
38. PebblePad. https://www.pebblepad.com.au/
39. Personal data. https://www.audiencedatasharing.org/about/glossary-of-terms/sensitive-personal-data
40. Robyn, D. and Richard, W. (2009). "RIMS: the research impact measurement service at the University of New South Wales", Australian Academic and Research Libraries, 40(2), pp. 76-87.
41. Si, L., Zeng, Y., Guo, S. and Zhuang, X. (2019). "Investigation and analysis of research support services in academic libraries", The Electronic Library, Vol. 37 No. 2, pp. 281-301. https://doi.org/10.1108/EL-06-2018-0125
42. Silvennoinen-Kuikka, Helena (2018). A strategic look at research support and open science services at our library. https://libraryconnect.elsevier.com/print/
43. Thomas, J. (2011). "Future-proofing: the academic library's role in e-research support", Library Management, 32(1/2), pp. 37-47.

Chapter Six

Collaborative Research

SUMMARY: Collaborative research has emerged as an entire field of study and understanding among researchers due to increasing complexity of researchers' work, digital environment and ethics. The following components have been brought together to frame the chapter:

- Introduction
- Collaborative Situations
- Collaborators' Expectations
- Written Agreements
- Collaborative Research and Formalized Agreements
- Business/Financial Issues of Collaborative Research
- Liability Issues in Collaborative Research
- Responsible Research and a Possible Co-Author
- Responsible Conduct of Research and Documentation
- Research collaboration Measurement
- Types of Collaborations
- Research data management in Collaborative Research
- Ethics in Collaborative Research
- Data Management and Protection
- Collaborative Research and Research Integrity
- Academic Policies
- Collaborations and Components
- Good Practices in Collaborative Research
- Issues for collaborators in Collaborative research
- Fostering Research Collaboration
- Research Integrity and Ethics Policy

INTRODUCTION

Collaborations among researchers are visible in several forms. The range of continuum is found from the classic partnership between two faculty members from the same academic organization to the factors such as collaboration due to a another's resources (may be a biological strain, some equipment, or an e-resource such as database). The expectations in a collaborative relationship relate to the rights as well as responsibilities shared by the collaborators. The term "collaboration" may have direct or indirect involvement of people involved giving it different meanings. Without proper communication and lack of transparency, the problems may arise in a collaborative research work. The concerned issues can range from the access to as well as use of the generated data, to the rights of intellectual property.

The expectations, queries and communication are the keys to a good collaboration in research among people. Sometimes, a written agreement takes shape before initiating the research collaboration. The organizations, collaborators belong or the funding agencies demand written agreements to formalize the research collaboration with the help of administrative staff members. The clear or written communication regarding the research collaboration is significant in the following situation:

- the number of collaborators is high
- interdisciplinary nature of research
- a number of academic institutions and corporate organizations are involved.

COLLABORATIVE SITUATIONS

As seen from the preceding examples, faculty and other researchers collaborate in many ways. Collaboration is defined: "To work jointly with others or together especially in an intellectual endeavor" (Merriam-Webster's 11th Collegiate Dictionary). The definition opens a broad umbrella under which we can place many forms of collaboration:

- Researchers in the same laboratory or academic department may work together on a sponsored project.
- There may be equal contributions in collaboration, or someone may lead while another is contributing expertise on a component or aspect of the project.
- They may be members of different departments in the same organization.
- The researchers may be from same discipline, or from various disciplines forming an interdisciplinary project.
- Researchers may collaborate on a complex set of questions across disciplines.

COLLABORATORS' EXPECTATIONS

Different expectations of collaborators and lack of proper communication leads to problems, sometimes in collaborative researches. The sufficient and efficient communication or expression of interests and roles are required to resolve the differences in expectations. To consider collaboration, it should be substantial intellectual contribution. There may be variation in understanding the "significant intellectual contribution". The characteristics of research relationship, any problem or disputes over authorship, and issues of IPR are usually observed. There are few facets related with collaborators' expectations, such as:

- Growth of interaction in collaboration
- Free and clear communication
- Expected contribution
- Role of administrative staff

WRITTEN AGREEMENTS

The informal communication and understanding among collaborators may not be the easy ways to complete the collaborations in research. In complex research projects, it is necessary to make each party's rights clear in writing. It is a good practice to have written agreements when external research collaborators and sponsors are involved. The following aspects of collaboration require attention for written responsibilities:

Authorship and Credit : The aspects related with authorship and credits to be given involve issues such as inclusion of authors, orders of authors, authority for presentation of results and publication, etc.

Research Accountability : The research accountability involves issues of access to original data, etc. and discussions of the results.

When collaboration is being done by a number of persons from different organizations, then few research-related issues arise due to institutional rights and responsibilities, including:

Intellectual Property : The issues involve rights to "patentable inventions", jointly owned by multiple organizations, understanding the difference between copyright and patents, issues of ownership, and license problems.

Use of Data : The access and use of data which is owned by institution or researchers require attention for clear communication and agreement among researchers. Sharing of data takes place while applying for grants, publishing of results etc. reflecting the contributions of the collaborators.

Data Retention and Preservation : Once the completion of data collection and analysis takes place, it is required to maintain and preserve the data. Sometimes data is retained for future verification, record of the research results and inventions. Agreements related to data retention, or destruction at a certain stage is helpful for understanding among the researchers.

COLLABORATIVE RESEARCH AND FORMALIZED AGREEMENTS

There are few other types of agreements though may be collaborative in nature yet clearly used in non-collaborative business transactions, which are:

Data Sharing Plans : Sometimes data developed under a sponsored project is to be made available for access. There may be instances where data sharing plan is not an understanding of collaboration, yet it facilitates the possibility for further collaborations on the basis of data having been shared.

Material Transfer Agreements : The "material transfer agreement" (MTA) helps in situation when one collaborator owns research materials and has to share the material with collaborator as requested. Though not acts of collaboration are the "MTAs", yet this contractual relationship is supportive in case of sharing the material between two research parties. The terms and conditions of the MTA are identical irrespective of existence of true research collaboration. Various issues addressed through MTAs are: (a) an acknowledgement that the provider retains ownership over the original material and any duplicates of the material created by the recipient, (b) an agreement concerning who owns other materials created through the use of the material, (c) and the responsibility for liability that may occur in the conduct of research using the material.

Facility Use Agreements : To use some equipment or the laboratory space, the "facility use agreement" is helpful with clear conditions. Such agreements are concerned with insurance and liability issues, the ownership of IPR, and the cost of access along with any other conditions.

BUSINESS/FINANCIAL ISSUES OF COLLABORATIVE RESEARCH

In the collaborative research, the written communication

and agreements include business and financial aspects. The financial or business issues can be addressed carefully and agreed upon due to written agreements. In case of any disagreement or dispute, the agreements can help in resolving the issues, there are types of agreements:

Subaward : This agreement guides about the work, budget, costs (permissible and not permissible), payments provisions, financial reports submission and the dispute resolving methods.

Consulting Agreement: A consulting agreement helps in formalization of collaboration. Usually the consulting agreements guide the hiring and payments of an individual (s) under collaborator. The "satisfactory completion of a well-defined scope of work" is responsible for payments. The person(s) hired for work retains no rights to the works, data or any intellectual property.

Facility Use Agreement: This agreement guides about the charges associated with use of the facilities and equipment at another collaborator's institution. The calculation of charges for facilities is based upon certain conditions.

MTA : This agreement provides information about the liability resulting from the usage of the material being transferred. Liability issues include cost issues, handling costs, return of leftover material etc.

LIABILITY ISSUES IN COLLABORATIVE RESEARCH

Liability for damages associated with collaborative research project invites attention for the related organizations. Though the liable instances may not be assumed in advance yet potential liabilities can be listed. Negligence, misconduct or any other aspect may harm collaboration. The collaborative research demands due care to avoid malpractices, misconduct or ignorance in terms of budgeting estimations, expenditures, misappropriations, mishandling of the materials or equipments, etc., liabilities occurring due to any factors invite lawsuits and penalties. It is essential to understand the policies, regulations, and administrative procedures to complete the collaborative research.

RESPONSIBLE RESEARCH AND A POSSIBLE CO-AUTHOR

Interests of the Affected Parties : The contributors from different sections of an organization, who have been active in a research work, would be sharing the authorship. The same case may be when more than one, organizations are involved for a joint research work.

Obligations : There is obligation to ensure the appropriate credit to the contributors and honoring the agreement, if any, to those who contribute to publications that originate from any research laboratory, to have clear communication among colleagues, administration etc.

Ethical Issues : The ethical issues are related with the obligations researchers have and honoring the written agreements.

Consequences of Actions : Unclear agreements, unmanaged contributions, etc. create problems in collaborative researches. Open communication, clear contributions and agreements among the researchers help to solve the authorship issues.

RESPONSIBLE CONDUCT OF RESEARCH AND DOCUMENTATION

Interests of the Affected Parties : The funding agencies are supportive to skilled, productive and ethical researchers.

Obligations : The complete research proposals, and applications should be submitted. The obligations on the part of researchers include the practices ethical standards, using data carefully with the proper permission etc.

Consequences of Actions : The documentation work in collaborative research take consideration of applications, research proposal, any data presented, its sources, written permissions, etc. The ethical aspects should be taken care of. Any agreement required for the documentation work and components is helpful in avoiding any confusion or penalties, later on.

RESEARCH COLLABORATION MEASUREMENT

The adequacy of measuring the 'collaboration' can be judged through various levels, such as co-authorship, in terms of inter-institutional and international collaboration. The co-authorship may be considered as a "partial indicator of collaboration". The commonness of research collaborations is observed through research grants applications, research network building, research partnerships, and co-authorship, etc. It is observed that the early career researchers gain more in collaborations by involvement and learning skills. Though there are collaborations among researchers in various fields, yet the methods to collaborate with industry, or at international level, are different. Keeping their requirements in view, the researchers can receive:

- Advice on collaboration with industry
- Guidance on functional and fruitful research collaborations
- The significance of collaborations at higher level

Producing highly visible research : The research is pivotal force of a researcher's work and aim and the engagement in multidisciplinary research often, demands collaborations. The output of such kind of research is considered as high-impact and quality work.

Innovative academic collaborations : Diversity in academic backgrounds brings the innovative ideas to the surface. The researchers receive different ideas and relating to their field in a relevant manner present solutions to many research problems.

Academia-industry collaborations : Collaborations between academic organizations and industry partners requires different perspectives. The kinds of research projects designed and agreements take shape are complex in nature.

TYPES OF COLLABORATIONS

The term "collaboration" indicates about the equal partnership and contribution in research for the purpose of mutual interests and fruitful research. In current times, collaborations are beyond simple academic partnerships for research work in the terms of co-authorship. Research collaborations have taken the shape of various kinds of partnerships due to educational or industrial background of researchers, their belonging to differing stature, the sponsorship and funding status, etc. The collaborators may belong to capacity or designation such as any research staff members, post-graduate students, post-doctoral fellows, and corporate employees. Creation and knowledge of agreements for the collaborative research work among the researchers is must; responsibilities, protection in the collaboration should be formalized by the agreement. The setting up of "subawards", or any other types of collaborative agreements, can be used to formalize the collaboration among the researchers.

Some examples in research collaboration relationships are as following:

- Two research groups from the same institution yet different sections to work on a project without any external funding. Their contribution is observed in the equal division of work with responsibility to review the work output with the aim to publish the results
- A research collaboration will be said when an academic research group and a member from industry work together in a research project.

- Creating a group for data collection for a funded research work.
- Participation of a researcher in another institution's research facility at regular intervals over a period of time.
- Collaboration between researchers of two different academic fields needing each other's expertise for testing or analysis, etc. and later combining the research results for publication.
- Combining the independent research at various nations being conducted by funded or independent researchers to study the research impact at global level. This collaboration involves the combination of data at later stage, once each researcher completes the work and add it to the common purpose.

RESEARCH DATA MANAGEMENT IN COLLABORATIVE RESEARCH

Research data management involves, sometimes, the availability, accessibility of funded data. The aspects such as data should be discoverable and usable for others are also related. Researchers need awareness, understanding and knowledge to follow the processes for research data management. The discovery of advantages of sharing research data is associated with reproducibility issues. This facilitates to build on the further research. The researchers need to share and explore the data citing, various components of data management plans. To be a part of collaborative research, the research data management supports the researchers in knowing the following:

- Significance of data sharing
- Steps of data management plans
- Awareness of the sharing solutions

The needs of research data management make a researcher learn the following:

Manage and publish research data : Data management and publishing has extended the advantages beyond the recognition of researcher; the promotion of transparent research has been achieved. The chances of research collaboration are augmented due to data sharing and reproducibility.

Storage, sharing and using data : The researchers should explore the methods of data storage and organization. This learning helps in data sharing and contributing in collaboration, thus increasing the research reproducibility.

Good research data management plan : The data management plan needs clear understanding of various components such as research data collection, organization, use of software or any technical platform, etc. The plan also includes aspects such as how this data may be shared. The researchers should know need of data management plan.

Citing data and significance : The significance of data citation is observed in building the strong research, this also supports the chronological developments in a particular academic fields and showing the strength of research.

ETHICS IN COLLABORATIVE RESEARCH

The formation of publishing reputation is based upon the good research work and ethical practices followed by the researchers. The steps to be taken since the manuscript or document preparation to the final stage of publishing and submitting are crucial and need to followed in ethical contexts. Existing guidelines should be exercised and in case of any failure, the consequences are faced once a researcher does not meet the obligations. Rules and practices of authorship, copyright permissions and issues of plagiarism require attention of researchers. Researchers in individual works or in collaboration should observe the following:

- What are publishing ethics

- Understanding and knowledge of the rules Content ownership and copyright permissions

Collaborative research among colleagues either across the same organization or other external institutions provides opportunities for "cross-disciplinary innovation". Collaboration also brings common platforms to understand the common accepted norms spread and practiced across the various disciplines, organizations and nations. Understanding the variations in research practices and reaching to an agreement before the research commences, to lead ahead of time. Such precautions and measures help to avoid potential disagreements among researchers. The following considerations are here to examine:

- Issues of authorship, patterns, and potential contributors
- Ethical codes of conduct, organizational guidelines, and publishers' policies.
- Cross-institutional research
- Legislation aspects
- Common practices and terminologies across the disciplines

The research and publishing ethics can be understood as following:

Plagiarism : The issues of similarity and plagiarism are common, yet there are ways to avoid it. The seriousness of plagiarism should be taken into cognizance as it has affected the researchers and research works worldwide.

Authorship : The level of contribution and agreements among the fellow researchers in a research work, project or paper determines the authorship in a publication. The understanding among the collaborators is very instrumental in order to avoid any problems at later stage.

Content ownership : Issues related to own the content

related to research work is often a matter of publishing problems. The ownership issues and copyright aspects are very significant components in publishing the research report, etc. The ownership may be retained on the part of researchers, funding agencies, parent organizations or publishers, according to terms and conditions laid before the commencement of work.

Adherence to publication ethics : The organizational policies, funding agencies guidelines and publishers rules are structured platforms for providing the avenues of sharing the research outcomes. The related policies, guidelines and rules are framed in such a way that promote research sharing, results publishing, promoting the interdisciplinary research, etc.

Knowledge of permissions : The researchers ought to know rules, permissions, and ways to strictly follow the ethical standards in collaborative research and publishing.

DATA MANAGEMENT AND PROTECTION

Research integrity is intricately woven in the research processes. The policies and guidelines support the researchers for sticking to the correct path and avoiding the practices which may create bigger problems. In this context, the data management is essential to keep a tab on activities taking place during research. The data management covers data collection, its storage and categorization (field notes, various forms such as consent forms, and including audio files). Inclusion of electronic data needs proper archiving. Properly management of data is required throughout the research life cycle, and later too. Data management includes essential archiving as well as data destruction at correct time. The integrity of research depends much upon data management. Poor data management is harmful for the integrity of the research. This may overshadow the impact/advantages related with the research output. The data handling should be done with due care keeping the relevant state legislation and organizational policies in planning. Research data management goes on during entire research lifecycle, where organizational research data policy and management tools can play a significant role. There are various niches to light upon, such as:

Items in Research Data Management : This kind of knowledge helps in understating the area and items to be covered under research data management during research life cycle.

Data Protection : This area is related with the tools for data protection, such as software, and any related legislation.

Transferring of data : The rules and awareness should be provided to researchers for the transfer mechanisms, ways and consequences.

Intellectual Property Rights : The proper awareness and guidance on various IPRs can be provided time to time to the researchers.

Information Security

A very crucial area to train the researchers, apart from their academic knowledge they should be aware of information security aspects. While the organizations provide much quality information and training for research data management, the basic concepts of data should also be known to the researchers. The aspects such as what data is; types and formats, storage and access of data are few of the areas to be explored by the researchers. Knowledge of data and its attributes will support the data management.

COLLABORATIVE RESEARCH AND RESEARCH INTEGRITY

The collective efforts of researchers from various departments, institutions and governments, at higher level form the collaborative research. Since a number of researchers involve in work frequently from multiple organizations on a number of projects simultaneously, the "maintenance" of various ethical practice becomes essential and difficult, as well. The academic, professional backgrounds and stages of their careers pose challenges in the form of research expectations form the colleagues associated in conducting research.

In case of any conflicts, the opportunities to communicate may remove the instances of further problems. The application of reasonable, consistent and open communication supports the various solutions in a research environment, these are: the access to the information, use of equipment, reporting hierarchy, and sharing of resources. These areas are the "conflict zones" which may require attention in research collaboration. Growth of interdisciplinary and multi-organizational research has created a complex situation. The review of research collaborations in the large scenario is a challenging task due to involvement of a number of organizations belonging to different subject backgrounds and in functional or geographical nature. Ethical issues pertaining to authorship in collaborative research are complex. Understanding and conventions related to authors' names for research publication may vary in various subject fields. The factors such as "significant intellectual contribution" and "significant scientific contribution" are responsible for being an author in publications.

The Research Integrity requires not only the training but also a framework to support the researchers developing a culture of research integrity. Research integrity in the researchers demands the knowledge and skills for the research tasks. The use of relevant research methods, well organized data management, practicing ethical measures, etc. The following ways throw light upon:

1. The assistance to researchers to maintain the integrity throughout the research lifecycle.
2. The training methods to understand and evaluate the research needs according to their research types.

ACADEMIC POLICIES

The academic policies in the context of collaborative research are significant. The responsible conduct of research (RCR) has created its niche in academic training. For example, Georgia Tech has RCR polices; Academic Policies, and RCR Compliance Policy:

RCR Academic Policy for Ph. D. Scholars : This RCR training is an intensive method to provide necessary skills to equip with integrity qualities.

RCR Academic Policy for Post Graduate scholars : This policy is the expansion of doctoral students' policy. Masters' students have to complete the RCR training course.

Research collaboration can be done in an efficient and professional manner if certain guidelines are followed. According to authors, Robyn Keast and Michael Charles from *Southern Cross University,* the idea of visibility of more collaboration between academia and industry as it would be helpful to "find solutions to real world problems and create jobs and growth". According to their view, "between 50% and 75% of all inter-organizational collaborations fail. And failure is expensive", as the collaboration is not an easy task. The following observations can help in making the collaboration established:

1. Identification of need to collaborate : Real need of collaboration should be judged by the researcher at own as to identify the areas or resources required.

2. Realizing the responsibilities in collaboration : The aspects related with research collaboration are the finding fellow contributors, organizational permissions, funding and the measurements of cost-effectiveness. It is the obligation of researcher to ensure such components while initiating the research collaboration.

3. Assessment of collaborators : Finding suitable research partners is not an easy task due to varied nature of research interests, organizational permissions, expectations, and required skills. It is significant to receive relevant expertise in the collaboration.

4. Extending the collaboration relationships : The research collaborations with the routine colleagues may derive the needed academic trust yet the external collaborations induce innovation in thinking, methods, skill-sets and input.

5. Identification of common research goals : Setting up of collaboration with the researchers begins with the proper communication of desired goals, methodologies, negotiation of terms and conditions, use of resources, equipments, etc. Even after the setting of terms and conditions, there should be provisions for any problems to be solved with understanding and responsibilities keeping the common interests and goals in mind.

6. Nurturing the collaborative relationships : The research collaborations are based on face-to-face relationships trusts instead of transactional agreements.

7. Value of stakeholders : Identification of experts in a research collaboration leads to the advantages to be achieved by the research collaboration and the organization(s) involved. This is effective in running the research projects to keep the interest alive and achieve the goals. The high-level authority and sponsorship demands the maintenance of ethical standards, research funding to keep the research collaboration functional.

8. Reviewing the team : Though the research collaborations begin with preparation and there may be conflicts among the researchers and affect the productivity. Such situations require review of the activities, processes and finding solutions.

9. Maintaining the good practices : To keep the collaboration in a good form, there is need to understand the nature, rules and goals of collaboration. This is necessary to know the methods of working, collaborative values and the aims in vision.

10. Continuous monitoring and evaluation : The measurements of achieved success practices are possible through regular monitoring of the research projects, comparing with the timelines and future plans.

COLLABORATIONS AND COMPONENTS

The research needs have motivated and compelled the researchers to establish the research collaborations. According to Kamp (2011), the organizational alliances are the strong collaborations. These alliances are visible in the form of "industry collaborations", or "public private partnerships" (PPPs) serving the areas such as ICT sector, banking, and government sector. Researchers and professionals from different organizations collaborate with clearly defined "common goals" to achieve the collaborative common outcomes. The structure of collaborative teams can be understood as one big team composed of subgroups or smaller representative teams from external or other organizations. The subgroups in a collaborative team form along "the organizational boundary lines" and governed by the individual organizational background and functional roles. Diversity in the background often leads to cultural and conceptual differences in the collaborative works, affecting the performance. The conflicts can be observed in the following ways:

a. determination of functional roles and responsibilities

b. methodologies and mechanisms to work

c. differences at personal level

The search of solution can be achieved by discussions, motivations and aim to reach the common goal of the collaboration. In this context, the common goals function as factors for motivating the team members and the allotment of work with clear roles functions as "structural solutions". Understanding and working on relevant "ground rules and structures" are must for collaboration to pace in desired direction. Also the concern of a team should be about "us" and common goals, not the individualistic approach. The collaborative team should work as one group instead of several sub-groups.

Sometimes a clear common goal is absent yet the component structures can play a significant role in creating a goal at one team level. Performance of component structure can be summed up to achieve the collaborative purpose. The division and sharing of costs/revenues can be done at structural level. When there are clear assignments and tasks divided among the subgroups, their contributions are visible without overlapping of the responsibilities, and the performance can be measured efficiently finally to combine and see the goal of collaboration. The role of "In-site learning" is also significant as it provides opportunity to the new team members to learn the work at its origin. It may not be applicable in each case of collaboration yet may be exercised wherever it can bring better results.

The opportunity before the participating organizations to emphasize the common goals to the members of collaborative teams gives the mechanism to discuss conflicts and find solutions. This gives birth to "reflexivity" which is a significant structural solution to improve the collaborative relationships by describing the work organization and clear roles to play. It is always challenging to form a collaborative team of multiple organizations and the participating members of different organizations due to difference in work and policy culture.

GOOD PRACTICES IN COLLABORATIVE RESEARCH

The collaborations in researches are often visible at very high level and intricately woven at various levels. These levels can be observed as collaborations between developing and developed nations, and multiple institutions from the same nation, too. There are thousands of examples of collaboration among researchers from different academic fields for research and innovative (R&I) projects. There may be problems or issues due to the physical distance between collaborating researchers, and few other factors for misunderstanding. These factors often named as cultural (social and work, both, language, and political). Effective collaboration can be initiated and maintained through honest and open communication at regular interval and whenever required since the stage of planning. The areas for communication involve:

- respective roles and responsibilities,
- methods, technology usage, and analytical techniques,
- practice of best available standards

The following aspects are discussed as acceptable practices in collaborations:

1. Understanding the goals at broader level : The researchers should make efforts towards the academic or research goals as well as strengthen the collaborative goals to maintain the goodwill and reputation for the future collaborations.

2. Confidentiality agreement : The maintenance of academic, industrial practices and confidentialities is significant to cover the research and collaborative ideas.

3. Definitions of roles and responsibilities : Clear communication (sometimes required in written manner) is important in complex research collaborations. These communications include information about exact responsibilities of collaborators, roles of contributors, guidance roles with realistic approach. A written agreement for the project lifetime should consider the following issues:

- A project time-frame and component milestones
- Functional roles and responsibilities in the collaboration team, the specific information of leader of the projects and various other roles in the sub-groups
- Ownership of IP rights and access rights
- Confidentiality, resource sharing, data sharing and procedure for reporting and investigating the research misconduct
- Financial issues, transport of materials
- Conflicts of interest
- Authorship and publication practices

4. Integrity of collaboration : The participating team members need to follow the practices and procedures to ensure the integrity, access and stewardship of the research data

5. Precautions for ethical dilemma : Researchers should understand the foreign collaborator(s) and terms and conditions of the employing institution(s), the end-users of the R&I and, and local key decision-makers.

6. Language solutions : It is significant to arrange the solutions in case of different languages among the collaborating researchers. The care in translation should be taken in order to avoid any problem in communication, academic writing, etc.

7. Strengthen the cultural contexts : The need to strengthen awareness of culture and regulatory context is to avoid any differences in hierarchy in team responsibilities or data quality, and approaches to authorship, etc.

For example, at the University of Sheffield, UK, the practices in international collaborations are as following:

1. To receive advice from "experts in foreign affairs and international development" in context with local knowledge;
2. Following the research ethics by reporting and

investigating witnessed or suspected incidents of research misconduct.

ISSUES FOR COLLABORATORS IN COLLABORATIVE RESEARCH

Due to interdisciplinary research and need of external expertise, researchers frequently collaborate. This requires formation of "project management group" and effective communication at early stage with other collaborators including the following aspects:

- Understanding the goals of research collaboration, concerned project and responsibilities
- Resource-sharing in the context of data, information resources and equipments.
- Early disclosure of conflicts of interest
- Collection of research data and later storage and sharing mechanisms
- Process, criteria and credits in authorship
- financial management and transport management, if any, including the organizations' policies
- Address to intellectual property rights and ownership issues
- training and supervision
- Following the funder and relevant regulatory matters

FOSTERING RESEARCH COLLABORATION

The following components and steps are taken together to foster the collaboration in research:

- Finding the research Expertise
- Collaborating or participating research centers and organizations
- knowledge of Interdisciplinary Resources
- Proposal Development for collaborative research

- Guidance for research Grants
- Setting up the research development plan
- Budgetary estimation and preparation of budget
- Supporting Documentation knowledge and preparation
- Budget expenditure and proper reporting

The competitive strength is due in part to support of research collaboration within the community, and our partners around the world. Goal is to provide faculty and staff with the collaborative tools and networks necessary to support the research enterprise.

RESEARCH INTEGRITY AND ETHICS POLICY

To understand and stick to research integrity, various university policies are framed and researchers follow the codes of practice, which can be explained as following:

- Academic integrity in research policy
- Conflict of interest policy
- Policy on the ethical conduct of research involving human participants and personal data
- Data supporting research Policy on the management
- Data protection policy
- Intellectual property policy
- Safety in fieldwork policy
- Use of animals in scientific research policy
- Public interest disclosure policy

The research ethics policies help in guiding the researchers to follow the correct procedures. To help them further, the designing of checklist helps in research. Once this information is supplied to research scholars/collaborators, the precautions can be taken at the initial stage of research work. The following checklist can be useful for the researchers:

Basic concepts of good practices in research : At this stage, the researchers should be informed about organizational resources for use.

Subject-specific policies/guidelines : The awareness about the discipline-specific codes of conduct must be given to scholars.

Funding agencies : Universities and other organizations may provide funding agencies related relevant information of funding terms and conditions.

Authorship : The requisite information about the requirements of being an author of publication, attribution, publication strategies related to project and guidelines of journals etc.

Conflict of interest : The awareness of concept of "conflict of interest" in research can be provided with the supply of documents related University's policy. Such documents help in understanding of "potential conflicts" and good management.

Research involving participants : Researchers should be provided training of dealing with involvement of human participants, and "personal data or materials".

Licences and permissions : Requirement of any licences and permissions to use certain materials etc. should be judged and imported/exported timely from relevant communities as well as government agencies.

Research data as well as records management : The research data, generated records management requires knowledge and understanding of storage, further identification, data protection, accessibility, archiving arrangement, and confidentiality/privacy issues are significant aspect for planning.

Intellectual property : This aspect is significant in context of funded research, data collection and storage, research notes, consent forms, etc.

Supervisory meetings and Mentoring : The regular monitoring and meetings keep the progress in check.

REFERENCES

1. Ailes, C., Roessner, D., Feller, I. and K. Ailes, (1997). 'The Impact on Industry of Interaction with Engineering Research Centers,' Final Report to the National Science Foundation, Engineering Education and Centers Program, The Science and Technology Policy Program, SRI International, Washington, DC.
2. Ambos, T. C., Mäkelä, K., Birkinshaw, J. and D'Este, P. (2008). When does university research get commercialized? Creating ambidexterity in research institutions. Journal of Management Studies, 45(8), 1424–1447.
3. Animal experiments. https://www.kyoto-u.ac.jp/en/research/research-compliance-ethics/animal-experiments.html
4. Beverly L. Clarke (1964). Multiple authorship trends in scientific papers, Science 143 (3608), pp. 822-824
5. Beaver, D. B. (2001). Reflections on scientific collaboration (and its study): Past, present, and future. Scientometrics, 52(3), pp. 365–377.
6. Behrens, Teresa R. and Gray, Denis O. (2000). 'Unintended Consequences of Cooperative Research: Impact of Industry Sponsorship on the Climate for Academic Freedom and Other Graduate Student Outcomes', Research Policy 30(2), pp. 179-199.
7. Best practices for Coordination and Set-up of Cost Shares https://uwnetid.sharepoint.com/sites/OR-Campus/ SiteCollection Documents/Interdisciplinary%20Resources/ORC-BestPractices-for-Coordination-and-Setup-of-Cost-Share.pdf
8. Bozeman, Barry and Corley, Elizabeth (2004). "Scientists' Collaboration Strategies: Implications for Scientific and Technical Human Capital", Research Policy 33(4), pp. 599-616..
9. Bozeman, B., & Gaughan, M. (2011). How do men and women differ in research collaborations? An analysis of the collaboration motives and strategies of academic researchers. Research Policy, 40(10), 1393–1402.
10. Bridge Funding. uw.edu/research/or/bridge-funding-program/
11. Burnham, J., (1997). 'Evaluating Industry University Research Linkages,' Research Technology Management 40(1), 52-55.
12. Bruneel, J., D' Este, P. and Salter, A. (2010). "Investigating the factors that diminish the barriers to university–industry collaboration." Research Policy, 39(7), pp. 858–868.

13. Chompalov, I., Genuth, J., and Shrum, W. (2002). The organization of scientific collaborations. Research Policy, 31(5), 749–767.

14. Collaborative for Research Education. https://www.washington.edu/research/training/core

15. Collaborative Proposal Development Resources. https://www.washington.edu/research/collaboration/collaborative-proposal-resources/

16. Collaborative research. https://researchsupport.admin.ox.ac.uk/governance/integrity/collaboration

17. Collaborative research with Kyoto University. https://www.kyoto-u.ac.jp/en/research/collaboration

18. Conflict of interest. https://researchsupport.admin.ox.ac.uk/governance/integrity/conflict

19. Conflict of interest management. https://www.kyoto-u.ac.jp/en/research/research-compliance-ethics/conflict_of_interest

20. Cronin, B. (2001). Hyperauthorship: A postmodern perversion or evidence of a structural shift in scholarly communication practices? Journal of the American Society for Information Science and Technology, 52(7), pp. 558–569.

21. Cummings, J. N., and Kiesler, S. (2005). Collaborative research across disciplinary and organizational boundaries. Social Studies of Science, 35(5), pp. 703.

22. Establish a Research Center uw.edu/research/establish-a-research-center-or-institute/ Guidelines for Establishing Organized Research Units (ORUs) https://uwnetid.sharepoint.com/sites/OR-Campus/ SiteCollectionDocuments/ Interdisciplinary%20Resources/ORC-UWGuidelines-for-Establishing-ORUs.doc?d=w59ace5a962ba4b319bc32745d82f1268

23. Faria, J. R., and Goel, R. K. (2010). Returns to networking in academia. Netnomics, 11(2), 103–117.

24. Feller, I. (1997). 'Technology Transfer from Universities,' in J. Smart ed., Higher Education: Handbook of Theory and Research, Vol. XII, New York: Agathon Press, pp. 1-43.

25. Fostering Research Collaboration uw.edu/research/collaboration/

26. Fox, Mary F. and Catherine A. Faver (1984). 'Independence and Cooperation in Research: The Motivations and Costs of Collaboration', Journal of Higher Education 55(3), pp. 347-359.

27. Frame, J. Davidson and Mark P. Carpenter (1979). "International research collaboration". Social Studies of Science 9, pp. 481-497.

28. FUNDING OPPORTUNITIES uw.edu/research/resources/funding-opportunities/

29. Garg, K. C., and Padhi, P. (2001). A study of collaboration in laser science and technology. Scientometrics, 51(10), pp. 415–427.

30. Godin, Benoit and Gingras, Yves (2000). "Impact of Collaborative Research on Academic Science", Science and Public Policy 27(1), pp. 65-73.

31. Godin, Benoit (2003). 'The Impact of Research Grants on the Productivity and Quality of Scientific Research', INRS Working Paper 2003, National Sciences and Engineering Research Council of Canada (NSERC).

32. Gordon, Michael (1980). "A Critical Reassessment of Inferred Relations Between Multiple Authorship, Scientific Collaboration, the Production of Papers and Their Acceptance for Publication", Scientometrics 2, pp. 193-201.

33. Guidance for NIH Institutional Training Grants. https://www.washington.edu/research/collaboration/guidance-for-nih-institutional-training-grants/

34. Guidance for NIH T32 Institutional Training Grants uw.edu/research/collaboration/guidance-for-nih-institutionaltraining-grants/

35. Handbook for Leaders of Organized Research Units https://uwnetid.sharepoint.com/sites/OR-Campus/

36. SiteCollectionDocuments/Interdisciplinary%20Resources/ORCCenters-and-Institutes-Handbook.doc?d=wbe369a3facc248b8abf37e8cf07c8d36

37. Heffner, A.G. (1981). "Funded Research, Multiple Authorship, and Sub-authorship Collaboration in Four Disciplines", Scientometrics 3(1), pp. 5-12 .

38. Heinze, T., and Bauer, G. (2007). "Characterizing creative scientists in nano-S&T: Productivity, multidisciplinarity, and network brokerage in a longitudinal perspective". Scientometrics, 70(3), 811–830.

39. Interdisciplinary Resources. https://www.washington.edu/research/collaboration/interdisciplinary-resources/

40. Interdisciplinary Resources uw.edu/research/collaboration/interdisciplinary-resources/

41. Jeong, S., Choi, J. Y., and Kim, J. (2011). "The determinants of research collaboration modes: Exploring the effects of research and researcher characteristics on co-authorship." Scientometrics, 89(3), pp. 967–983.

42. Kamp, Martijn van der (2011). Collaborating and colliding: when alliances go wrong.

43. Katz, Sylvan J. and Martin, Ben R. (1997). "What is Research Collaboration?." Research Policy 26(1), pp. 1-18.

44. Keast, Robyn, Charles, Michael (2016). Ten rules for successful research collaboration, Southern Cross University.

45. Kyoto University Institute for Advanced Study (KUIAS). https://www.kyoto-u.ac.jp/en/research/

46. Lee, Y.S. (1996). 'Technology Transfer' and the Research University: A Search for the Boundaries of University-Industry Collaboration," Research Policy, 25, pp. 843-863.

47. Liao, C. H., & Yen, H. R. (2012). Quantifying the degree of research collaboration: A comparative study of collaborative measures. Journal of Informetrics, 6(1), pp. 27–33.

48. Limited Submissions Opportunities depts.washington.edu/research/funding/limited-submissions

49. Matching Funds uw.edu/research/or/matching-funds-request/

50. McCauley, James E. (1963). Multiple authorship, Science 141 (3580) pp. 579.

51. Melin, Goran (2000). "Pragmatism and Self-organization: Research Collaboration on the Individual Level", Research Policy 29(1): 31-40

52. Pao, Miranda Lee (1982). "Collaboration in computational musicology", Journal of the American Society for Information Science 33 (1), pp. 38-43.

53. Proper use of research grants. https://www.kyoto-u.ac.jp/en/research/research-compliance-ethics/proper-use-of-research-grants

54. Publication and authorship, Good research conduct guidance on publication, authorship and peer review. https://researchsupport.admin.ox.ac.uk/governance/integrity/publication

55. Research Affiliation Agreement and Template https://uwnetid.sharepoint.com/sites/OR-Campus/ SiteCollection Documents/Interdisciplinary%20Resources/Research_Affiliation_Agreement_Template_and_Process.doc?d=w1e45a6b005c 948abab4a435d534edac8

56. Research Centers and Institutes uw.edu/research/collaboration/centers-and-institutes/

57. Research compliance & ethics. https://www.kyoto-u.ac.jp/en/research/research-compliance-ethics/Research integrity. https://

researchsupport.admin.ox.ac.uk/governance/integrity

58. Research integrity rules and reporting. https://www.kyoto-u.ac.jp/en/research/research-compliance-ethics/research-integrity-rules-reporting/research-integrity-rules-reporting.html
59. Research misconduct. https://researchsupport.admin.ox.ac.uk/governance/integrity/misconduct
60. Responsible Academic Research Policies. https://rcr.gatech.edu/compliance-policy
61. Responsible Conduct of Research. https://rcr.gatech.edu/
62. Royalty Research Fund (RRF) uw.edu/research/or/royalty-research-fund-rrf/
63. RCR Academic Policy for Doctoral Students. https://rcr.gatech.edu/doctoral-policy
64. Rogers, Juan and Bozeman, Barry (2001). "Knowledge Value Alliances: An Alternative to R&D Project Evaluation", Science, Technology and Human Values 26(1), pp. 23-55.
65. Shared Research Facilities and Resources. https://www.washington.edu/research/shared-research-facilities-resources/
66. Subramanyam, K. Citation and significance, New Library World 76, pp. 227-228.
67. Subramanyam, K. and Stephens, (1982). Elsie M. Research collaboration and funding in biochemistry and chemical engineering, International Forum on Information and Documentation 7 (4) 26-29
68. Sylvan, J. Ben, Katz, Martin, R. What is research collaboration? https://doi.org/10.1016/S0048-7333(96)00917-1Get rights and content
69. Thorsteinsdottir, O. Halla (2000). "External Research Collaboration in Two Small Science Systems", Scientometrics 49(1), pp. 145-160
70. Web Resources Fostering Research Collaboration uw.edu/research/collaboration/ Guidance for NIH T32 Institutional Training Grants uw.edu/research/collaboration/guidance-for-nih-institutional training-grants/ Barry.

Chapter Seven

Open Data

SUMMARY : The "Open data" has been an initiative and movement for the research purposes across the word. Various nations have framed policies and guidelines to augment the open data usage. The chapter has been framed to encapsulate the conceptual information in the following manner:

- Introduction
- Defining Open Data
- Open Data and Knowledge Creation
- Open Data and Limitations
- Open data and Innovation through Liquid Information
- Open Data Kit
- Open Data and Certain Conditions
- Various Steps to Open Data
- Project Open Data
- Open Data Community and Events
- The Open Data Research Network
- Open Data Initiative
- World Bank Open Data
- Registry of Open Data on AWS
- OPEN DATA and India

INTRODUCTION

The concepts and myths of "Open Data" have been creating new waves of learning in the academic and worldly scenario. There are several examples which help us in understanding the areas where open data is already playing great yet subtle roles. The reasons behind data becoming "open" are obvious in the contexts of access, availability and applications in myriad areas. The aspects such as various sorts of data, why can be open or can't be open. In open data, the criterion and focus is on opening up on the "non-personal data", i.e., data without containing information related with specific individuals. Open data is as defined (https://opendefinition.org/) by the Open Definition, "Open data is data that can be freely used, re-used and redistributed by anyone - subject only, at most, to the requirement to attribute and sharealike". The full Open Definition (https://opendefinition.org/okd/) gives crisp and precise information in the summarized manner:

- Availability and Access
- Re-use and Redistribution
- Universal Participation

All the above attributes are possible, due to the feature of interoperability in the digital data. Interoperability can be understood as the ability of diverse systems to inter-operate and make multiple system functional altogether. The capacity to interoperate among the systems and inter-mixing the different datasets makes the data open. The working composition of elements is interrelated so that interoperability can support open data. In the complex systems, the ability to "plug together" all the elements is necessary.

DEFINING OPEN DATA

With the creation of the Open Knowledge Foundation in 2005, a succinct explanation and knowledge about open data has been spread to provide both and a detailed definition of open data. In the words of Laura James (2013), "as the open data movement grows, and even more governments and organisations sign up to open data, it becomes ever more important that there is a clear and agreed definition for what open data means if we are to realise the full benefits of openness, and avoid the risks of creating incompatibility between projects and splintering the community."

The conditions are there to understand the "open" attribute related with data. Data from any sources or about any concept may be open in nature given in certain conditions. The release of data under an open licence can be done for free use. This release is for the information use benefits of public and by the public. Though release of data by the government sector and various organizations has been observed in the availability of budget information or geographical information as maps, etc., at larger level, the researchers have started sharing the research output in the form of publications. Various types of organizations such as academic institutes, community groups, non-governmental organizations, and individuals are sharing the data in "open" manner. The subject areas include science information, academic information, economics and transport related data, cultural information, and libraries, etc. The "open" attribute can be applied to various kinds of information sources and data (even to big data and "small data" i.e. images, and text, etc.).

The understanding of open data invites attention towards the aspects and attributes related with it. The intention of open data is to augment collaborating, enhance sharing and scaling as open data to reach the larger communities. The two facets of open data according to full Open Definition (https:/ /opendefinition.org/okd/) are as following that make it clear:

Legal openness : This is related with getting, building and sharing the data in legally permissible ways. The role of appropriate (open) license is observed in providing legal openness. The open licence allows the data for free access, reuse and making data available in public domain.

Technical openness: The technical openness means the removal of technical barriers for using the data. Various formats and accessibility should be in such manner that it makes data open for community use, including machine readability.

Various aspects such as open data are useable by anyone, irrespective of their academic status, location, or particular purpose, etc. The removal of any restrictions is possible due to open data. The amount of open data availability makes the ease of work possible. Free of charge availability for communities or very minimal charging of production cost related with data are appreciated. Other aspects are the availability of digital nature in downloadable formats in easy ICT environments. Permissions and possibilities to use the data according to requirement are facilitated through open data. Open data allows the re-use, redistribution and intermixing of data. The Open Definition gives a way to use the data and various permissions yet the acknowledgements cannot be ignored. The source of data should be given credit. Further sharing of data should be done in as open data after creation of new datasets, declaring if any changes were made.

The significant motives behind the effective open data are as following:

- **Availability of data:** communities can access and avail the data for their use.
- **Re-use of data and further Redistribution :** reuse and sharing the data for further use.
- **Universal Participation :** the data is for use among the communities to make it available universally.

The "Open Definition" is governed by an Advisory Council since 2007. This council has been taking care of documentation and related materials with the mission to facilitate the open knowledge community. The compliance of licences with the Open Definition is the responsibility of the advisory council. The council is maintained by the appointment of members from community based on knowledge and competence. The open definition is available in more than 30 languages for awareness among communities. The relationship of the Open Definition to specific sets of principles for openness – such as the Sunlight Foundation's 10 principles and Tim Berners-Lee's 5 starsystem, why having a shared and agreed definition of open data is so important, and how one can go about "doing open data".

Understanding Open Data

Many aspects of open data are simple to comprehend. The data that is accessed, used and shared by anyone is open data. Bodies at various levels such as governmental organizations, corporate, and individuals are providing and using open data. These initiatives are concerned with social factors, economic purposes and environmental benefits. The knowledge about open data among communities is related with the understanding of:

- basic concepts of open data
- understanding data in comprehensive manner
- the conditions and mechanism that make data open
- requirements and benefits of open data

The availability of open data is ensured by a common understanding of technical platforms including "machine-readable format". The licensing processing related with open data is a must compo net which makes it real open by permissions to use in the required way such as transformation of data, combination of data and sharing it further.

OPEN DATA AND KNOWLEDGE CREATION

The role of open data in creation of new knowledge is significant as open data contributes in conversion into the information, later taking shape of new knowledge. The availability of open data helps in transformation of raw material to knowledge.

Data: The "raw material" which is the basis of derivation and origin of information and knowledge. Various items and entities form data; images, descriptions, figures, facts about anything are data.

Information : Once the data is given a context and direction, it takes form of information. All the related entities are combined to become single information. The gathering and interrelation of data support in formation of information.

Knowledge : The derived systematic information is known as knowledge as it personalized for the intended needs. Hidden aspect of knowledge relates to the conversion of information into the desired choices for decision making of a person or group.

OPEN DATA AND LIMITATIONS

The availability of data and certain attributes making it open in nature are followed by few limitations which are as following:

Limitation : Data should be without any limitations to be used in various ways. The preventions from limitations include users, methods, modifications, combinations and sharing.

Cost : The access is governed by the cost involved with creation, maintenance and publication of data. It is assumed that a reasonable reproduction cost is charged to keep the open data purpose alive and functional. Sometimes the reproduction cost is negligible for most of the datasets. In this context, it should be observed that live data and big data have different cost perspectives.

Reuse : Even the commercial use is permitted, once the data is open in nature. The measurement of data is done by estimating the purpose and mechanism of use. The related facets such as data format, its structure and machine readability are significant in aggravating the use among communities.

Need of Open Data : The benefits to the researchers and the outcomes to governments, societies, and businesses are innumerable. The further discussion is as following:

- **Transformation in government and societies :** The transparency in governance leads to better policies and services to societies.
- **Building Corporate opportunities :** New opportunities for businesses and corporate affairs are brought upon through open data. The interfaces and connection with customers are facilitated. The outcomes of open data can be easily observed in transportation facilities,
- **Protection of environment :** Building of global infrastructure on the basis of World Wide Web and d open data platforms has provided support for sharing information and creation of warning systems. These warnings and careful approaches are related with the disaster management as well as peoples' impact on environment.

Sharing of Open Data

To remember in mind, the open data is that data for anyone to access, use and share; the data in the form of numbers, maps, texts, and photos that form the raw material for information. For the users, open data should be free of restrictions for its use. Communities need open data to unlock social, environmental and economic values by providing access to millions of datasets and make governments more transparent and accountable. Thus, open access and free use of data, i.e. making data open for people without restrictions creates new value by augmenting the potential. The diversity of advantages to the governments, researchers, and communities include the improvement in services, economic growth etc.

Open data is data that can be freely used, re-used and redistributed by anyone – subject only, at most, to the requirement to attribute and sharealike. –Open Data Handbook

The sharing of open data is exponentially fruitful to communities:

- augmenting the scientific collaboration and research reproducibility,
- transparent governance t and corporate affairs
- enhancing the research and innovation
- discovery of solutions to social progress.

Potential value of data is discerned beyond the organizational and geographical boundaries. The legal aspects are related with open data are observed though the use of standard, authorized legal tools for copyright management and reuse of data. Use of Creative Commons licenses to facilitate data sharing is common among various organizations. In this context, the CC0 Public Domain Dedication is significant in exploring and maximizing the re-use of data. This helps in understanding the permissions and restrictions related to use of highly factual data and resources. CC0 covers entire range of copyright and database rights. The adoption of "Open data policies" enhances and ensures access to data in various forms such as raw material, research and scholarly outputs. The application of CC licenses is visible in facilitation of data-specific repositories for users.

OPEN DATA AND INNOVATION THROUGH LIQUID INFORMATION

Open data is propelling innovation by replacing the conventional decision-making. It has been observed that open data that is basically "machine-readable information" has emerged as a great platform due to its potential:

- empowering citizens,
- changing how government works, and

- improving the delivery of public services.

According to McKinsey report, "seven sectors alone could generate more than $3 trillion a year in additional value as a result of open data, which is already giving rise to hundreds of entrepreneurial businesses and helping established companies to segment markets, define new products and services, and improve the efficiency and effectiveness of operations".

The Open-data Opportunity

Open data has become a tool to understand and break down the information gaps across information generating organizations. The application of open data practices has motivated organizations to share benchmarks and leading the follow of best practices to increase productivity. MGI's Michael Chui (in James Manyika, et. al.2013) discusses the economic potential of open data and how governments and businesses can unlock it. The clear potential of open data to explore economic value by application of advanced analytics to knowledge. The large amount of data, including government data, has been made available to communities." Open data is propelling innovation by replacing the conventional decision-making. Open data is mixed with proprietary data sets and provides data-driven approaches. Open-data analytics is an effective instrument to uncover users' preferences. This is related with improvement in output by uncovering anomalies and variations, leading to efficient and reliable processes. The combination of effective technology and instrumental expertise is needed for data usage though it requires efforts from various stake holders such as governments, corporate organizations, academic institutions and people. The policy framing including aspects such as protect privacy, protection of intellectual properties, technical standards for data-flow speed, etc. It is observed that companies and members of communities show reluctance in sharing data due to factors e.g. privacy and proprietary nature of information.

POTENTIAL VALUE AND APPLICATIONS OF OPEN DATA

The roles played by open data are visible in many areas since the last decade. The areas related with global economy where the open data can imprint its success by application are as following:

Education : The academic scene and research areas can be benefited by open data application. The education context is highly demanding the applications and use of open data.

Transportation : The information in the form of open data are crucial for decision making.

Consumer products : The powers in the hands of consumers are increased by the induction of open data.

Electricity : The areas such are electricity are not remaining untouched by open data application.

Oil and gas : The natural resources knowledge and sharing is increased by using open data for sharing the information, for further research and usage.

Health care : The healthcare facilities are enhanced by the sharing of information through open data in the contexts of increasing research and facilities sharing among communities.

Consumer finance : One of the major market related process that can be impacted positively by the open data applications.

Identification of Methods to Create Economic Values

There are certain ways that are helpful in identifying the creation of economic value in few areas. There are few potential barriers which have created problems in adoption of open data practices that are to be removed. The application of certain steps is supportive in capturing value through open data to achieve the growth by innovation driven industries. The following aspects provide more glimpses about the value creation by open data, as:

- Potential economic value in terms of benefits for customers.
- Augmenting big data's effects in the perspectives of transparency, experimentation; customization of products and services.
- Creation of business opportunities and enhancing the productivity, improvements in products and services among the existing and new companies.
- Community and consumer oriented by providing the transparency in prices and opening new channels for company-consumer interactions, and improving quality of goods and services.
- Understanding and forecasting the risks in context with the reputational issues, the potential consumer backlash, and identifying the risk areas.
- Governments' role and barriers to be identified for such policy making that can enhance use and sharing of open data among the communities in the perspectives of legal and regulatory frameworks.

The advantages of open data are self-implicating and advancing by increasing the individuals' perception about the benefits received, thus improving the accuracy of the information, and accelerating the momentum by cultivating the "open-data ecosystem" by framing favorable policies. The application of technologies for data collection, analysis, and sharing of data are providing platforms for open data.

OPEN DATA KIT

The support of various members of open communities and platforms of open source has been instrumental in developing "Open Data Kit" (https://opendatakit.org/community/). The open data kit is "user-focused and deployment-centric". The "Open Data Kit" is supporting a large number of community people in areas such as collecting, managing, and using the data. Various organizations such as CDC, USAID, the Red Cross and Red Crescent, and Google, WHO, the Carter Center are using such kits. The toolkits are useful (mobile data collection) in various information prediction areas including climate conditions in forests, democratic aspects, and others such as tracking outbreaks. These open data tool kits are useful in following ways:

Data collection for decision making: including various formats, and classification, organization, languages and of course, the offline work.

Using at several platforms : the out of box approach is very significant for the users as it can be used in customized way across the devices in the form of mobile, or desktop tools.

Suitable start and scaling : the open data tools kits are devised in a way for ease of usages and scaling can be done in highly technological environment.

OPEN DATA AND CERTAIN CONDITIONS

Along with the governmental policies and practices, certain measures are applicable to make the data "open". The specific approaches related to the organization or government for releasing the data is concerned with kind of data and targeted users. According to the foundation's California Open Data Handbook, which was published in collaboration with Stewards of Change Institute, has given following terms and conditions:

Technically open : Data should be available in "a machine-readable standard format, which means it can be retrieved and meaningfully processed by a computer application".

Legally open : It should be "licensed in a way that permits commercial and non-commercial use and re-use without restrictions".

The "technically open" expresses the easy access of data

for the intended users. In case of "developers and programmers" the data is presented in the form of "application programming interface" (API); while the academic users can be provided in structured fashion for bulk downloading, and the common people the open data should be available in such formats that can be used without specific technical requirements. The open data packaging should be in various file formats to be useful diverse potential users. The legal aspects related with open data are making it available for "universal participation." No legal aspects should isolate its usage and sharing among users of various academic and technical backgrounds.

The unrestricted use and common liability fears are few aspects demanding attention for awareness among communities. The unrestricted use relates to interoperability further as "Interoperability denotes the ability of diverse systems and organizations to work together (inter-operate). In this case, it is the ability to interoperate — or intermix — different data sets." The initial terminology related with "open data" emerged around 2009, yet after these many years the governments and organizations are faming rules, revising them and we can say that it is still the time to shape up the "open data" policies. The vision towards the "value of open data" is related with the building support for open data not only among policy-makers but also the citizens. The open data brings transparency in various components of state such as government, and citizen engagement, which support in data-driven decisions. The disconnected documents should be replaced with open data for the communities. The simplification of data and processes can be done by standardizing and publishing the data.

VARIOUS STEPS TO OPEN DATA

The steps to make data are full of complexities due to technical aspects, technological platforms and policies in the contexts, yet there are few basic steps:

Choosing Data Set : Choosing a data set can be supported by certain guidelines and accessing few open data resources.

Attaching Open License : To avoid ambiguity and augment usage of open data, the open licenses play a great support. The proactive approach is much in need for encouraged use of open data. The guiding information and connecting links to open licenses should reach to more number of communities.

Data formatting for the communities : The format of data should be according to the needs of users, which include programmers, developers, researchers, and civic hackers in the form of APIs, text, spreadsheet and zip files. The availability of FTP servers as well as other networking systems is required.

Discovery of data : Discovery of open data through "a centralized hub" acting as a single platform for downloading open data. The discovery of open data is possible with the awareness of kinds of available data and the formats.

PROJECT OPEN DATA

How the governments are playing roles and responsibilities in the open data scenario, few examples are before us. In the USA, on January 14, 2019, the "Evidence Act" was signed. This is related with "Evidence-Based Policymaking Act" including the OPEN Government Data Act. There are provisions of tools, following best practices, and some schema standards; and furthermore:

Considering the information as asset : For any government, the data is considered as significant resource which functions as strategic asset for the stakeholders. The strengthening democracies and bonding among the communities including the relations of state to its public are happening due to "open data", its availability and use. The example is release of weather and GPS data by the governments for the people has let the industries emerge and benefiting themselves as well as the common people through the tools. The "open data policy" of US government is the reflection of a constructed approach towards the management and release of data among the organizations. The "Project Open Data" is a comprehensive platform for accessing the code and tools. The provisions of various tools and case studies are supportive for the organizations in context with adoption of Open Data Policy. This is a step towards unlocking the potential of data generated by government and creating a community resource. Conceptual guidance about open data: The open data definitions and guiding principles are helpful for users, which include information about:

- Few set of open data principles - The set of open data principles.
- Knowledge of standards, specifications, and formats which are influential in proliferation of
- The information about the datasets, APIs in the Project Open Data Metadata Schema

The guiding principles for implementation : The implementation guidance can be useful, supportive and informative for the workforce behind the open data practices.

Public Data Listing : This is a guiding tool publishing related to publishing the "Open Data Catalog" at the agency.gov/data page.

Documenting APIs : The documentation on "documenting APIs" helps in the preparation and maintenance of data catalogs.

Open Licenses : The information on the "open license guidance" is supportive for the implementation purposes.

Various Tools : There are few "ready-to-use solutions" in the forms of tools for the organizations to implement the open data. The common platforms such as "Labs.Data.gov" invite developers to contribute improvements and support such initiatives.

Data Catalog Tools

Project Open Data Dashboard : It is a dashboard to check the status of /data and /data.json for different organizations.

Data.json validator : A "validator" to check the guidance and compliance with the "Project Open Data schema".

Data.json File Merger : This tool permits the "combination of multiple data.json files." It takes data files from various component organizations.

ckanext-datajson : It is "CKAN extension" to generate "agency.gov/data.json" catalog files.

Inventory.data.gov : This tool is useful in data management of "Enterprise Data Inventory" and "Public Data Listing JSON files".

DKAN : This is an open data portal which modeled on CKAN. The "DKAN" is considered a stand-alone Drupal distribution. This portal is helpful to establish open data portal as well as modules, "DKAN Dataset and DKAN Datastore."

Datahub.io : This is a service related with hosting data publicly provided by the "Open Knowledge Foundation."

Esri Geoportal Server : This supports "automated harvesting" from various other open catalog sources by "supporting ISO/FGDC/DC/... metadata with mapping to DCAT to support agency.gov/data.json listings in addition to providing OGC CSW, OAI-PMH and OpenSearch".

GeoNode : This is an open source "spatial data infrastructure" (SDI). It is helpful for organizations to publish their geographic data in "open" and "standard open formats". GeoNode uses pycsw (a tool for discovery of open data) to publish standard ISO metadata.

Converter Tools

Database to API : This tool generates RESTful APIs from

the contents of a database table by providing JSON, XML, and HTML.

CSV to API : The RESTful APIs from static CSVs are generated.

JSON-to-CSV Converter : It converts data.json files to a "spreadsheet-friendly format" through the CSVkit functions as a command line suite of utilities.

ESRI2Open : This tool developed by ESRI that converts "spatial and non-spatial data form ESRI only formats" to the Open Data formats.

Various Data Tools

Spatial Search : This tool helps in querying geographic entities by latitude and longitude, and extract data.

API Sandbox : This API Sandbox is an interactive "API documentation systems".

HMDA Tools : These are tools for importing and analyzing HMDA (Home Mortgage Disclosure Act) data.

Tabula : This tool helps in finding data tables inside PDF files, the tables in PDF files can be converted into Excel spreadsheets, as well as CSVs.

OPEN DATA COMMUNITY AND EVENTS

The efforts at various levels count many contributions in the open data movement and awareness. The goal of such programs is establishing connection between technologies and communities with the objective of making open data available. Various programs and events are as following:

Data Jam : this event was related with interaction in the areas of open data sets between developers, subject matter experts and communities.

Datapalooza : the "open press celebration" was related with awareness creation of government open data releases in context with open data tools, corporate organizations.

Hackathon : to strengthen the roles of technology community, this program facilitated them in team building and finding solutions.

Such programs and events are supportive in expanding the awareness among common people. The qualitative goals of such programs and events are in the directions of leadership of open data, its awareness among people, IT modernization, and data sharing. There are number of avenues for channeling the open data awareness and participation, such as: website, social Media and interagency meetings. The best practice for such events and programs include consistent design across print and digital materials, in the language of the community, ideas from technologists, the subject matter, types of communities, and feedback mechanism. The organizers seek ways to maintain communication and meet the challenges to create awareness among the community by maintaining the website and identifying a tangible goal at the beginning of the open data program and event.

THE OPEN DATA RESEARCH NETWORK

The overall developments and communities' involvement have generated many ideas and platforms such as "the Open Data Research network." The governments, technological institutes and corporate organizations have found reasons and directions for engaging with open data. The areas and directions are publishing and using datasets in order to promote innovation in research, growth and developments leading to democratic change and societies. This network has been playing role in connecting researchers to explore the open data initiatives and its impact. This network is a joint project of "IDRC and the Web Foundation." The Open Data Research Network has been instrumental in "Exploring the Emerging Impacts of Open Data in Development Countries (ODDC)" programme. This network has been supportive in providing information such as:

Transparent Chennai study on civic data in water, sanitation and health : *http://www.opendataresearch.org/content/2015/777/transparent-chennai-study-civic-data-water-sanitation-and-health.html.* Since 02nd Dec 2015

Researchers and Open Data Barometer : *http://www.opendataresearch.org/content/2015/773/call-researchers-open-data-barometer.html.* Since 01st Jun 2015

Open Data Research Symposium : *(http://www.opendataresearch.org/content/2015/772/draft-agenda-open-data-research-symposium.html).* Since 21st Apr 2015

Open data for International Women's Day Making data work to bridge the gap in women's political representation http://www.opendataresearch.org/news/2015/open-data-international-womens-day-making-data-work-bridge-gap-women%EF%BF%BD%2580%2599s-political.html. Since 07th Mar 2015

Mapping existing open data research : *http://www.opendataresearch.org/news/2015/mapping-existing-open-data-research.html.* Since 19th Jan 2015.

Mapping existing open data research

- 2015 Open Data Research Symposium http://www.opendataresearch.org/project/2015/symposium.html
- New action research programme to build on ODDC project in Africa and Asia. *http://www.opendataresearch.org/content/2014/746/new-action-research-programme-build-oddc-project-africa-and-asia.html.* 12th Nov 2014

Various projects in different nations related with open data are as following:

The Web Foundation : Exploring the Emerging Impacts of Open Data in Developing Countries – http://www.opendata research.org/project/2013/oddc.html

Step Up Consulting : Opening the Gates: Will Open Data Initiatives Make Local Governments in the Philippines

More Transparent? – http://www.opendataresearch.org/project/2013/step.html

iHub Research : Understanding the impacts of Kenya open data applications and services – http://www.opendataresearch.org/project/2013/ihub.html

Freedom Forum : Exploring the use and impacts of open budget and aid data in Nepal – http://www.opendataresearch. org/project/2013/freedomforum. html

The Energy and Resources Institute : Open government data for regulation of energy resource industries in India – http://www.opendataresearch.org/project/2013/teri.html

Research team : Opening the Cities: Open Government Data in Local Governments of Argentina, Brazil and Uruguay – http://www.opendataresearch.org/project/2013/jcv.html

Instituto de Estudos Socioeconomicos - INESC : Open data, public budget and its relations to people's rights in Brazil – http://www.opendataresearch.org/project/2013/inesc.html

University of Cape Town : The use of open data in the governance of South African higher education – http://www.opendataresearch.org/project/2013/uct.html

Transparent Chennai, Institute for Financial Management and Research, India : The quality of civic data in India and the implications on the push for Open Data – http://www.opendataresearch.org/project/2013/tc.html

The Web Foundation & The Open Data Institute : Open Data Barometer – http://www.opendataresearch.org/project/2013/odb.html

OPEN DATA INITIATIVE

Among the various initiatives, the Open Data Initiative (ODI) has emerged as a platform in the shape of an effort to combine data from organizations like Adobe, Microsoft, SAP, and few other third-party systems. This joint effort has emerged as creation of "customer's data lake". The guiding factors are as following:

- Every organization owns and maintains complete, direct control of all their data
- Customers can use AI to get insights from unified behavioral and operational data
- Partners can easily leverage an open and extensible data model to extend solutions

The provisions by ODI are as following:

Data accessibility across organization : By removing the cross-system data silos, creating the structured information and transforming the information ecosystem.

High level technological Insights : The use of predictive analytics with the help of AI, machine learning can be found supportive in decision-making in context with products and services.

The Open Data Initiative functions on the basis of Common data model and "common data lake" as to increase interoperability among companies such as Adobe, Microsoft, SAP, and other third-party systems; and facilitating the discovery of data through intelligent apps.

WORLD BANK OPEN DATA

World Bank Open Data is a venture to provide access to global development data. There are resources such as:

Open Data Catalog : This tool provides access to World Bank datasets, pre-formatted tables, and other resources.

DataBank : This visualization tool contains collections of time series data on a variety of topics.

Microdata Library : This tool is helpful in providing access to data collected through sample surveys.

World Development Indicators : This platform is

accessible for the information *related with* development indicators.

Open Finances : This tool facilitates users reach to raw data *of* World Bank Group's finances.

Projects & Operations : The researchers can find information about the World Bank's lending projects from 1947 to the present.

Open Data Toolkit : This toolkit is helpful in creating awareness about the open data and its implementation techniques.

REGISTRY OF OPEN DATA ON AWS

In the registry by AWS, the datasets are provided by a "variety of third parties under a variety of licenses", the following details are given:

Sentinel-2 : A land monitoring constellation of two satellites for "SPOT and Landsat missions" since 2018.

Landsat 8 : Provides collection of satellite imagery of all land on Earth generated by the "Landsat 8 satellite."

Terrain Tiles : This dataset provides bare-earth terrain heights.

NEXRAD on AWS : This dataset is related with real-time and archival data from the "Next Generation Weather Radar" (NEXRAD) network.

SpaceNet : Since August 2016, this innovation project has been imagery with co-registered map features.

eBird Status and Trends Model Results : To know bird occurrence and abundance at a high spatiotemporal resolution, the dataset is very useful.

Global Database of Events, Language and Tone (GDELT) : This is world's broadcast, print, and web news in over 100 languages.

Open NeuroData : To find multiple neuroimaging

datasets across multiple modalities and scales, this dataset is very helpful.

National Renewable Energy Laboratory's (NREL) PV Rooftop Database This is a lidar-derived, geospatially-resolved dataset of suitable roof surfaces.

Amazon Customer Reviews Dataset : The "Amazon Customer Reviews" (a.k.a. Product Reviews) Provides access to more than 130+ million customer reviews as part of this dataset.

Community Earth System Model Large Ensemble (CESM LENS) : Dataset is comprised of 40-member ensemble of "climate simulations" for the duration of 1920-2100 through the application of historical data (1920-2005).

Encyclopedia of DNA Elements (ENCODE) : The National Human Genome Research Institute (NHGRI) funded "Encyclopedia of DNA Elements" (ENCODE) Consortium is an international collaboration of research groups.

ECMWF ERA5 Reanalysis : The dataset is helpful in providing atmospheric meteorological parameters.

1000 Genomes : It is one of the most detailed catalogues of human genetic variation.

The Massively Multilingual Image Dataset (MMID) : This multilingual dataset of images is paired with the words they represent collected at the University of Pennsylvania.

DigitalGlobe Open Data Program : This is related with "pre and post event high-resolution satellite imagery" in support of emergency planning, and risk assessment.

OPEN DATA AND INDIA

The "Open Government Data" (OGD) Platform India - data.gov.in – has emerged as a platform to support and create awareness about "Open Data initiative of Government of India". Various components of Government of India Ministries are using this portal for publishing datasets, and documents, etc. The aim of this initiative was to augment transparency and create avenues for innovative governance. To harness the growing potential of Open Data and its usage among the public have been the concern of Indian government. The governments' willingness to open the data is directly associated with the improved internal efficiency and effectiveness. The areas which observe the increase are transparency, and economic growth. The opportunities for Open Data in India are discerned in the following ways:

- the availability of a vast resource of data;
- a stable, open source platform for open government data;
- rich technological expertise and knowledge; and
- opportunities to design specific data sciences programmes in educational institutions.

The challenges in the open data scenario in India are in the form of requirement of infrastructure, eliminating digital divide, addressing the privacy issues, and the technicalities of data (format etc.). After the US and UK, India was one of the first countries to join the Open Data movement. Since 2012, Indian government became active in open data initiatives by framing "National Data Sharing and Accessibility Policy" (NDSAP) in March 2012. The NDSAP has been a disclosure of "all sharable, non-sensitive datasets in open formats by various ministries, departments, subordinate offices, organizations and national government agencies as well as individual states." this policy is intended to establish the principles of openness, quality, machine-readability and transparency. Various Indian states have taken initiatives for open data and its availability for the concerned.

REFERENCE

1. API Sandbox. http://project-open-data.github.com/api-sandbox
2. CC0 Public Domain Dedication. https://creativecommons.org/publicdomain/zero/1.0/

3. California Open Data Handbook. http://www.stewardsofchange.com/what-we-do/Documents/Open%20Data%20Handbook%20-%20WEB.pdf

4. Chakraborty, Simonti (2018). Open Data Policy of the Government of India: What has it achieved? http://www.cbgaindia.org/teams/simonti-chakraborty/#programme

5. Choosing Data Set. http://www.govtech.com/data/Got-Data-Make-it-Open-Data-with-These-Tips.html

6. ckanext-datajson. https://github.com/HHS/ckanext-datajson

7. Data.json validator. http://labs.data.gov/dashboard/validate

8. Data.json File Merger. http://data.json.file.merger.ongithub.com/

9. Datahub.io. http://datahub.io/

10. DKAN. http://drupal.org/project/dkan

11. Esri Geoportal Server. https://github.com/Esri/geoportal-server/

12. ESRI2Open http://github.com/project-open-data/esri2open

13. Freedom Forum http://www.opendataresearch.org/project/2013/freedomforum.html

14. GeoNode. http://geonode.org/

15. HMDA Tools. https://github.com/cfpb/hmda-tools

16. http://www.amazonteam.org/act-pilots-open-data-kit-odk-enable-indigenous-partners-seamlessly-collect-field-data-their-native

17. http://democracyinternational.com/resources/2017-final-monitoring-report-of-the-albanian-assembly-elections

18. https://www.scoop.it/topic/data-revolution-by-dr-lendy-spires?page=3

19. https://registry.opendata.aws/

20. https://news.cs.washington.edu/2014/11/18/paul-g-allen-tackles-ebola-with-10000-odk-equipped-smartphones/

21. http://www.ifrc.org/en/news-and-media/news-stories/americas/bolivia/bolivian-red-cross-and-ifrc-visits-border-between-bolivia-and-brazil—72334/

22. https://www.google.com/earth/outreach/success-stories/chief-almir-and-the-surui-tribe-of-the-amazon/

23. https://www.cdc.gov/ophss/chiic/projects/2014/ideas/using-open-data-kit-odk-for-rapid-data-collection-transport-visualization-and-management-of-malaria-data-in-siaya-county-kenya.html

24. http://blog.cartercenter.org/2012/08/06/carter-center-on-leading-edge-of-technology-use-in-election-observation/
25. http://www.emro.who.int/som/somalia-news/somalia-to-conduct-second-round-of-focused-polio-vaccination-activity-in-banadir-and-lower-and-middle-shabelle-regions.html
26. https://www.agrilinks.org/blog/partnership-open-source-technology-opens-door-improved-survey-data
27. iHub Research. http://www.opendataresearch.org/project/2013/ihub.html
28. Instituto de Estudos Socioeconomicos - INESC. http://www.opendataresearch.org/project/2013/inesc.html
29. Inventory.data.gov. https://inventory.data.gov/
30. JSON-to-CSV Converter. CSVkit. http://csvkit.readthedocs.org/en/latest/scripts/in2csv.html
31. Laura James (2013). Defining Open Data October 3, 2013. https://blog.okfn.org/author/laura/
32. www.Labs.Data.gov
33. Manyika, James, Chui, Michael, Farrell, Diana, Van Kuiken, Steve, Groves, Peter and Doshi, Elizabeth Almasi (2013). Open data: Unlocking innovation and performance with liquid information. (October 2013, Report) https://www.mckinsey.com/our-people/michael-chui
34. Manyika, James et. al. (2013). https://www.mckinsey.com/our-people/james-manyika
35. Mckinsey Report (2013). https://www.mckinsey.com/our-people/james-manyika
36. Mapping existing open data research http://www.opendataresearch.org/news/2015/mapping-existing-open-data-research.html 19th Jan 2015
37. New action research programme to build on ODDC project in Africa and Asia. http://www.opendataresearch.org/content/2014/746/new-action-research-programme-build-oddc-project-africa-and-asia.html. 12th Nov 2014
38. OAI-PMH. http://www.openarchives.org/pmh/
39. OGC CSW. http://www.opengeospatial.org/standards/cat
40. Open data. https://opendefinition.org/
41. OPEN DATA and India. https://data.gov.in/
42. Open Data. Descrier. http://descrier.co.uk/

43. Open data. CC BY 2.0. https://creativecommons.org/licenses/by/2.0/
44. Open Data Handbook. http://opendatahandbook.org/guide/en/what-is-open-data/
45. Open Data Kit. https://opendatakit.org/community/
46. Open Data Research Symposium http://www.opendataresearch.org/content/2015/772/draft-agenda-open-data-research-symposium.html (21st Apr 2015)
47. OpenSearch. http://www.opensearch.org/"
48. Open data for International Women's Day Making data work to bridge the gap in women's political representation http://www.opendataresearch.org/news/2015/open-data-international-womens-day-making-data-work-bridge-gap-women%EF%BF%BD%2580%2599s-political.html. 07th Mar 2015
49. Open Data Research Symposium http://www.opendataresearch.org/project/2015/symposium.html
50. Open License. https://opendefinition.org/licenses/
51. Project Open Data Dashboard. http://labs.data.gov/dashboard/
52. Pycsw. http://pycsw.org/
53. Research team http://www.opendataresearch.org/project/2013/jcv.html
54. Researchers and Open Data Barometer: http://www.opendataresearch.org/content/2015/773/call-researchers-open-data-barometer.html 01st Jun 2015
55. Spatial Search. https://github.com/project-open-data/Spatial Search
56. Step Up Consulting: http://www.opendataresearch.org/project/2013/step.html
57. Tabula. http://tabula.technology/
58. Various projects in different nations related with open data are as following:
59. The Energy and Resources Institute. http://www.opendataresearch.org/project/2013/teri.html
60. The full Open Definition. https://opendefinition.org/okd/
61. The Web Foundation & The Open Data Institute http://www.opendataresearch.org/project/2013/odb.html
62. The Web Foundation: http://www.opendataresearch.org/project/2013/oddc.html

63. Tim Berners-Lee's 5 starsystem. https://www.w3.org/DesignIssues/LinkedData.html

64. Transparent Chennai, Institute for Financial Management and Research, India. http://www.opendataresearch.org/project/2013/tc.html

65. Transparent Chennai study on civic data in water, sanitation and health: http://www.opendataresearch.org/content/2015/777/transparent-chennai-study-civic-data-water-sanitation-and-health.html. 02nd Dec 2015

66. University of Cape Town. http://www.opendataresearch.org/project/2013/uct.html

67. What Data are You Talking About?http://opendatahandbook.org/guide/en/what-is-open-data/#what-data-are-you-talking-about. https://opendatahandbook.org/guide/en/what-is-open-data/

Chapter Eight
Digital Humanities

SUMMARY : Developments and applications of ICT tools in humanities have altered the scholar' patterns in research. Various aspects, tools, and techniques have been discussed as following:

- Introduction
- Development Phases in Digital Humanities
- The Digital humanities and Initial Scholarship
- Technical Aspects in Digital Humanities
- Developments and Versions of Digital Humanities
- Example of CDH
- Scholars' Needs and Solution
- Skills and Competences for Digital Humanities
- Humanities and Digital Tools Application
- Tools for Incorporating Digital Humanities
- Technical Evaluation for Digital Humanities Projects
- Platforms for Publishing Digital Humanities
- Perspectives from Libraries
- Various Approaches, Libraries and Digital Humanities

INTRODUCTION

In the shape of "Digital Humanities," research and scholarly activities are overlapping and using the digital methods in the context of arts and humanities researchers. It can be observed that the use of computers was initiated in the art and humanities subject in the early years of 1040s, leading to humanities computing applications during 1964 at University of Cambridge. The Literary and Linguistic Computing Centre was established in this direction to support and develop the current "digital humanities". The focus on computational methods application in the complex structures found in the primary materials was created and the outcome was "Text Encoding Initiative". This was later included in preparation of large "machine-readable textual corpora," and "historical workstation" in Germany. During 1980s Association for Computers and the Humanities (ACH), came into action for the various innovation in the field. In the early 1990s, the World Wide Web, and other areas such as creation of non-textual files supported the augmented collaboration between the arts and humanities and digital technologies. The significance of digital preservation of metadata and multimedia content is observed. The presence and availability of various tools to provide "automatic and semi automatic capture" is supportive in digital preservation metadata for (Cantara, 2006) the digital humanities scholarship. Large-scale digitization activities at libraries promoted access, and the commercial platforms also jumped into it. According to McGann (2011), "the whole of our cultural inheritance has to be recurated and reedited in digital forms and institutional structures". This digitization was not the only option but also Geographic Information Systems (3D visualization) came into existence. Reid (2011) found out that the "fundamental rupture between digital and print humanities lies in the turning of a materialist, object-oriented analysis upon the practices of humanistic scholarship". Various aspects to understand and define the concept of digital humanities are as following:

- "At its core digital humanities is more akin to a common methodological outlook than an investment in any one specific set of texts or even technologies.... Yet digital humanities is also a social undertaking. It harbors networks of people who have been working together, sharing research, arguing, competing, and collaborating for many years.... a culture that values collaboration, openness, nonhierarchical relations, and agility" - Kirschenbaum (2011).
- "The phrase Digital Humanities... describes not just a collective singular but also the humanities in the plural, able to address and engage disparate subject matters across media, language, location, and history. But, however heterogeneous, the Digital Humanities is unified by its emphasis on making, connecting, interpreting, and collaborating" - *Digital Humanities* by Anne Burdick, Johanna Drucker, Peter Lunenfeld, Todd Presner, Jeffrey Schnapp.
- "DH values collaboration, plurality, investigation of human culture, and the disruption of and reflection on traditional practices and is concerned with not just the use of digital technology for humanities projects but how the use of digital technology for humanities projects changes the user's experience." - THATCamp LAC 2012 (This definition emerged at collaboratively during the conference in a "Glossary of the Digital Humanities" @Google doc).

In the words of Adam Crymble, digital humanities is related to, "A willingness to engage in new modes of exploring humanities problems using interdisciplinary approaches that may go beyond the comfort level of traditional scholars in your core discipline but that seek truth and understanding with all the rigours of academic research." Various other definitions and discussions revolve around the developments in the form of Web 2.0 and various web tools available for the digital research environment. Such developments have pushed the increased use of digital tools, and provided an approach to shift focus on conceptual issues. The emphasis has been laid on holistic approach and projects in humanities. With the availability of digital aggregators, the research environment has focused upon resource inclusion on the basis of certain policies and guidelines. Many common practices of review, assessments and evaluate the scholar-created digital projects are significant for further use and proliferation. The inclusion of metadata and provisions of index facilitate the information retrieval in the federated and discovery platforms.

Development Phases in Digital Humanities

Various development phases are understood in the chronological growth and application of digital humanities. It begins with the 1940s and leads to the current times, with the large research coverage and tools. During 1949 to 1970s, the initial stages were observed in the works of 1949-1970: DH in Computing Centers. During mid of the last century, Wisbey founded the "Centre for Literary and Linguistic Computing" in Cambridge (1963), followed by "Computers and the Humanities" (now "Language Resources and Evaluation") (1966) by Wilhelm Ott and emergence of "Association for Literary and Linguistic Computing conference" (1970). The period of next two decades till early 1990s, is known as Foundation of various Scholarly Societies which contributed in digital humanities. This period began since 1973 by establishing The Association for Literary and Linguistic Computing, followed by founding of the "Association for Computers and The Humanities" in 1978. Later during 1985, the Perseus Project initiated at Harvard University, and in the next year the "Digital Scholarship in the Humanities" was founded in 1986. In the year 1986, SGML specification was released, which was followed by Text-Encoding Initiative and Humanist in 1987.The Electronic Beowulf Project and H-Net began in 1991 and 1992 respectively. Later the role of libraries began and various initiatives were taken in the form of Etext Center (1992) at Virginia, release of Mosaic (1993), STG (Scholarly Technology Group - currently the "Center for Digital Scholarship") The first edition of the TEI guidelines (1994) and first draft of XML spec (1996) were released. In the end of 1990s MITH was founded (1999). The new developments were seen in the foundations of HASTAC (2003) and "Blackwell Companion to Digital Humanities" (2004).

The mainstream digital humanities emerged since the mid of new millennium during 2005-2012. Various achievements such as: DH Mainstreamed Blake Archive, Electronic Textual Editing (by MLA, 2006), Cyber-infrastructure for Humanities and Social Sciences (ACS report, 2006), NEH Office of Digital Humanities (2006), CLIR Survey of Digital Humanities Centers (2008), and "One Culture: Computationally Intensive Research in the Humanities and Social Sciences" (2012). These developments in the form of drafts, establishments, conferences, and technological aspects have been instrumental in the current stage of digital humanities.

THE DIGITAL HUMANITIES AND INITIAL SCHOLARSHIP

The digital humanities have been playing great support in the diverse arena of learning, scholarship and academic serviced. Various pioneering tasks have been performed since the early times of last mid-century. The developments of collaborative, innovative and inter-disciplinary methods in the direction applying the "humanities computing" have been observed. During 2004, publishing of "*Blackwell Companion to Digital Humanities" has initiated the wider awareness and use of this term.* The foundation of "*Alliance of Digital Humanities Organisations*" (ADHO) in 2005 later emphasized the adoption of "Digital Humanities". The innovative methods to analyze and disseminate the humanities research in a digital form has become the digital humanities. The digital landscape implemented in the humanities has given insights to offer and address the issues such as authenticity, identity and authority.

The early scholars and initiatives have demonstrated the promise and potential of digital technologies in identification and finding answers for critical questions in the humanities. The "digital humanities" has helped in identification of representations of researches and scholarly production of literature. The developments have emerged as "digital and critical, inclusive and connected." Various aspects such as diversity of researchers, discipline specialization, and roles played by organizations at public research have opened new vistas in digital humanities. Digital humanities extends across organizations' types and their spaces and serving, diverse range of institutions participatory action.

The Components and Research in Digital Humanities

The creation of digital space for dialogues and discovery in the humanities' researches followed by few more steps to utilize the benefits of digital humanities. Beginning with research initiative and the articulation of the questions or problems, these research questions are addressed in the process and course of action. According to Fitzpatrick (2011), "The particular contribution of the digital humanities, however, lies in its exploration of the difference that the digital can make to the kinds of work that we do as well as to the way that we communicate with one another." The roles and inclusion of digital humanities can be observe as "a scholarship and pedagogy that are collaborative and depend on networks of people and that live an active 24-7 life online" (Kirschenbaum, 2010). Chen, Chen, and Liu (2017) talked about "automatic text annotation system (ATAS)" which enhances the resources collection through "Linked Data (LD)". This technique helps in "automatically annotating ancient texts" related with digital humanities research. Such tools are supportive in referring to resources while interpretation of ancient texts. The advancement in the development of tools and techniques has enhanced the digital

The research support systems and learning programs are carried out through high-level incubation advice. The additional collaborations and "knowledge Transfer opportunities" are similar to Digital Humanities, transcending the "disciplinary boundaries". The beginning components are as following related with the digital humanities:

Code : Coding is the initial step in the digital humanities what digital practitioners begin with (Davidson, 2011). Coding is the initial intellectual contributions into the digital humanities related projects.

Community : Communities collaborate, edit, develop and share the technological advancements by contributing in the digital humanities on the basis of shared interests. Communities work on a perpetual platform to share ideas on similar purposes and values (Scheinfeldt, 2010).

Distant Reading : The distant reading relates to digital humanities with text mining and it has been considered" as a field that has more association with men authors" (Klein 2018).

Diversity and Inclusion : The in-depth ties are reflected through the digital humanities. The relation among the topics such as "race, project, projects, gender, women, feminist, transformed, studies, color, black, koh, postcolonial," is found scattered in the documents and engaged with the diversity and representation in digital humanities (Barnett, 2014), leading to transformation.

Thus the four components related with digital humanities are defining its nature as well as the framing of the concept. In discerning closely the digital humanities, two more aspects emerge as the "Humanities", the subjects and disciplines related with human cultural (i.e. arts, literature, philosophy etc.); and the application of digital technologies.

TECHNICAL ASPECTS IN DIGITAL HUMANITIES

Digital humanities permits and facilitates the researchers to visualize the intricate connections and patterns. The intersection of humanities computing can be understood as digital humanities. The roles of humanities disciplines and computing can be seen in reverse order to understand the influence of humanities on computing. Thus the interdisciplinary nature of humanities subjects and computation tools application are the basic facets of digital humanities. This approach has been influential in the scholarly understanding, analysis and discoveries in the humanities researches; with the help of various tools including text mining, data mining, and digital mapping. Chen and Tsay (2017) emphasized that "collaboratively annotating digital texts allow users to add valued information, share ideas and create knowledge." Their efforts are visible in the development of "collaborative annotation system (CAS) with four types of multimedia annotations including text annotation, picture annotation, voice annotation and video annotation". These components support embedding into any HTML Web pages and have a shared mechanism among multiple users with the adoption of "asynchronous JavaScript (Ajax) and a model-view-controller framework". This tool has been able to support digital curation and crowdsourcing as digital curation can be practiced by the digital humanities scholars. Scholarship in the Digital Humanities is comprised of scholarly activities, application of new technologies and expanding the traditional routes of humanities research:

- The sharing of collections to access (e.g., maps, visualizations and exhibitions, etc.).
- The augmentation of expression though the use of digital media (e.g., human-computer interaction, as well as cultural informatics).

- The advent of digital tools in the classroom.

DEVELOPMENTS AND VERSIONS OF DIGITAL HUMANITIES

The distinctions among the types of digital humanities and versions are available in the form of the related actions and digital methods. There are distinctions such as the computing humanities, kinds of blogging humanities and forms of multimodal humanities; in this context, according to McPherson:

Computing humanities : This type of humanities focus on "building tools, infrastructure, standards and collections".

Blogging humanities : It is concerned with the "production of networked media" and peer-to-peer writing.

Multimodal humanities : This type of digital humanities is responsible for "scholarly tools, databases, networked writing." This includes "peer-to-peer commentary" and visual media.

This typology is comprehensive and provides value of networked media, without single out "the digital as an object of analysis", further, Davidson (2008) identified following version or phases of digital humanities; "Humanities 1.0 and Humanities 2.0" on the similar patterns of Web 1.0 and Web 2.0. According to her, "Humanities 2.0 is distinguished from monumental, first-generation, data-based projects not just by its interactivity but also by openness about participation grounded in a different set of theoretical premises, which decenter knowledge and authority". The technology is a key participant in various activities such as:

- the "decentering of authorship",
- credentialing practices,
- reward systems,
- interdisciplinarity, and
- collaboration.

The clear assumption of change and trajectory relates to various "epistemic traditions and goals", dealing with collaboration and identification of common goals in the digital humanities. The Digital Humanities Manifesto 2.0 (2009) share the view: "Digital Humanities is not a unified field but *an array of convergent practices* that explore a universe in which: a) print is no longer the exclusive or the normative medium in which knowledge is produced and/or disseminated; instead, print finds itself absorbed into new, multimedia configurations; and b) digital tools, techniques, and media have altered the production and dissemination of knowledge in the arts, human and social sciences" (Presner et al., 2009). It is observed that "while technical digital humanities teams now have a vastly more sophisticated range of options than previous generations, including corporate-grade cloud services and free online services, this has done little to ease the problem of maintainability or sustainability - especially for high quality digital scholarship. Idiosyncratic solutions to specific research questions in this emerging field have left us with a legacy corpus developed from the 1990s into the 2000s, which raises new challenges in terms of sustainability (Smithies et al., 2019). Discerning the past, the "*Blackwell Companion to the Digital Humanities*", illustrates the "ambivalent interrelation" between humanities computing and digital humanities in the context of coexistence of these two fields, "The digital humanities, then, and their interdisciplinary core found in the field of humanities computing, have a long and dynamic history best illustrated by examination of the locations at which specific disciplinary practices intersect with computation" (Schreibman et al., 2004). The consequences of various changes and developments have reflected in the implications of digital media for research into various areas such as cultural studies theme, including disciplinary forms of knowledge. The pre-constituted knowledge in the humanities amounts to literary studies, history, philosophy, psychoanalysis, sociology, and so on. According to Hall, digital media has been capable to induce change (Hall, 2008). The "inclusive and broad notion" of digital humanities on a strategic level, functions as an asset due to broad scope and engagement.

EXAMPLE OF CDH

The Digital Humanities at Cambridge Digital Humanities (CDH) has been a comprehensive example to what humanities can take shape in the perspective of computation. The innovative tools and methods applied in the humanities research data have provided opportunities. The increased chances and platforms for collaborative and mutually creative research process have been possible due to digital humanities in humanities and social science disciplines. The following efforts at Cambridge Digital Humanities are unlocking the transformative powers of research since 2017, with the help of following:

CDH Research : the focal point to enable the projects, programs and other activities etc.

CDH Lab : supporting in "high-level project incubation advice" with the help of research support service.

CDH Learning : provides training in research methods and skills for digital scholarship.

CDH Network : to support the community and identity at the university.

Strategic Initiatives and Research through CDH

The University of Cambridge has formulated the strategy through the following aspects and establishments:

The Cambridge Centre for Digital Knowledge (CCDK) : related with digitization process for humanities, and growth of a "digital humanities discipline" by promoting access, perpetuate well-worn approaches, and transcending of technologies.

The Cambridge Big Data Strategic Research Initiative: to support the researchers deal with large amount of data by applying "Big Data to solve challenging problems for society".

Leverhulme Centre for the Future of Intelligence (CFI): a platform for new interdisciplinary community, technologists and the policy makers to build a team to achieve the digital humanities goals.

Cambridge Centre for Digital Built Britain: delivering a smart digital economy by providing a partnership between the Department of Business, Energy & Industrial Strategy and the University of Cambridge.

International Image Interoperability Framework (IIIF): responsible for developments and implementations of Application Programming Interfaces (APIs).

SCHOLARS' NEEDS AND SOLUTION

The scholars have to face a lot of innovation and application of technologies in the humanities. Zhang, Liu, Mathews (2014) have identified the common cores of digital humanities (DH) between humanities and library professionals due to the observed efforts taken in the form of developing new services and digital tools. The innovative approach, collaborative nature of digital humanities work and various channels are the factors to involve the librarians with digital humanities scholars. The other factors include development of tools, data sets, "unbalanced geographical and disciplinary distribution" and lack of integration in the digital humanities aspects. The future roles in the form of: creator and contributor; mediator and interpreter; "hybrid scholar"; etc, can be played by of LIS professionals. These scholars require some understanding as following:

- To find and use Datasets in the Digital Humanities
- techniques to understand and use Humanities Data
- Recognizing the text of a .pdf (with the help of software,

such as FreeOCR -Windows Software) searching and utilizing Geospatial Data? Finding and using Statistical Data

- Finding discipline specific primary resources such as Classics, and Language & Literature

Primary Source Repositories by Place and Type

- The Halifax Regional Municipality Archives
- OpenImages
- VADS or Visual Arts Data Service
- Europeana
- The Internet Archive
- The Digital Public Library of America
- Library of Congress
- A Vision of Britain Through Time
- David Rumsey Map Collection
- NHGIS: National Historical Geographic Information Systems

Digital Libraries and Book Repositories

Resources for learning:

CUNY Guide to Digital Humanities : This resource provides information related with Digital Humanities projects and resources in the form of wiki platform.

Digital Humanities Resources for Project Building : A comprehensive platform in the shape of an online archive. This archive provided various guides and tools for digital humanities.

The Programming Historian : This open-access archive provides knowledge of digital techniques for Humanities research in the form of lessons on APIs, GIS, and Data Management.

UCLA Center for Digital Humanities : This platform

provided introductory materials for beginners in Digital Humanities.

SKILLS AND COMPETENCES FOR DIGITAL HUMANITIES

According to the 2005 Summit on Digital Tools held at the University of Virginia observed, "Only about six percent of humanist scholars go beyond general purpose information technology and use digital resources and more complex digital tools in their scholarship" (Summit, 2006). Although this observation is from long ago, the current times also witness the need of awareness and possession of skills among the scholars. The various skills and competences including the technical and psychological abilities are as following:

Work in interdisciplinary teams : it needs the capacity to understand the teamwork and the designing of processes in the digital environments.

Capacity for digital learning : the plasticity of thinking in order to identify, and apply new digital techniques to professional practice.

Publishing guidelines : using open access, managing personal research data, and knowledge management.

Understating of regulations on authorship, reproduction as well as dissemination of digital objects.

Use of digital tools : the knowledge and capacity of application of digital tools for the purpose of data analysis, data processing and preservation.

Including mining "text corpora".

Knowledge of designing and preparation of research project : to contribute in the field of digital humanities.

HUMANITIES AND DIGITAL TOOLS APPLICATION

The factors for use of digital tools inhumanities are as given:

Distant Reading : This is the process and means of discovering trends among the related topics scattered among the genres, and across the networks, connections throughout the vast published literature. The distance reading involves computer processes (text and topic analysis) to find out the patterns about information (Distant Reading, 2011).

Visualization : The use of geospatial and text visualization methods in digital humanities supports to understand place and space in primary texts, correlating the operation of historical social networks leading to display of quantitative trends discovery.

Tools in the Digital Humanities

The tools in digital humanities are the mechanisms to indulge and get the work done. The "experimental and prototypical work" produced by digital tools of first generation have come so far. The digital tools now have quality interfaces and supporting documentation. The designing of tools should consider as following:

- Inclusion of ideas from humanities users
- Clear design and accessible documentation
- Emphasis on methodological value
- Clear indications of limitations of the tool
- Supporting "combinatorial approaches" to humanities data

In the areas of textual analysis, visualizations, mapping, data management, and publishing in the digital humanities, the following description shows few of the areas and related tools:

Visualization Tools

D3js : "D3.js is a JavaScript library for manipulating documents based on data by using HTML, SVG and CSS.

Gapminder World : This is a comprehensive tool for

teachers to view preloaded data using visualization software.

Google Fusion Tables (Beta) : It is an "experimental data visualization web application" helpful in collecting, ,sharing data tables and visualizing the data as maps, timelines and charts which can be published later.

Prefuse Information Visualization Toolkit : It is a set of software tools for visualization framework for the Java programming language.

Visual Understanding Environment (VUE) : This is an Open Source project provides tools for integrating digital resources.

Walrus : A tool for visualizing "large directed graphs in three-dimensional space" of both local and global perspective.

R-Project : An integrated suite of software facilities for data manipulation, calculation and graphical display.

PiktoChart : "Freemium", easy to use "infographic creator."

Paper Machines : It is a plugin for Zotero to prepare "topic-modeling analysis" or humanities researchers.

Textal : It is a smart phone app to analyze websites, tweet streams, & documents such as graphs and statics generation and visualization.

Few more visualization apps and tools are as following:

Adobe Color CC : the color palettes for visualizations.

Airtable : a kind of spreadsheet for data organization.

Awesome Table : for display of data in functional views (directories, Gantt chart views, Google Maps, card views)

Bl.ocks : a simple viewer for "sharing code examples" which are hosted on GitHub Gist.

Cytoscape : an open source software platform for visualizing complex networks and problem domains, including bioinformatics, and semantic web".

D3js : aJavaScript library for manipulating documents based on data using HTML, SVG and CSS.

Data Basic: a suite of easy-to-use web tools for beginners.

Data Illustrator : for "infographics and data visualizations" without programming

Gapminder : to view preloaded data.

Gephi: for data analysts and manipulate the "structures, shapes and colors" to help appear the inside patterns.

Graph Commons: to transform the data into interactive maps.

LucidChart : to create online flowcharts, diagrams, etc.

Palladio: a web-based platform for complex, and multi-dimensional data.

SVG Crowbar : it is a "Chrome-specific bookmarklet" to extract SVG nodes and accompanying styles from an HTML document.

Tableau : to help in connecting the data files scattered throughout the spreadsheets and producing data visualizations.

Twitter Analytics and Visualization Tools : e.g. Portwiture, Twitonomy, MentionMap and Tweetstats etc.

Voyant Tools : very powerful tools to help in a web-based text reading and analysis.

Raw Graphs: for creating "vector-based visualization" based on data

Simile : a platform for "open-source web widgets" meant for data visualizations.

Tools for Content Management

DH Box: This tool is meant for streamlining installation processes. It is very efficient platform to provide digital humanities laboratory.

DH Press : A tool for mashup. This is very supportive in visualizing the diverse material in digitized form related with humanities.

Drupal : An open source content management platform

Drupal for Humanists : A highly customized for use in the humanities.

HistoryPin : To share images history spread across time and space on maps and timelines.

Mukurtu : A grassroots project to manage, and exchange the digital heritage.

NeatLine : To tell stories with the help of maps and timelines.

Omeka : An open source web-publishing platform.

ViewShare : A platform to generate interactive maps, and timelines by the Library of Congress.

3D Modeling, Photogrammetry, AR & VR

A-Frame.io : A web framework for building virtual reality experiences.

Kubity : A cloud-based cross-platform application for instant messaging of 3D files across multiple devices.

Photoscan : For "photogrammetric processing" of digital images and generates "3D spatial data".

SketchUp : 3D modeling software.

Open Image and Multimedia Collections

Best Practices for Attribution : A platform and resource for "how to credit Creative Commons resources".

British Library Image Collection : a large amount of image realted data is available, over one million images from 17th, 18th, and 19th century books on Flickr. This collection is available with metadata into the public domain.

Flickr Creative Commons : Flickr users offering their

work under a Creative Commons license.

Freesound : A database of "Creative Commons" Licensed sounds.

US Library of Congress Flickr Stream : This is about the Library of congress Flickr collection of digitized photos.

Various Collaboration Tools

Trello : Web-based project management application for keeping track of tasks.

Evernote : This is a suite of software for note-taking and archiving.

Timeline Tools

Chronos Timeline : To represent time-based data "switching easily between vertical and horizontal orientations, researchers can recontextualize" historical data.

TimeGlider : It is a web-based timeline builder

TimeToast : A great tool for creating timelines to web-based interactive social media platforms such as website or blog.

Mapping Tools

ArcGis Explorer Online : A client-tool for using "ArcGIS maps online".

MapAList : For creating "customized Google maps" from lists of addresses.

QGIS : A "geographic information systems" (GIS) application for "data viewing, and analysis capabilities".

CartoDB : a cloud-based geospatial and mapping software

Google Maps : For mapping and visualizing geospatial data.

Text analysis and Data Mining tools

Voyant : text analysis suites for Digital Humanities to upload texts and observe "word counts, co-occurrences, keyword frequency, collocations, relationship between words", and more.

MALLET : For Topic Modeling; identification of topics contained in texts.

Google Books Ngram Viewer : To analyze keyword occurrence found in the "Google books corpus".

Voyant-tools.org : "Voyant" Tools is a web-based reading and analysis environment for digital texts.

Wordle : A robust word cloud generator.

Culturomics - Google Ngrams Addon : An add-on to download data sets.

Time Magazine Corpus : Offers access to American Mainstream Cultural Text Analysis of the Time Magazine Archive (1923-2006).

Juxta : A cross-platform tool to collate, compare, and analyze textual objects.

Calibre : A free and open source e-book library management application.

HathiTrust Research Center : For computational access for nonprofit and educational users to published works in the public domain.

Hermeneutica : A platform of text mining tools.

Intelligent Archive : A Java application for managing "corpora of texts for stylometry".

TAPoR 2.0 : a platform for tools used in "sophisticated text analysis" and retrieval.

Text & Video Annotation Tools

- Annotation Studio
- AntVidHypothes.is

- Thing Link
- LookAt
- Manifold

TOOLS FOR INCORPORATING DIGITAL HUMANITIES INTO THE CLASSROOM

DH101 - UCLA's Intro to Digital Humanities Curriculum : This online coursebook is comprised of information of digital approaches along with lessons and tutorials.

Digital Pedagogy in the Humanities : Concepts, Models, and Experiments (from MLA): This is a curated collection of "reusable and remixable pedagogical artifacts" for humanities scholars by the Modern Language Association.

Find Open Educational Resources (OER) Teaching Tools : Reusing existing Open Educational Resources (OER) through openly licensed media elements

OER Commons : OER Commons is a single point of access of over 30,000 items that are publicly available through "Creative Commons" licensing.

Zotero - DH Syllabi : A platform for syllabi/ curriculum planning documents, networked pedagogies, etc.

NotaBene : A tool to annotate course material online

TEI Encoding Initiative : A consortium responsible for "development of standard" for the representation of texts in digital form.

Time Mapper : A tool for creation of timeline from a spreadsheet.

Word Seer : A text analysis environment with the combination of visualization, and information retrieval, natural language processing.

TECHNICAL EVALUATION FOR DIGITAL HUMANITIES PROJECTS

An important consideration for all Digital Humanities projects is the evaluation. Various assessment aspects are related and many questions can be taken up by funding agencies, parent organizations, etc. Hoeve (2018) found out the "noticeable absence of references to the inclusion of genealogy and family history studies within the field of digital humanities" and observed the extended inclusiveness in the form of "production-coding and cultural analysis" in genealogy among digital humanities. The significance of genealogy as family history can serve in the technological advancement. The practice of" production to cultural analysis corresponds with the transition of production and coding (influenced by humanities computing) to the inclusion of experimental cultural research adopted" in the digital humanities due to use and presence of technological tools. The availably of databases, techniques such as text encoding, and data-text mining support the studies. The provisions in the shape of graphic information systems and DNA mapping have been significant in coding. The methods of demographic study and crowdsourcing have been able to relate the cultural connections and visualizing the innovative scholarship. Pratono et. al. (2020) involve "observation of social enterprises that concern digital humanities projects and crowdfunding for financing the projects" by an interpretative approach and they found out that "Adopting the crowdfunding platform encourages social enterprises to reshape social missions, share the risk with stakeholders and "hire professional workers with flexible work arrangements to attract specific donors and investors". The sustaining and successful Digital Humanities projects require planning and follow up of the timelines. The few aspects are as following:

Platform : There are few aspects related with the platform which can be assessed in the contexts of software updates, responsible staff, adding new content, need of technical skills, (e.g. web form vs. hand coding), hosting of project, costs and provision of resources and renewals.

Sustainability : The sustainability of a project is associated with use of existing campus resources including hardware, software licenses, languages, open source software, connect with other projects, requirement of extensive custom programming, data availability for reuse, common formats, documentation, and update.

PLATFORMS FOR PUBLISHING DIGITAL HUMANITIES

Anvil Academic : For born-digital and born-again-digital research publishing in the humanities.

Digital Culture Books : An imprint of the University of Michigan Press since 2006, functions as an incubator for "new publishing models" in the humanities and social sciences.

Institute for the Future of the Book : A platform for publishing with independent branches of Institute in New York, London and Brisbane.

Media Commons Press : A platform for promoting the digital publication.

Open Humanities Press : For publishing open access e-books.

Public Knowledge Project : A multi-university initiative developing (free) open source software.

Scalar : A product of the "Alliance for Networking Visual Culture" for the publishing at the University of Southern California.

University of California eScholarship : Open-Access scholarly publishing services.

PERSPECTIVES FROM LIBRARIES

The libraries have reconstructed created new resources and services to deal with the patterns of digital humanities.

Almost a decade ago, the serving "symbiotic relationship" was observed in the Digital Scholarship at Brown (2010) to meet the "digital cultural heritage," related with "digital management and access to cultural heritage" on a larger level. A similar example is the "DigiCult" in Europe, EU-funded research related with "cultural heritage, digital libraries and digital preservation." Libraries function as "humanities laboratory" as basic infrastructure in the forms of "humanities-based information" and digital technologies. The libraries have been playing roles in provisions of collections, texts handling and tools building, and providing research collaboration to humanities scholars. With the help of "Log Analysis of Internet Resources in the Arts and Humanities (LAIRAH); Warwick et al. (2008) concentrated upon significance of information resources and digital finding aids. The role of information providers in the form of libraries, websites and research centres by the provisions of digital and print resources is fruitful for humanities scholars. Zorich (2008) prepared a working definition of digital humanities for the Council on Library and Information: "A digital humanities center is an entity where new media and technologies are used for humanities-based research, teaching, and intellectual engagement and experimentation. The goals of the center are to further humanities scholarship, create new forms of knowledge, and explore technology's impact on humanities-based disciplines". Following the above definition, various activities are interrelated and functional in the area of digital humanities:

1. Builds digital humanities collections for scholarly purposes
2. Creates tools for authoring, analyzing collections, data or research processes and management
3. Generation of intellectual products
4. Providing digital humanities training and creating awareness through conferences and seminars on digital humanities topics

5. Providing research support in humanities and "humanities computing and digital scholarship"
6. Creation of specific area for experimentation in humanities
7. Rendering technology solutions to humanities departments

Information visualization techniques and roles of academic librarians (Chen, 2019) have been studied in this aspect on the basis of content analysis. This method includes data mining, and natural language processing. Neatrour, Callaway, and Cummings (2018) have endeavored to determine "if the digital humanities technique of topic modeling would reveal interesting patterns in a corpus of library-themed literature focused on the future of libraries and pioneer a collaboration model in librarian-led digital humanities projects". The support being provided librarians in digital humanities can be enhanced by training and changed approaches. With the "latent Dirichlet allocation style topic modeling on the corpus using the programming language R", they received word-clouds and visualized topics.

VARIOUS APPROACHES, LIBRARIES AND DIGITAL HUMANITIES

The dynamic link between digital humanities and libraries is expansion of the digital humanities. The archiving roles and spaces of libraries are shifting towards the innovative and project spaces for digital humanities. The collaborations between information service providers, library professionals and subject experts and specialists have observed in the role "an information professional may also pursue subject research and perform digital humanities work, and vice versa" (Porter, 2014). The "library labor" in the digital humanities has endeavored to find out the role of library staff as providing "service" to humanities scholars, or as "professional peer".

For Digital Humanities, most libraries provide digital services in "understaffing and underfunding" situations. The OCLC report "Does Every Research Library Need a Digital Humanities Center?" also invited attention to understand and identify scholars' research needs. It is observed that digital humanities research and practice of librarianship is highly intricate in nature. In this context, Poole (2016) stated that "digital humanities stands greatly to impact the Information and Library Science (ILS) professions (and vice versa) as well as the traditional humanities disciplines" and various contours of digital humanities due to structure and epistemology. The interdisciplinary and collaborative nature of digital humanities has been the associating factors with ILS.

The observations about the library collaborations with the areas of digital humanities are prominent yet undermined by the factors such as structure of academic libraries, lack of resources, and organizational support. In the words of Poremski (2017), "The current landscape of DH librarianship shows a profession that is not entirely prepared to meet the needs of its users. [...] Given the nature of our profession, we rise to meet this challenge with enthusiasm, even if our levels of funding and support may not be as high as our hopes. DH librarians appear to be making do with what they have available to them but require additional aid, both institutionally and professionally".

The consideration of library work as "service work" and librarians' role as peer collaborators, it may be understood that librarians are intermediaries between digital humanities experts and novice researchers as DH collaborations. The roles and responsibilities librarians have to derive and "focus on the digital realization of scholarship and the access, organization, and preservation of sustainable digital research content working with various campus partners" (Webster, 2019) in the digital humanities, along with "infrastructure must be leveraged and policy developed or clarified for optimal collaboration between librarians and DH" (Poole and Garwood, 2018) thus, bringing all the components of academic system in the direction of digital humanities.

REFERENCES

1. A Vision of Britain Through Time. http://www.visionofbritain.org.uk/
2. A-Frame.io. *https://aframe.io/*
3. Adam Crymble (2005). *https://github.com/hepplerj/whatisdigital humanities*
4. Alliance of Digital Humanities Organisations (ADHO 2005). https://adho.org/
5. *Adobe Color CC. https://color.adobe.com/create/color-wheel/*
6. *Airtable. https://airtable.com/*
7. Association for Computers and the Humanities. http://www.ach.org/
8. *Awesome Table. https://awesome-table.com/galleryBl.ocks*: a simple viewer for "sharing code examples" which are hosted on GitHub Gist.
9. Barnett, F. M. (2014). "The Brave Side of Digital Humanities." *Differences* 25 (1): 64–78. *https://doi.org/10.1215/10407391-2420003.*
10. Blackwell -Companion to Digital Humanities (2004). http://digitalhumanities.org/companion/
11. Blake Archive. MLA's CSE. *http://www.blakearchive.org/blake/*
12. *British Library Image Collection on Flickr. http://www.flickr.com/photos/britishlibrary*
13. Brown (2010). (*Humanist* 23.636, February 12, 2010)
14. Callaway, Elizabeth Turner, Jeffrey Stone , Heather, Halstrom , Adam (2020). The Push and Pull of Digital Humanities: Topic Modeling the "What is digital humanities?" DHQ: Digital Humanities Quarterly, 14(1).
15. Calibre. *http://calibre-ebook.com/*
16. Cambridge Big Data Strategic Research Initiative. *https://www.bigdata.cam.ac.uk/*
17. *Cambridge Centre for Digital Built Britain. https://www.cdbb.cam.ac.uk/*
18. *Cambridge Centre for Digital Knowledge (CCDK). http://www.crassh.cam.ac.uk/programmes/the-concept-lab-cambridge-centre-for-digital-knowledge*

19. *Camille Villa* (2015). Technical Evaluation for Digital Humanities Projects. April 3rd, 2015. *https://digitalhumanities.berkeley.edu/users/camille-villa-digital-humanities-assistant*

20. Cantara, Linda (2006). "Long term preservation of digital humanities scholarship." https://www.emerald.com/insight/content/doi/10.1108/10650750610640793/full/pdf?title=longterm-preservation-of-digital-humanities-scholarship

21. CartoDB. *https://cartodb.com/*

22. CDH Research. https://www.cdh.cam.ac.uk/research

23. CDH Lab. https://www.cdh.cam.ac.uk/lab

24. CDH Learning. https://www.cdh.cam.ac.uk/learning

25. CDH Network. *https://www.cdh.cam.ac.uk/network-0*

26. Chen, Chih-Ming and Tsay, Ming-Yueh (2017). "Applications of collaborative annotation system in digital curation, crowdsourcing, and digital humanities." The Electronic Library, vol. 35 no. 6

27. Chen, Chih-Ming Chen, Yung-Ting and Liu, Chen-Yu (2017). "Development and evaluation of an automatic text annotation system for supporting digital humanities research." Library Hi Tech, vol. 37 no. 3

28. Chen, Hsuanwei Michelle (2019). "Information visualization skills for academic librarians: A content analysis of publications and online LibGuides in the digital humanities." Library Hi Tech, vol. 37 no.

29. Claire Warwick, Terras, Melissa Galina, Isabel Huntington, Paul and Pappa, Nikoleta (2008). "Library and information resources and users of digital resources in the humanities." Program, vol. 42 no. 1

30. CLIR Survey of Digital Humanities Centers (2008). *http://www.clir.org/pubs/abstract/pub143abst.html*

31. Cordell, Ryan (2015). How Not to Teach Digital Humanities (2015). http://ryancordell.org/teaching/how-not-to-teach-digital-humanities

32. Cyberinfrastructure for Humanities and Social Sciences (ACS report, 2006). http://www.acls.org/programs/Default.aspx?id=644

33. *Cytoscape. http://www.cytoscape.org/*

34. David Rumsey Map Collection. http://www.davidrumsey.com/

35. Davidson, Cathy N. (2008). "Humanities 2.0: Promises, Perils, Predictions". *PMLA* 123: 3, pp. 707-717.

36. Davidson, Cathy (2011). "Advice to DigHum Job Candidates: Don't Lead With HTML. *HASTAC* (blog)." *https://www.hastac.org/blogs/*

cathy-davidson/2011/01/13/advice-dighum-job-candidates-dont-lead-html.

37. De Wilde, Max, Helsinki, Simon Hengchen (2017). "Semantic Enrichment of a Multilingual Archive with Linked Open Data". DHQ: Digital Humanities Quarterly, 11(4).
38. Defining Digital Humanities. https://www.cdh.cam.ac.uk/cdh/what-is-dh
39. DH101 - UCLA's Intro to Digital Humanities Curriculum. http://dh101.humanities.ucla.edu/
40. Digital Humanities. https://www.libraries.rutgers.edu/services-for-researchers/digital-humanities
41. *Digital Scholarship in the Humanities.* http://dsh.oxfordjournals.org.proxy.lib.duke.edu/
42. *Digital Humanities* by Anne Burdick, Johanna Drucker, Peter Lunenfeld, Todd Presner, Jeffrey Schnapp https://mitpress.mit.edu/sites/default/files/titles/content/9780262018470_Open_Access_Edition.pdf
43. Digital Pedagogy in the Humanities: Concepts, Models, and Experiments (from MLA). *https://digitalpedagogy.mla.hcommons.org/*
44. Distant Reading. *http://www.nytimes.com/2011/06/26/books/review/the-mechanic-muse-what-is-distant-reading.html?_r=0*).
45. *DH Box. http://dhbox.org/*
46. *DH Press*: a tool for mashup and visualize a variety of digitized humanities-related material.
47. *Drupal. https://drupal.org/*
48. Edmond, Jennifer (2018). "How Scholars Read Now: When the Signal *Is* the Noise". DHQ: Digital Humanities Quarterly, 12(1).
49. Electronic Textual Editing (MLA, 2006). http://www.tei-c.org/About/Archive_new/ETE/Preview/index.xml
50. Europeana. http://www.europeana.eu/portal/
51. Flickr Creative Commons *http://www.flickr.com/creativecommons/*
52. *FreeOCR. http://www.paperfile.net/*
53. Freesound. *http://freesound.org/*
54. Google Books Ngram Viewer. https://books.google.com/ngrams
55. Google Maps. *https://support.google.com/maps/answer/3045850?hl=en&guide=21670&rd=2*
56. HathiTrust Research Center:
57. HASTAC (2003). *http://hastac.org/*

58. Hermeneutica. *http://hermeneuti.ca/*

59. *HistoryPin. http://www.historypin.com/*

60. Hoeve, Casey Daniel (2018). Finding a place for genealogy and family history in the digital humanities. Digital Library Perspectives, vol. 34 no. 3.

61. *https://acrl.ala.org/dh/2014/02/12/what-if-we-do-in-fact-know-best-a-response-to-the-oclc-report-on-dh-and-research-libraries/.*

62. *http://drstephenrobertson.com/blog-post/finding-questions/.*

63. https://mkirschenbaum.files.wordpress.com/2011/01/kirschenbaum_ade150.pdf

64. Intelligent Archive. https://www.newcastle.edu.au/research-and-innovation/centre/education-arts/cllc/intelligent-archive

65. *International Image Interoperability Framework (IIIF). http://iiif.io/*

66. Jerome Bruner, The Process of Education (Cambridge, MA: Harvard University Press, 1960), quoted in Noel Entwistle, Teaching for Understanding at University (Basingstoke, UK: Palgrave Macmillan, 2009).

67. Juxta. *https://www.nines.org/about/software/juxta/*

68. Fitzpatrick, Kathleen (2011). *The Chronicle of Higher Education*, May 8, 2011. *http://chronicle.com/article/The-Humanities-Done-Digitally/127382/*

69. Kirschenbaum, M.G . (2010). "Hello Worlds (Why Humanities Students Should Learn to Program)." *https://mkirschenbaum.wordpress.com/2010/05/23/hello-worlds/.*

70. Kirschenbaum, M. (2004). "Interface, Aesthetics, and Usability". In Susan Schreibman, Ray Siemens and John Unsworth, eds., "*A Companion to Digital Humanities*". New York: Blackwell Publishing, 2004. pp. 523-542

71. Kirschenbaum, M. (2010). ADE Bulletin, 150, pp. 55-59. https://www.ade.mla.org/ADE-Bulletin.

72. Klein, Lauren (2018). "Distant Reading after Moretti." *http://lklein.com/2018/01/distant-reading-after-moretti/.*

73. Kubity. *https://www.kubity.com/*

74. *Leverhulme Centre for the Future of Intelligence (CFI). http://lcfi.ac.uk/*

75. Library of Congress. http://www.loc.gov/library/libarch-digital.html

76. MALLET. *http://mallet.cs.umass.edu/*

77. Machielse, Christopher (2012). 5 Ways to Use Your iPad to Teach in

the College Classroom (2012). *http://info.lecturetools.com/blog/bid/52506/5-Ways-to-Use-Your-iPad-to-Teach-in-the-College-Classroom*

78. Mann, Joshua L. (2018). "How Technology Means: Texts, History, and Their Associated Technologies." DHQ: Digital Humanities Quarterly, 12(3).

79. McGann, J (2011). "On Creating a Usable Future", *Profession*, pp. 182-95

80. Neely, Ben. Using Technology as a Learning Tool, Not Just the Cool New Thing. *http://www.educause.edu/Resources/EducatingtheNetGeneration/UsingTechnologyasaLearningTool/6060*

81. Mukurtu. *http://mukurtu.org/about/*

82. Neatrour, Anna L. , Callaway, Elizabeth and Cummings, Rebekah (2018). "Kindles, card catalogs, and the future of libraries: a collaborative digital humanities project." Digital Library Perspectives, vol. 34 no. 3

83. *NeatLine. http://neatline.org/*

84. NEH Office of Digital Humanities (2006). *http://www.neh.gov/odh/*

85. NHGIS: National Historical Geographic Information Systems. http://nhgis.org/

86. *OER Commons. https://www.oercommons.org/*

87. *Omeka. http://omeka.org/*

88. One Culture: Computationally Intensive Research in the Humanities and Social Sciences" (2012). "http://www.clir.org/pubs/reports/pub151"

89. Open Humanities Press. Open access e-books. http://openhumanitiespress.org/

90. OpenImages. http://www.openimages.eu/

91. Papadopoulos, Costas, Schreibman, Susan (2019). "Towards 3D Scholarly Editions: The Battle of Mount Street Bridge", DHQ: Digital Humanities Quarterly, 13 (1).

92. Parry, M. (2016). Evolving Business Models to Support the growth of technology-based start-up firms. WTR, 5(2).

93. Perseus Project. http://www.perseus.tufts.edu/hopper/

94. Photoscan. *http://www.agisoft.com/*

95. Poole, Alex H. (2016). "The conceptual ecology of digital humanities." Journal of Documentation, vol. 73 no. 1

96. Poole, A.H., and Garwood, D.A. (2018). "'Natural Allies': Librarians, Archivists, and Big Data in International Digital Humanities Project Work". *Journal of Documentation*, 74 (4), pp. 804-826.

97. Porter, D. (2014). "What If We Do, In Fact, Know Best?: A Response to the OCLC Report on DH and Research Libraries"

98. Poremski, M.D. (2017). "Evaluating the landscape of digital humanities librarianship". *College & Undergraduate Libraries*, 24 (2-44), pp. 140-154.

99. Pratono, Aluisius Hery , Prima, Delta Ardy , Flora, Nur, Sinaga, Nita Taruli , Permatasari, Anggraeni Ariani, Mintarti and Han, Ling (2020). Crowdfunding in digital humanities: some evidence from Indonesian social enterprises. Aslib Journal of Information Management, vol. 72 no. 2 DOI: https://doi.org/10.1108/AJIM-05-2019-0123

100. Presner, Todd, et al. (2009). "HyperCities: Building a Web 2.0 Learning Platform". In A. Natsina and T. Tagialis, eds., *Teaching Literature at a Distance*. London & New York: Continuum Books, 2010.

101. Public Knowledge Project. Multi-university initiative developing (free) open source software. https://pkp.sfu.ca/

102. Reid, Alexander (2011). "Social Media Assemblages in Digital Humanities: from Backchannel to Buzz." Teaching Arts and Science with the New Social Media

103. Scalar. Alliance for Networking Visual Culture. http://scalar.usc.edu/

104. SketchUp. *https://www.sketchup.com/*

105. Schaffner, J., & Erway, R. "Does Every Research Library Need a Digital Humanities Center?" Dublin, Ohio: OCLC Research (2014). *http://www.oclc.org/content/dam/research/publications/library/2014/oclcresearch-digital-humanities-center-2014.pdf.*

106. Scheinfeldt, Tom (2010). "Stuff Digital Humanists Like: Defining Digital Humanities by Its Values." *Found History. https://foundhistory.org/2010/12/stuff-digital-humanists-like/.*

107. Schreibman, Susan, Siemens, Ray and Unsworth, John (2010). "The Digital Humanities and Humanities Computing: An Introduction". In Susan Schreibman Ray Siemens and John Unsworth, *A Companion to Digital Humanities*. Malden: Blackwell, 2010. pp. xxiii-xxvii.

108. Smithies, James, Westling, Carina, Sichani Anna-Maria, Mellen, Pam (2019). "Managing 100 Digital Humanities Projects: Digital Scholarship & Archiving in King's Digital Lab." DHQ: Digital Humanities Quarterly, 13 (1).

109. STG (Scholarly Technology Group - currently the "Center for Digital Scholarship. http://www.stg.brown.edu/

110. *SVG Crowbar. http://nytimes.github.io/svg-crowbar/*

111. TAPoR 2.0. *http://www.tapor.ca/*

112. *Tableau. http://www.tableau.com/*

113. Tanya Clement. Teaching DH: On Pedagogy and Digital Humanities. http://blogs.ischool.utexas.edu/teachingdh/ -

114. Text-Encoding Initiative. *http://www.tei-c.org/*

115. THATCamp LAC (2012). http://thatcamp.org/

116. The Internet Archive. https://archive.org/index.php

117. The Digital Public Library of America. *http://dp.la/*

118. The Halifax Regional Municipality Archives *http://www.halifax.ca/archives/*

119. Time Magazine Corpus. https://corpus.byu.edu/time/

120. Turan, Julia (2016). "How Exactly Do the 'digital Humanities' Mix Science with the Arts?" *Our Cells Our Selves*. February 9, 2016. *https://juliaturan.com/2016/02/09/how-exactly-do-the-digital-humanities-mix-with-the-arts/.*

121. *Twitter Analytics and Visualization Tools. http://twittertoolsbook.com/10-awesome-twitter-analytics-visualization-tools/*

122. University of California eScholarship. *https://escholarship.org/*

123. US Library of Congress Flickr Stream. https://www.flickr.com/photos/library_of_congress/

124. VADS or Visual Arts Data Service. http://www.vads.ac.uk/about/

125. *ViewShare. http://viewshare.org/*

126. Voyant. *http://voyant-tools.org/*

127. Voyant-tools.org. *https://voyant-tools.org/*

128. Webster, Jessica Wagner (2019). "Digital Collaborations: A Survey Analysis of Digital Humanities Partnerships Between Librarians and Other Academics." Digital Humanities Quarterly, 13 (4). http://digitalhumanities.org/dhq/vol/13/4/000441/000441.html

129. Wordle. *http://wordle.net/*

130. Yuen, Steve (2010). Exploring the use of social technology in the college classroom. *http://scyuen.wordpress.com/2010/04/05/exploring-the-use-of-social-technology-in-the-college-classroom/*

131. Zhang, Ying, Liu, Shuand Mathews, Emilee (2014). "Convergence of digital humanities and digital libraries." Library Management, vol. 36 no. 4/5

132. Zorich, Diane M. (2008). *"A Survey of Digital Humanities Centers in the United States"*. Washington DC: Council on Library and Information Resources.

Bibliography

1. ACRL (2015). "Environmental scan 2015." www.ala.org/acrl/sites/ala.org.acrl/files/content/publications/whitepapers/EnvironmentalScan15.pdf.
2. Adam Crymble (2005). https://github.com/hepplerj/whatisdigitalhumanities.
3. Ailes, C., Roessner, D., Feller, I. and K. Ailes, (1997). "The Impact on Industry of Interaction with Engineering Research Centers," Final Report to the National Science Foundation, Engineering Education and Centers Program, The Science and Technology Policy Program, SRI International, Washington, DC.
4. Alain, Ambrosi, Valérie, Peugeot and Daniel, Pimienta (2005). Multicultural perspectives on information societies. C & F Éditions.
5. Almudena, Moreno Mínguez and Ballesteros, Enrique Crespo. The Digital Divide in Education in the Knowledge Society. Encyclopedia of Networked and Virtual Organizations.
6. Ambient Intelligence. https://www.igi-global.com/chapter/ambient-intelligence/13337.
7. Ambos, T. C., Mäkelä, K., Birkinshaw, J., and D'Este, P. (2008). When does university research get commercialized? Creating ambidexterity in research institutions. Journal of Management Studies, 45(8),

1424–1447.

8. Arms, William Y. (2000). Digital Libraries. MIT Press in January 2000.
9. Arquilla, J. and Ronfeldt, D. (2001). "'The advent of netwar (revisited)". In Networks and Netwars: The Future of Terror, Crime, and Militancy Edited by: Arquilla, J., Ronfeldt, D. and Rand, Santa Monica. 1–25.
10. Ashenfelder, Mike (2013). "The Library of Congress and personal digital archiving." In D. Hawkins (ed.), Personal Archiving: Preserving Our Digital Heritage. Medford, NJ, USA: Information Today, Inc. Available as an ebook through IUPUI.
11. Ayres, R.U., Williams, E. (2004). "The digital economy: Where do we stand?" Technological Forecasting and Social Change, 71 (4), pp. 315-339, 10.1016/j.techfore. 2003.11.001.
12. Barnett, F. M. (2014). "The Brave Side of Digital Humanities." Differences 25 (1): 64–78. https://doi. org/10.1215/10407391-2420003.
13. Bartolo.https://journals.tdl.org/jodi/index.php/ jodi/article/view/119/hdl.handle.net/2249.2/jodi-151.
14. Beaver, D. B. (2001). Reflections on scientific collaboration (and its study): Past, present, and future. Scientometrics, 52(3), pp. 365–377.
15. Behrens, Teresa R. and Gray, Denis O. (2000). 'Unintended Consequences of Cooperative Research: Impact of Industry Sponsorship on the Climate for Academic Freedom and Other Graduate Student Outcomes', Research Policy 30(2), pp. 179-199.
16. Bell, D. (1973). The coming of post-industrial society: A venture in social forecasting. New York: Basic Books.
17. Berkeley Digital Library SunSITE. http://sunsite.

berkeley.edu/ARL/definition.html.

18. Bert, Markgraf (2019). Characteristics of a Good Management Information System. Rev. by Michelle Seidel.

19. Beverly L. Clarke (1964). Multiple authorship trends in scientific papers, Science 143 (3608), pp. 822-824.

20. Bracero History Archive. http://braceroarchive.org/

21. Brendan, Loughridge. Knowledge management, librarians and information managers: fad or future? https://www.emeraldinsight.com/author/Loughridge%2C+Brendan.

22. Bishop, A. P., Mehra, B., et al. (2003). "Participatory Action Research and Digital Libraries: Reframing Evaluation". Digital Library Use: Social Practice in Design and Evaluation, edited by A. P. Bishop, N. A. Van House and B. Buttenfield (Cambridge, MA: MIT Press), 161-189.

23. Bollen, K., Cacioppo, J., Kaplan, R., Krosnick, J. A., and Olds, J. L. (2015). Social, Behavioral , and Economic Sciences Perspectives on Robust and Reliable Science. Report of the Subcommittee on Replicability in Science Advisory Committee to the National Science Foundation Directorate for Social, Behavioral, and Economic Sciences.

24. Bowen, P., J. Hash, and M. Wilson (2007). Information Security Handbook: A Guide for Managers: Information Security, National Institute of Standards and Technology (NIST) Special Publication (SP) 800-100, Rev. 3.

25. Bozeman, B., and Gaughan, M. (2011). How do men and women differ in research collaborations? An analysis of the collaboration motives and strategies of academic researchers. Research Policy, 40(10), 1393–1402.

26. Bozeman, Barry and Corley, Elizabeth (2004). "Scientists' Collaboration Strategies: Implications for Scientific and Technical Human Capital", Research Policy 33(4), pp. 599-616.

27. Broman, K., Cetinkaya-Rundel, M., Nussbaum, A., Paciorek, C., Peng, R., Turek, D., and Wickham, H. (2017). Recommendations to Funding Agencies for Supporting Reproducible Research. American Statistical Association.

28. Brown (2010). Humanist 23.636, February 12, 2010.

29. Brown, Nathan (May/June 2015). "Helping members of the community manage their digital lives: developing a personal digital archiving workshop." D-Lib Magazine, 21(5/6). Available online.

30. Brown, R.A., Wolski, M. and Richardson, J. (2015). "Developing new skills for research support librarians", The Australian Library Journal, 64 (3), pp. 224-234.

31. Bruneel, J., D' Este, P. and Salter, A. (2010). "Investigating the factors that diminish the barriers to university–industry collaboration." Research Policy, 39(7), pp. 858–868.

32. Budapest Open Access Initiative (BOAI) (2002). www.budapestopenaccessinitiative.org/read.

33. Burnham, J., (1997). 'Evaluating Industry University Research Linkages,' Research Technology Management 40(1), 52-55.

34. Butler, K. and Byrd, J. (2016). "Research consultation assessment: perceptions of students and librarians", Journal of Academic Librarianship, 42(1), pp. 83-86.

35. Callaway, Elizabeth Turner, Jeffrey Stone , Heather, Halstrom, Adam, (2020). The Push and Pull of Digital Humanities: Topic Modeling the "What is digital humanities?" DHQ: Digital Humanities Quarterly, 14(1).

36. Camille Villa, (2015). Technical Evaluation for Digital Humanities Projects. April 3rd, (2015). https://digitalhumanities.berkeley.edu/users/camille-villa-digital-humanities-assistant.

37. Cantara, Linda (2006). "Long term preservation of digital humanities scholarship." https://www.emerald.com/insight/content/doi/10.1108/10650750610640793/full/pdf?title=longterm-preservation-of-digital-humanities-scholarship.

38. Chakraborty, Simonti (2018). Open Data Policy of the Government of India: What has it achieved? http://www.cbgaindia.org/teams/simonti-chakraborty/#programme.

39. Chen, Chih-Ming and Tsay, Ming-Yueh (2017). "Applications of collaborative annotation system in digital curation, crowdsourcing, and digital humanities." The Electronic Library, vol. 35 no. 6.

40. Chen, Chih-Ming Chen, Yung-Ting and Liu, Chen-Yu (2017). "Development and evaluation of an automatic text annotation system for supporting digital humanities research." Library Hi Tech, vol. 37 no. 3.

41. Chen, H., Ng, T., Martinez, J., and Schatz, B. (1997). "A concept space approach to addressing the vocabulary problem in scientific information retrieval: An experiment on the Worm Community System". Journal of the American Society for Information Science, 48(1), 17-31.

42. Chen, Hsuanwei Michelle (2019). "Information visualization skills for academic librarians: A content analysis of publications and online LibGuides in the digital humanities." Library Hi Tech, vol. 37 no.

43. Chompalov, I., Genuth, J., and Shrum, W. (2002). The organization of scientific collaborations. Research Policy, 31(5), 749–767. Bruneel, J., D'Este, P., & Salter, A.

(2010). Investigating the factors that diminish the barriers to university–industry collaboration. Research Policy, 39(7), pp. 858–868.

44. Claire Warwick, Terras, Melissa Galina, Isabel Huntington, Paul and Pappa, Nikoleta (2008). "Library and information resources and users of digital resources in the humanities." Program, vol. 42 no. 1.

45. Cleveland (1998). "Characteristics of digital libraries." (In) Integration of digital libraries in e-learning. https://www.tlu.ee/~sirvir/Information%20and%20Knowledge%20Management/Integration%20of%20digital%20libraries%20in%20e-learning/characteristics_of_digital_libraries.html.

46. Cornell University Library (2011). "Toward 2015: Cornell University Library Strategic Plan, 2011-2015", available at: www.library.cornell.edu/sites/default/files/CUL_Strategic_Plan_2011-2015%28re-numbered%29_1.pdf (accessed 11 January 2018).

47. Corrado, Edward M. and Moulaison, Healther Lea (2014). Digital Preservation for Libraries, Archives, and Museums. Rowman & Littlefield.

48. Cosmas L. Zavazava, Projects and Knowledge Management https://news.itu.int/#topicsscroll.

49. Costantino, G., Crowley, B., Morin, R., and Thomas, E. (2011). "Heeding the Call: User Feedback Management and the Digital Library". Microform & Digitization Review, 40(4), 146-157.

50. Cox, A.M. and Pinfield, S. (2014). "Research data management and libraries: Current activities and future priorities", Journal of Librarianship and Information Science, 46 (4), pp. 299-316.

51. Croft, B., Cook, R. and Wilder, D., (1995). "Providing Government Information on the Internet: Experiences with THOMAS," in Proceedings of the Digital Libraries

Conference DL'95, Austin, TX. June 10-12, pp. 19-24.

52. Cronin, B. (2001). Hyperauthorship: A postmodern perversion or evidence of a structural shift in scholarly communication practices? Journal of the American Society for Information Science and Technology, 52(7), pp. 558–569.

53. Culnan, M. J. (1984). The dimensions of perceived accessibility to information. Journal of the American Society for Information 36, pp. 302-308.

54. Cummings, J. N., and Kiesler, S. (2005). Collaborative research across disciplinary and organizational boundaries. Social Studies of Science, 35(5), pp. 703.

55. Davidson, Cathy (2011). "Advice to DigHum Job Candidates: Don't Lead With HTML. HASTAC (blog)." https://www.hastac.org/blogs/cathy-davidson/2011/01/13/advice-dighum-job-candidates-dont-lead-html.

56. Davidson, Cathy N. (2008). "Humanities 2.0: Promises, Perils, Predictions". PMLA 123: 3, pp. 707-717.

57. De Wilde, Max, Helsinki, Simon Hengchen (2017). "Semantic Enrichment of a Multilingual Archive with Linked Open Data". DHQ: Digital Humanities Quarterly, 11(4).

58. Delanty, Gerard (2001). Challenging knowledge: the university in the knowledge society. Open University Press, Buckingham. ISBN 9780335205783.

59. Dempsey, Lorcan (2015). Introduction: rules and roles. In N. Allen (ed.), New Roles for the Road Ahead: Essays Commissioned for ARCL's 75th Anniversary. ACRL.

60. Denise, A. D. Bedford, Jennifer K. Donley, Nancy Lensenmayer, (2015). "The Role of Librarians in a Knowledge Society: Valuing Our Intellectual Capital Assets", in (ed.) Current Issues in Libraries, Information

Science and Related Fields (Advances in Librarianship, Volume 39) Emerald Group Publishing Limited, pp.81 - 113.

61. DeRidder, Jody L. and Matheny, Kathryn (July/August 2014). What do researchers need? feedback on use of online primary source materials. D-Lib Magazine, 20(7/8).

62. Diani, M. (2000). 'Social movement networks virtual and real'. Information, Communication & Society, 3(3), pp. 386–401.

63. Dowlin, K.E. (1984). The electronic library. Neal-Schuman.

64. Douglass, J. A. (1998). "Shared Governance at UC: An Historical Review", Center for Studies in Higher Education, University of California, Berkeley http://ishi.lib.berkeley.edu/cshe/jdouglass/gov.html.

65. Drucker, P. (1993). Post-capitalist society. Harper Business.

66. Edmond, Jennifer (2018). "How Scholars Read Now: When the Signal Is the Noise". DHQ: Digital Humanities Quarterly, 12(1).

67. Etzkowitz, H., Webster, A., Gebhardt, C., and Cantisano Terra, B. R. (2000). The future of the university and the university of the future: Evolution of ivory tower to entrepreneurial paradigm. Research Policy, 29, 313–330.

68. Faria, J. R., and Goel, R. K. (2010). Returns to networking in academia. Netnomics, 11(2), 103–117.

69. Feller, I. (1997). 'Technology Transfer from Universities,' in J. Smart ed., Higher Education: Handbook of Theory and Research, Vol. XII, New York: Agathon Press, pp. 1-43.

70. Fitzpatrick, Kathleen (2011). The Chronicle of Higher Education, May 8, 2011.

71. Fox, Edward A. (2011). Guidelines and Resources for Teaching Digital Libraries. JCDL 2011 Tutorial. PowerPoint Presentation.

72. Fox, E. A., et al. (1993). "Users, user interfaces, and objects: Envision, a digital library". Journal of the American Society for Information Science, 44(8), September: 480-491.

73. Fox, Edward A., Yang, Seungwon, Ewers, John, Wildemuth, Barbara, Pomerantz, Jeffrey P., Oh, Sanghee (2011). 1-a (10-c): Digital Library Curriculum Development Module. Collaborative Research: Curriculum Development: Digital Libraries. Available: http://curric.dlib.vt.edu/modDev/modules/DL_1-a_2011-05-11.pdf.

74. Fox, Mary F. & Catherine A. Faver (1984). "Independence and Cooperation in Research: The Motivations and Costs of Collaboration", Journal of Higher Education 55(3), pp. 347-359.

75. Frame, J. Davidson and Mark P. Carpenter (1979). "International research collaboration". Social Studies of Science 9, pp. 481-497.

76. Freeman, C., Perez, C. (1986). "The diffusion of technical innovations and changes in techno-economic paradigm." Science Policy Research Unit University of Sussex, Brighton.

77. Fuchs, C. (2016). "Reading Marx in the information age", Vol. 1, Routledge. http://fuchs.uti.at/wp-content/uploads/Grundrisse.pdf.

78. Garg, K. C., and Padhi, P. (2001). A study of collaboration in laser science and technology. Scientometrics, 51(10), pp. 415–427.

79. Garrett, R. Kelly (2006). "Protest in an Information Society: a review of literature on social movements and new ICTs". Information, Communication and Society,

9:2, pp. 202-224.

80. Gates, B. (1999). Business @ the speed of Thought: Succeeding in the digital economy. Grand Central Publishing.

81. Gessner, G.G., Eldermire, E., Tang, N. and Tancheva, K. (2017). "The research lifecycle and the future of research libraries: a library of apps", Proceedings of the ACRL 2017, pp. 533-543.

82. Godin, Benoit (2003). 'The Impact of Research Grants on the Productivity and Quality of Scientific Research', INRS Working Paper 2003, National Sciences and Engineering Research Council of Canada (NSERC).

83. Godin, Benoit and Gingras, Yves (2000). "'Impact of Collaborative Research on Academic Science", Science and Public Policy 27(1), pp. 65-73.

84. Gordon, Michael (1980). "A Critical Reassessment of Inferred Relations Between Multiple Authorship, Scientific Collaboration, the Production of Papers and Their Acceptance for Publication", Scientometrics 2, pp. 193-201

85. Grant, R.M. (1996). "Toward a knowledge-based theory of the firm." Strategic Management Journal, 17 (1996), pp. 109-122, 10.1002/smj.4250171110.

86. Haddow, G. and Mamtora, J. (2017). "Research support in australian academic libraries: services, resources, and relationships", New Review of Academic Librarianship, 23 (6), pp. 1-21.

87. Harrington, E. G. (2019). Academic libraries and public engagement with science and technology. Cambridge, MA: Chandos Publishing.

88. Harrington, Eileen (2019). Expanding the impact of research. https://libraryconnect.elsevier.com/print/

89. Hawkins, Donald T., (ed.) (2013). Personal Archiving:

Preserving Our Digital Heritage. Medford, NJ, USA: Information Today, Inc.. Available as an ebook through IUPUI. http://site.ebrary.com.proxy.ulib.uits.iu.edu/lib/iupui/detail.action?docID=10778521&p00=digital+preservation.

90. Heffner, A.G. (1981). "Funded Research, Multiple Authorship, and Sub-authorship Collaboration in Four Disciplines", Scientometrics 3(1), pp. 5-12.

91. Heinze, T., and Bauer, G. (2007). "Characterizing creative scientists in nano-S&T: Productivity, multidisciplinarity, and network brokerage in a longitudinal perspective". Scientometrics, 70(3), 811–830.

92. Hensley, M.K., Shreeves, S.L. and Davis-Kahl, S. (2013). "A survey of library support for formal undergraduate research programs", College and Research Libraries, 75(4), pp. 422-441.

93. Hofstadter, R. (1963). Anti-intellectualism in American life. Knopf.

94. Houghton, Bernadette (March/April 2015). Trustworthiness: self-assessment of an institutional repository against ISO 16363-2012. D-Lib Magazine, 21(3/4).

95. Jaguszewski, J.M. and Williams, K. (2013). "New roles for new times: transforming liaison roles in research libraries", available at: www.arl.org/storage/documents/publications/nrnt-liaison-roles-revised.pdf

96. Jeong, S., Choi, J. Y., and Kim, J. (2011). "The determinants of research collaboration modes: Exploring the effects of research and researcher characteristics on co-authorship." Scientometrics, 89(3), pp. 967–983.

97. Jerome Bruner (1960). The Process of Education

(Cambridge, MA: Harvard University Press, 1960), quoted in Noel Entwistle, Teaching for Understanding at University (Basingstoke, UK: Palgrave Macmillan, 2009).

98. Jia, D., Wang, M. and Sun, Q. (2017). "Study on the research support services in American University Libraries: based on an analysis on strategic plans texts of libraries", Library Development, 281(5), pp. 59-65.

99. Kamp, Martijn van der (2011). Collaborating and colliding: when alliances go wrong.

100. Katz, Sylvan J. and Martin, Ben R. (1997). "What is Research Collaboration?." Research Policy 26(1), pp. 1-18.

101. Keast, Robyn, Charles, Michael (2016). Ten rules for successful research collaboration, Southern Cross University.

102. Kim, B., Barua, A., Whinston, A.B. (2002). "Virtual field experiments for a digital economy: A new research methodology for exploring an information economy." Decision Support Systems, 32 (2002), pp. 215-231.

103. Kirchner, Joy, Diaz, José, Henry, Geneva, Fliss, Susan, Culshaw, John, Gendron, Heather & Cawthorne, Jon E. (February 2015). The center of excellent model for information services. Council on Library and Information Resources. http://www.clir.org/pubs/reports/pub163/pub163.pdf.

104. Kirschenbaum, M. (2004). "Interface, Aesthetics, and Usability". In Susan Schreibman, Ray Siemens and John Unsworth, eds., "A Companion to Digital Humanities". New York: Blackwell Publishing, 2004. pp. 523-542.

105. Kirschenbaum, M. (2010). ADE Bulletin, 150, pp. 55-59. https://www.ade.mla.org/ADE-Bulletin.

106. Kirschenbaum, M.G . (2010). "Hello Worlds (Why

Humanities Students Should Learn to Program)." https://mkirschenbaum.wordpress.com/2010/05/23/hello-worlds/.

107. Klein, Lauren (2018). "Distant Reading after Moretti." http://lklein.com/2018/01/distant-reading-after-moretti/.

108. Kostkova, P., and Madle, G. (2013). "What impact do healthcare digital libraries have? An evaluation of national resource of infection control at the point of care using the Impact-ED framework." International Journal On Digital Libraries,13 (2), 77-90.

109. Kozievitch, Nadia P. and Torres, Richardo da Silva (2014). Complex Objects. In E. Fox, R. Torres, Digital Library Technologies: Complex Objects, Annotation, Ontologies, Classification, Extraction, and Security. Synthesis Lectures on Information Concepts, Retrieval, and Services. Morgan & Claypool Publishers. Available as an ebook through IUPUI. http://site. ebrary.com. proxy.ulib.uits.iu.edu/lib/iupui/detail.action?adv.x=1&docID=10857385&f00=all&f01= subject&p00=digital+library&p01=%22Digital+ Libraries%22.

110. Krishnamurthy, M. (2008). "Open access, open source and digital libraries: a current trend in university libraries around the world", Program, Vol. 42 No. 1, pp. 48-55.

111. Laura James (2013). Defining Open Data October 3, 2013. https://blog.okfn.org/author/laura/

112. Lee, Y.S. (1996). "'Technology Transfer' and the Research University: A Search for the Boundaries of University-Industry Collaboration," Research Policy, 25, pp. 843-863.

113. Leizerov, S. (2000). "Privacy advocacy groups versus Intel: a case study of how social movements are tactically using the Internet to fight corporations". Social Science

Computer Review, 18(4), pp. 461–483.

114. Li Si, Yueliang Zeng, Sicheng Guo, Xiaozhe Zhuang (2019). "Investigation and analysis of research support services in academic libraries", The Electronic Library.

115. Liao, C. H., and Yen, H. R. (2012). Quantifying the degree of research collaboration: A comparative study of collaborative measures. Journal of Informetrics, 6(1), pp. 27–33.

116. Lyman, P., Varian, H., et al. (2003). How much information? http://www.sims.berkeley.edu/research/projects/how-much-info-2003/

117. Machielse, Christopher (2012). 5 Ways to Use Your iPad to Teach in the College Classroom (2012). http://info.lecturetools.com/blog/bid/52506/5-Ways-to-Use-Your-iPad-to-Teach-in-the-College-Classroom.

118. Madhusudhan, M., and Nagabushnam, V. (2012). "Use of web based library services in select university libraries in India: A study." International Journal of Library and Information Studies, 2 (1). Retrieved from http://ijlis.org/img/2012_2_issue_1/1_20.pdf.

119. Magee, C.L., Devezas, T.C. (2017). "An extension of dematerialization theory: Incorporation of technical performance increases and the rebound effect." Technological Forecasting & Social Change, 117, pp. 196-205.

120. Mann, Joshua L. (2018). "How Technology Means: Texts, History, and Their Associated Technologies." DHQ: Digital Humanities Quarterly, 12(3).

121. Manuel, Castells, Wallis, Annenberg and Barcelona, Gustavo Cardoso (2006). The Network Society From Knowledge to Policy, edited by Manuel Castells, Wallis Annenberg and Barcelona Gustavo Cardoso. https://www.dhi.ac.uk/san/waysofbeing/data/communication-zangana-castells-2006.pdf

122. Manyika, James, Chui, Michael, Farrell, Diana, Van Kuiken, Steve, Groves, Peter and Doshi, Elizabeth Almasi (2013). Open data: Unlocking innovation and performance with liquid information. (October 2013, Report) https://www.mckinsey.com/our-people/michael-chui.

123. Manyika, James et al. (2013). https://www.mckinsey.com/our-people/james-manyika.

124. Marginson, S. (2006). Putting 'public' back into the public universities. Thesis Eleven 84, 44–59. https://link.springer.com/article/10.1007/s10734-008-9123-7#ref-CR56.

125. Marlino, M., Sumner, T. R., et al. (2001). "The Digital Library for Earth System Education: Building Community, Building the Library". Communications of the ACM, special issue on Digital Libraries, May, 80-81.

126. Marx, K. (1958). The fragment on machines. http://thenewobjectivity.com/pdf/marx.pdf.

127. Masuda, Y. (1980). "The information society as post-industrial society". https://scholar.google.com/scholar_lookup?title=The%20information%20society%20as%20post-industrial%20society&publication_year=1980&author=Y.%20Masuda.

128. McCauley, James E. (1963). Multiple authorship, Science 141 (3580) pp. 579.

129. McGann, J. (2011). "On Creating a Usable Future", Profession, pp. 182-95.

130. Mckinsey Report (2013). https://www.mckinsey.com/our-people/james-manyika.

131. McLean and Lynch (2004). Reasons to integrate digital libraries and VLEs. in Integration of digital libraries in e-learning. https://www.tlu.ee/~sirvir/Information%20and%20Knowledge%20Management/Integration

% 20of%20digital%20libraries%20in%20e-learning/index.html.

132. McMartin. https://journals.tdl.org/jodi/index.php/jodi/article/view/119/hdl.handle.net/2249.2/jodi-148.

133. Md. Ashikuzzaman. Types of knowledge. http://www.lisbdnet.com/types-of-knowledge/

134. Melin, Goran (2000). "'Pragmatism and Self-organization: Research Collaboration on the Individual Level" , Research Policy 29(1): 31-40.

135. Naidoo, R., and Jamieson, I. (2005). Knowledge in the marketplace: The global commodification of teaching, learning in higher education. In P. Ninnes & M. Hellstén (Eds.), Internationalizing higher education: Critical explorations of pedagogy and policy (pp. 37–52). Dordrecht: Springer. https://link.springer.com/article/10.1007/s10734-008-9123-7#ref-CR50.

136. Neatrour, Anna L., Callaway, Elizabeth and Cummings, Rebekah (2018). "Kindles, card catalogs, and the future of libraries: a collaborative digital humanities project." Digital Library Perspectives, vol. 34 no. 3.

137. Neely, Ben. Using Technology as a Learning Tool, Not Just the Cool New Thing. http://www.educause.edu/Resources/EducatingtheNetGeneration/UsingTechnologyasaLearningTool/6060.

138. Nelson, R. (1991). National innovation systems. Oxford: Oxford University Press.

139. Nosek, B. A. (2017). Opening science. In R.S. Jhangiani & R. Biswas-Diener (Eds.), "Open: The philosophy and practices that are revolutionizing education and science" http://www.ubiquitypress.com/site/books/10.5334/bbc/download/1451.

140. OECD (2016). "New markets and new jobs. Background

report for the OECD ministerial meeting on the digital economy", 21–23 June 2016, Cancún, Mexico.

141. Pao, Miranda Lee (1982). "Collaboration in computational musicology", Journal of the American Society for Information Science 33 (1), pp. 38-43.

142. Parry, M. (2016). "Evolving business models to support the growth of technology-based start-up firms". World Technopolis Review, 5 (2), December.

143. Papadopoulos, Costas, Schreibman, Susan (2019). "Towards 3D Scholarly Editions: The Battle of Mount Street Bridge", DHQ: Digital Humanities Quarterly, 13 (1).

144. Parry, M. (2016). Evolving Business Models to Support the growth of technology-based start-up firms. WTR, 5(2).

145. Phillips, F. (2004). "Trading Down: The intellectual poverty of the new FTAs." Technological Forecasting & Social Change (2004), pp. 71-78.

146. Phillips, Fred, Yu, Ching-Ying, Tahir Hameed, Mahmoud Abdullah El, Akhdary (2017). "The knowledge society's origins and current trajectory." International Journal of Innovation Studies, Volume 1, Issue 3, pp. 175-191 https://doi.org/10.1016/j.ijis.2017.08.001.

147. Poole, A.H., and Garwood, D.A. (2018). "'Natural Allies': Librarians, Archivists, and Big Data in International Digital Humanities Project Work". Journal of Documentation, 74 (4), pp. 804-826.

148. Poole, Alex H. (2016). "The conceptual ecology of digital humanities." Journal of Documentation, vol. 73.

149. Poremski, M.D. (2017). "Evaluating the landscape of digital humanities librarianship". College & Undergraduate Libraries, 24 (2-44), pp. 140-154.

150. Porter, D. (2014). "What If We Do, In Fact, Know Best?: A Response to the OCLC Report on DH and Research Libraries".

151. Pratono, Aluisius Hery , Prima, Delta Ardy , Flora, Nur, Sinaga, Nita Taruli , Permatasari, Anggraeni Ariani, Mintarti and Han, Ling (2020). Crowdfunding in digital humanities: some evidence from Indonesian social enterprises. Aslib Journal of Information Management, 72 (2) DOI: https://doi.org/10.1108/AJIM-05-2019-0123.

152. Presner, Todd, et al., (2009). "HyperCities: Building a Web 2.0 Learning Platform". In A. Natsina and T. Tagialis, eds., Teaching Literature at a Distance. London & New York: Continuum Books, 2010.

153. Reid, Alexander (2011). "Social Media Assemblages in Digital Humanities: from Backchannel to Buzz." Teaching Arts and Science with the New Social Media.

154. Reidenberg, JR (1997). Lex informatica: The formulation of information policy rules through technology. Tex. L. Rev., 1997 - HeinOnline. https://heinonline.org/hol-cgi-bin/get_pdf.cgi?handle=hein.journals/tlr76&section=24.

155. Reitz, Joan M. (2014). Online Dictionary for Library and Information Science. Libraries Unlimited. Available: http://www.abc-clio.com/ODLIS/odlis_a.aspx.

156. Robyn, D. and Richard, W. (2009). "RIMS: the research impact measurement service at the University of New South Wales", Australian Academic and Research Libraries, 40(2), pp. 76-87.

157. Rodrigues, M.J (2002). "The new knowledge economy in Europe: A strategy for international competitiveness and social cohesion." UK: Edward Elgar.

158. Rogers, Juan and Bozeman, Barry (2001). "Knowledge

Value Alliances: An Alternative to R&D Project Evaluation", Science, Technology, & Human Values 26(1), pp. 23-55.

159. Sachs, J. D. (2004). "Sustainable Development: Editorial". Science, 304 (5671): 649.

160. Sally Burch. The Information Society / the Knowledge Society. https://vecam.org/archives/spip6232.html?page=auteur&id_auteur=220&lang=en&nemo=edm.

161. Sangale, D.B. (2015). "ICT application and web based services in Library and Information Science". ASM's International E-Journal on ongoing research in Management and IT, 9-14.

162. Schatz, B., Mischo, W., Cole, T., Hardin, J., Bishop, A., and Chen, H. (1996). Federating diverse collections of scientific literature, Computer, May, 28-35.

163. Schumpeter, J.A. (1943). Capitalism, socialism & democracy. London: Routledge.

164. Schaffner, J., and Erway, R. "Does Every Research Library Need a Digital Humanities Center?" Dublin, Ohio: OCLC Research (2014). http://www.oclc.org/content/dam/research/publications/library/2014/oclcresearch-digital-humanities-center-2014.pdf.

165. Scheinfeldt, Tom (2010). "Stuff Digital Humanists Like: Defining Digital Humanities by Its Values." Found History. https://foundhistory.org/2010/12/stuff-digital-humanists-like/.

166. Schreibman, Susan, Siemens, Ray and Unsworth, John (2010). "The Digital Humanities and Humanities Computing: An Introduction". In Susan Schreibman Ray Siemens and John Unsworth, A Companion to Digital Humanities. Malden: Blackwell, 2010. pp. xxiii-xxvii.

167. Shafritz, Jay M. and Ott, J. S. (1992). Classics of Organization Theory, third edition (Pacific Grove, CA: Brooks/Cole Publishing).

168. Sharifabadi (2006). Reasons to integrate digital libraries and VLEs. In Integration of digital libraries in e-learning. https://www.tlu.ee/~sirvir/Information%20and %20 Knowledge%20Management/Integration%20of %20 digital%20libraries%20in%20e-learning/index.html.

169. Sheridan, P. and Ballerini, J. (1996). "Experiments in multilingual information retrieval using the SPIDER system". Proceedings of ACM SIGIR Conference on Research and Development in Information Retrieval, 58-65.

170. Si, L., Zeng, Y., Guo, S. and Zhuang, X. (2019). "Investigation and analysis of research support services in academic libraries", The Electronic Library, Vol. 37 No. 2, pp. 281-301. https://doi.org/10.1108/EL-06-2018-0125.

171. Silvennoinen-Kuikka, Helena (2018). A strategic look at research support and open science services at our library. https://libraryconnect.elsevier.com/print/

172. Smithies, James, Westling, Carina, Sichani Anna-Maria, Mellen, Pam (2019). "Managing 100 Digital Humanities Projects: Digital Scholarship & Archiving in King's Digital Lab." DHQ: Digital Humanities Quarterly, 13 (1).

173. Subramanyam , K. Citation and significance, New Library World 76, pp. 227-228.

174. Subramanyam, K. and Stephens, Elsie M. (1982). Research collaboration and funding in biochemistry and chemical engineering, International Forum on Information and Documentation 7 (4), 26-29.

175. Sylvan, J. Ben, Katz, Martin, R. What is research collaboration? https://doi.org/10.1016/S0048-7333 (96) 00917-1Get rights and content.

176. Tett, G. (2016). "The productivity Imperative: Advice for the president-elect." Foreign Policy (2016), pp. 98-99. December.

177. Thomas, J. (2011). "Future-proofing: the academic library's role in e-research support", Library Management, 32(1/2), pp. 37-47.

178. Thorsteinsdottir, O. Halla (2000). "External Research Collaboration in Two Small Science Systems", Scientometrics 49(1), pp. 145-160.

179. Turan, Julia (2016). "How Exactly Do the 'digital Humanities' Mix Science with the Arts?" Our Cells Our Selves. February 9, 2016. https://juliaturan.com/2016/02/09/how-exactly-do-the-digital-humanities-mix-with-the-arts/.

180. Udland, M. (2017). United Airlines loses $950 million in market value as shares tumble.

181. UNESCO (2005). https://link.springer.com/article/10.1007/s10734-008-9123-7#ref-CR79.

182. Välimaa, J., Hoffman, D. (2008). Knowledge society discourse and higher education. High Educ 56, 265–285. https://doi.org/10.1007/s10734-008-9123-7.

183. Wójcik, M. (2019). "How to design innovative information services at the library?", Library Hi Tech, 37(2), pp. 138-154. https://doi.org/10.1108/LHT-07-2018-0094.

184. Webster, Jessica Wagner (2019). "Digital Collaborations: A Survey Analysis of Digital Humanities Partnerships Between Librarians and Other Academics." Digital Humanities Quarterly, 13 (4). http://digitalhumanities.org/dhq/vol/13/4/000441/000441.html.

185. Welch, A.N. and Wyatt-Baxter, K. (2018). "Beyond metrics: connecting academic library Makerspace assessment practices with organizational values", Library Hi Tech, 36(2), pp. 306-318, available at: https:/

/doi.org/10.1108/LHT-08-2017-0181 (accessed March 26, 2018).

186. Witten, Ian H., Bainbridge, David, and Nicholas, David (2010). How to Build a Digital Library. Morgan Kaufmann: Elsevier. Google Preview Available: https://books.google.com/books?id=HiJNbEy5f70C. Available as an ebook through IUPUI. http://site.ebrary.com. proxy.ulib.uits.iu.edu/lib/iupui/detail.action? docID=10344401.

187. Yang, Sharon Q and Dalal, Heather A. (2015). Virtual reference: where do academic librarians stand? Computers in Libraries, 35(5), 4-10.

188. Yuen, Steve (2010). Exploring the use of social technology in the college classroom. http://scyuen.wordpress.com/2010/04/05/exploring-the-use-of-social-technology-in-the-college-classroom/

189. Zhang, Ying, Liu, Shuand Mathews, Emilee (2014). "Convergence of digital humanities and digital libraries." Library Management, vol. 36 no. 4/5.

190. Zorich, Diane M. (2008). "A Survey of Digital Humanities Centers in the United States". Washington DC: Council on Library and Information Resources.

Index

D

T

U

V

W